WESTMAR COLLEGE L...

P9-CRI-009

The book traces the development of this search for spiritual renewal from the ancient Christian heretics of the Greco-Roman period to the mystics of the Middle Ages to the radical philosophers and "prophets of doom'" such as Schopenhauer and Nietzsche to the Symbolist and Spiritualist movements of the nineteenth century to the German Romantic and Wandervogel movements to the Zen beatniks of the 50s to the hippie counterculture of the 60s — all of which is seen as a culmination of a widespread revulsion against history and especially against the inescapable influence of historical events which the modern, like the ancient, Gnostic seeks to escape by retreating into a timeless, eternal world. Raschke examines the thought of influential twentieth-century writers such as C. G. Jung, Henri Bergson, Herman Hesse, Alan Watts, and Theodore Roszak, showing how modern gnosticism promises to become the dominant popular belief of our time.

Clearly and powerfully, *The Interruption of Eternity* deals with some of mankind's most profound issues. Its engaging and colorful prose places obscure concepts within the grasp of all who seek a new perspective on modern man and his world.

About the author

Carl A. Raschke is a professor in the Department of Religious Studies at the University of Denver, where he teaches courses in philosophy of religion, contemporary ethical problems, and the history of modern culture. He earned his doctorate from Harvard University and is the author of *Moral Action, God, and History in the Thought of Immanuel Kant* (1975) and is editor and co-author of *Religion and the Human Image* (1976).

The Interruption of Eternity

Modern Gnosticism and the Origins of the New Religious Consciousness

The Interruption of Eternity

Modern Gnosticism and the Origins of the New Religious Consciousness

Carl A. Raschke

Nelson-Hall ⌊nh⌋ Chicago

BL
98
.R37

Lines reprinted from "First Poems" from *Translations from the Poetry of Rainer Maria Rilke,* by M.D. Herter Norton, with permission of W.W. Norton & Company, Inc. Copyright 1938 by W.W. Norton & Company, Inc. Copyright renewed 1966 by M.D. Herter Norton. Permission for use outside the U.S. and Canada from Hogarth Press.

Lines reprinted from "Burnt Norton" from *Four Quartets,* by T.S. Eliot, with permission of Harcourt Brace Jovanovich, Inc. Permission to quote *Collected Poems 1909-1962* for use outside the U.S.A. from Faber and Faber Ltd., Publishers.

Reprinted with permission of Macmillan Publishing Co., Inc. from *Collected Poems* by William Butler Yeats: "Byzantium," copyright 1933 by Macmillan Publishing Co., Inc., renewed 1961 by Bertha Georgie Yeats; "The Second Coming," copyright 1924 by Macmillan Publishing Co., Inc., renewed 1952 by Bertha Georgie Yeats; "Among School Children," copyright 1928 by Macmillan Publishing Co., Inc., renewed 1956 by Georgie Yeats. Permission for use outside the U.S. from M.B. Yeats and Miss Anne Yeats.

Sonnets to Orpheus by Rainer Maria Rilke. Copyright 1960 by C.F. MacIntyre; reprinted by permission of the University of California Press.

Library of Congress Cataloging in Publication Data

Raschke, Carl A
    The interruption of eternity.

    Bibliography: p.
    Includes index.
    1. Religion—20th century. I. Title.
BL98.R37   291   79-16460
ISBN 0-88229-374-5

Copyright© 1980 by Carl A. Raschke

All rights reserved. No part of this book may be reproduced in any form without permission in writing from the publisher, except by a reviewer who wishes to quote brief passages in connection with a review written for broadcast or for inclusion in a magazine or newspaper. For information address Nelson-Hall Inc., Publishers, 111 North Canal Street, Chicago, Illinois 60606.

Manufactured in the United States of America

    10   9   8   7   6   5   4   3   2   1

98928

To Lori

Contents

Preface

Since the early 1970s considerable attention has been given by both scholars and journalists to the growth of countless religious and "spiritual" movements in the Western world which are at odds with the normative Jewish and Christian traditions of our culture. Different forms and adaptations of Hinduism, Buddhism, and Islamic mysticism have joined forces with the myriad practices of occultism in contributing to the making of what Robert Ellwood has termed an "alternative reality" for many members of our society. Quite recently the religious side of this trend has merged with the development (one should perhaps say *burgeoning*) of many new popular psychotherapies and popular techniques of meditation and mind control, the most important of which is Transcendental Meditation. All these together represent a momentous search within our culture for new and unprecedented systems of personal meaning which turn out to be prescriptions for *salvation,* but which at the same time betoken a widespread disenchantment with conventional religious and secular ideologies that in the past have satisfied similar purposes. Not a few observers have ritualistically dismissed these developments as "marginal" to real tendencies in the ongoing pattern of social change, but a Gallup poll at the end of 1976 (the first to analyze commitment to these movements statistically by a major, national public opinion research organization) indicated that the effect of such groups and philosophies on the shaping of individual attitudes is more consequential than previously thought.

In late 1972 I first began research for this book as a more or less straightforward investigation of the characteristics and origins of many of the new religious cults. I intended to work out a theoretical model that would be useful in helping to understand the phenomena in

ix

question, rather than merely describing what was going on. However, in the meantime there appeared a number of significant studies which accomplished for the most part what I had set about to do. Some surveyed the entire field of the turning to alternative religious outlooks, while others dissected particular groups as paradigm instances of the changes taking place. In the first category I would cite the following works: Robert S. Ellwood, *Religious and Spiritual Groups in Modern America* (Prentice-Hall, 1973), Charles Glock and Robert Bellah, *The New Religious Consciousness* (University of California Press, 1976), and my own lengthy article "The Asian Invasion of American Religion: Creative Innovation or a New Gnosticism" (American Academy of Religion, 1973). In the second case I would mention J. Stillson Judah, *Hare Krishna and The Counterculture* (John Wiley & Sons, 1974). As I undertook to begin the writing of this book in the summer of 1974 it became evident that an examination of contemporary happenings was not needed so much as a probe into the historical origins of the so-called "new religious consciousness." It is commonplace for both students and academics in our present-oriented world to become fascinated with certain discrete, but transient phenomena or events, to look at them inside out, without however attempting to place them within a larger scheme of understanding. Many professional and lay sociologists, of course, have submitted some valuable theses as to the reasons for the spread of the new religious consciousness in terms of the social crises of the past fifteen years; but virtually none of them have seriously analyzed it as part of a long-ranging historical pattern. Those "histories" of the tradition of the "alternative" religious viewpoint have by and large been only of the narrative kind, and have not tied the tradition to related cultural factors and transformations.

Thus I started groping toward some clues for the deeper, past origins of what is transpiring nowadays. In this book I proffer a tentative theory. I maintain that the "new religions" and their psychotherapeutic surrogates are mainly the cresting wave of forces that have been at work in Western culture for at least two hundred years, primarily since the eighteenth century, though the seeds were planted over two millennia ago. I argue that the actual phenomenon which one must inspect is what I term modern "Gnosticism" (and I am using the term "Gnostic" in a sense much broader than that employed by scholars interested in the ancient illuminist cults of the Graeco-Roman period which traditionally have borne the name and which were the chief competitors with the early Christian church, who branded them for posterity as noxious heresies). Modern Gnosticism encompasses not only the different underground religious communities, but also key attitudes on the part of certain intellectuals toward the nature of man, toward society and history. Such "Gnosticism," therefore, would cover the ideas of figures like the German Romantics, Friedrich Nietzsche, and Carl G. Jung. These latter day Gnostics, the book contends, must be understood as taking a rear-guard action against the "progress" of the modern, industrial world. They are in revolt against the course of modern history and seek salvation within the sphere of the timeless. Their passion is not for a life lived within all the ambiguities of human time, but for salvation beyond the plane of the temporal, in *eternity*. The title of the book, *The Interruption of Eternity,* thus suggests that there exists a significant way of looking at the world which seeks surcease from—a qualitative break in—the motion of time and history.

In conclusion, I would like to indicate my appreciation for those individuals and institutions who gave me assistance in the preparation of this work. First and foremost, I want to express thanks to Mrs. Gretchen Hawley, administrative assistant at the University of Denver, for her long labors of typing and editing. Secondly, I would like to thank the University of Denver itself for awarding me several faculty research grants to fund primarily clerical assistance and the gathering of information, and the German Academic Exchange Service which paid my way to Germany in the summer of 1974 to do archive research on Schopenhauer and nineteenth-century philosophy. Third, I wish to acknowledge gratitude to the following persons for various kinds of aid—Barbara Wihera, Edward Myers, Constance Foster, Elizabeth Mutters, M. Colleen McDannell, and Sharon Coggan for work as research assistants; Diane Gould and Alice Trembour for help in translating certain text passages from French and German; Sallee Morris, Sandra Sullivan, and Constance Gianulis for typing assistance. And finally I would like to thank my family—my wife Lori for patience, my son Erik for keeping me down to earth, and my mother Grace Raschke for help in preparation of the index.

Chapter 1

The Quest
for
Eternity

This is my strife:
dedicate to desire
through all days to roam.
Then, strong and wide,
with a thousand root-fibers
deep into life to gripe—
and through pain
far beyond life to ripen,
far beyond time!

—*Rainer Maria Rilke*[1]

THE TEMPORAL AND THE TIMELESS

There is a scene in Shakespeare's *King Henry IV, Part I* where the dying Hotspur rues the sudden end to his mortal career:

> But thought's the slave of life, and
> life time's fool;
> And time, that takes survey of all the world,
> Must have a stop.[2]

Hotspur's lament, of course, strikes a universal chord: "time that takes a survey of the world" is a baleful presence in man's life and must be "stopped." Indeed, the yearning of man throughout history to make time cease and thereby secure the bliss of eternity has been articulated by generations of religious seers, artists, and poets.

> Who can speak of eternity without a solecism,
> or think thereof without an ecstasy? Time
> we may comprehend, 'tis but five
> days older than ourselves.[3]

Similarly, Saint Augustine, in his perplexity and anguish about the frailties and finitude of humanity, once reflected: "I am not long-

1

suffering, because I am mortal. But thou hast it in thy power to become so; join thy heart to the eternity of God, and with Him thou shalt be eternal."[4] The "long-suffering" creature of mortal flesh thirsts after surcease from the pain, worry, and uncertainty which time-ridden existence irrevocably enforces. The simplest pleasures, the most homely accomplishents, relentlessly drift away in the flow of moments. Man searches for felicity, for an order and stability unravaged by the tide of change which wears down the peaks of joy and carries their sediment into the valley of remembrance. This vain struggle for an uncompromised happiness, a happiness which proves as precarious as each fleet instant of experience itself and which may, at last, give way to sorrow and despair, is the ironical condition of all beings immersed in their senses. One may recall a description by Soren Kierkegaard, the Danish philosopher, of the "esthetic" personality, the dupe of fate and becoming who fervently wishes to snatch a timeless delight from time itself. As Kierkegaard's "seducer," Johannes proclaims at sexual climax: "Everything finite and temporal is forgotten, only the eternal remains. The power of love, its longing, its happiness."[5] It is also implied in the Buddha's teaching of *tanha* (literally, "grasping," analogically, "desire") as both the sire of human misery and the stepchild of ignorance. Perhaps since time immemorial has man held the melancholy idea that his highest aspirations are perhaps impossible in the temporal world. Thus the philosopher Nietzsche through the mouth of his character Zarathustra passionately avows: "Joy wants eternity, wants deep, deep eternity."[6] Thomas Browne's *o altitudino* can only ring clear beyond the restless din of time and events. The tragedies and frustrations of common life point toward the conquest of time as a whole. As Kierkegaard says, "Suffering is training for eternity."[7] Human life constitutes a heroic endeavor to wrest the eternal out of the chaos of mundane experience.

The sense of eternity, etched indelibly in the myths and symbols of the world's religions, therefore, may provide an important clue not only to source of worship, but also to the fundamental predicament of mankind. The image of eternity, as we shall see, composes the Archimedean point of man's quest for meaning and order in an enigmatic universe; it becomes the central locus of perception and evaluation for both consciousness as a whole and for the more specific mode of time consciousness, from which the horizons of all reflection, intuition, and motivation are extended. If religion be defined in terms of what Paul Tillich called "ultimate concern," or the search for significance at the outermost boundaries of human awareness, then the sense of the eternal must somehow lie beneath the threshing floor of religious imagination. The search for eternity, therefore, constitutes the very origins of religion itself.

The philosopher Immanuel Kant once advanced the rather novel idea that time and space are the fundamental "forms" of sensation in which all phenomena appear and through which experience of the world becomes possible. Kant thus broke ground in philosophical discussions of the nature of time by treating temporal succession not as a feature of the external world but as a reflex of human consciousness itself. Although Kant presumably erred in his contention that the structure of time-consciousness remains inalterable and uniform among all intelligent creatures, his discovery that the time sense consists in the bedrock on which man's knowledge of himself and his surroundings is built has far-reaching implications. In one important respect, it may be assumed that the time sense is precisely what gives rise to what we denote as "consciousness." Although it is wise to hedge all speculations about the evolutionary origins of human consciousness in light of scant supportive evidence, the very character of "conscious" processes and behavior within man urges such a hypothesis. As G. W. F. Hegel observed long ago in his *Phenomenology of Mind,* consciousness is precisely that ability of man to separate subject from object, perceiver from the perceived, self from world; it is "reflection" on the relationship between these two poles of experience in order to arrive at a second-order knowledge of phenomena mediated through enduring concepts. "Consciousness finds that it immediately is and is not another consciousness, as also that this other is for itself only when it cancels itself as existing for itself. . . ."[8] The ability to retain impressions from one moment to the next, to distinguish their essential properties and to compare these properties by analogy with the forms of other existing objects, involves at least an elementary intuition of past and future; it implies the facility for anticipating new patterns of experience in association with firm memories of events that have gone before.

By the same token, Kenneth Boulding in a landmark study of perception among living species, argues how the "image" of time distinguishes man's superior mode of consciousness from the cognitive habits of other creatures. Boulding writes:

> Our image of time . . . goes far beyond that of the most intelligent of the lower animals, mainly because of our capacity for language and for record. It is doubtful whether the time image of the lower animals ever goes much beyond the immediate moment, and it is certainly confined to their private experience. A dog has no idea that there were dogs before him and there will be dogs after him. The human being, on the other hand, is firmly located in a temporal process. He has an image of the past which extends back far beyond the limits of his own life and experience, and he likewise has an image of the future. Closely associated with the time structure of his image is the image of the structure of relationships. Because we are aware of time, we are also aware of cause and effect, of contiguity and succession, of cycles and repetition. The image of man is also characterized by a much greater degree of self-consciousness and self-awareness than that of the lower animals. We not only know, but we know that we know. . . . Because of the extended time image and the extended relationship images, man is capable of "rational behavior," that is to say, his response is not to an immediate stimulus but to an image of the future filtered through an elaborate value system.[9]

Temporal awareness is what enables man to deal with his environment *symbolically,* to forge raw sensation into intelligible forms which can be used to interpret immediate perceptions, to acquire beliefs, and to construct ideal universes with no direct counterpart in day-to-day experience. Consciousness entails, therefore, both *projection* and *intention*—the power to set forth imagined or predicted experiences as well as to act in accordance with those experiences. Human consciousness comprehends what has already transpired in life and maps subsequent strategies of behavior in concert with the way it interpreted those previous happenings. The time sense renders human consciousness purposeful or goal-directed, thence constituting it as more than a series of automatic responses to environmental stimuli. The time sense liberates man from the tyranny of immediacy and, in consequence, enlarges his cognitive domain from simple three-dimensional space to a complex manifold of awareness which reckons change as the passage from potentiality to actuality and back to potentiality again.

Through his talent for "locating" events somewhere beyond the ever apparent now along a temporal axis, man is able to master his world and avoid becoming a passive victim of circumstances or a prisoner of instinct. Because man can judge what is yet to come in light of what he can remember having already taken place, he can also devise equipment to contend with new situations. The time sense enables man not just to "learn" ways of coping with emergencies through conditioned retroaction, as behaviorist experiments have suggested, but to make preparations "ahead of time" as well, before a demand or challenge is laid upon him. Man's fabrication of tools gives evidence of the time sense as governing human activity. A tool remains a random object until it has been employed regularly in the achievement of certain ends. For example, paleolithic man discovered that certain rocks, when chipped and chiseled into sharp points and then bound to a stick, could be used to kill elusive quarry. The invention of spears and arrow shafts was not a capricious exercise in trial and error, as when a chimpanzee *happens* to find that by swinging a rod it can bring down a bunch of bananas from the top of its cage. The chimpanzee would not think of obtaining an arsenal of rods for this endeavor. But man contrives such tools for doing specific tasks in the future by retaining the knowledge that they have worked before. Not only does he recall how delicious roasted meat tasted on a fire, but he preserves and perfects methods for making or using fire when the occasion arises.[10]

The logical principle which serves to guide primitive resourcefulness and technique, of course, is that of *causation*. In order to compose a means whereby certain "lessons" of experience can be translated into practical utensils, man must discern some analogy between a prior sequence of events and a later one. However, the disclosure of such an analogy rests on cognizance of succession in time, of repeated patterns of connection between separate occurrences. As Jean Piaget remarked, "time is inherent in causality."[11] The grasp of causality, on the other hand, undergirds the manipulative, purposeful intelligence of the human race.

The order of time relations follows a natural rhythm of life, an ongoing series of causally related experiences which nurture a familiar and predicable universe. In short, time becomes coherent when things go on and on as we would expect them to, when our elementary assumptions about what will probably happen next under particular conditions are not violated. Many animate species, from migrating birds to autumn leaves, have "internal clocks" which orient them to changes in the position of the stars, the intensity of sunlight, and so on.

Although these biological time mechanisms do not correspond necessarily to the more sophisticated time sense in man, they at least illustrate how temporal sensitivity is established in various organisms through coordinating metabolic processes with rhythmic alterations in the outward environment.[12] For *homo temporalis*, though, the problem of coordination involves not merely an adjustment to simple changes of state in the natural world, but the attunement of his pattern of belief and expectation with empirical evidence about many phenomena from when the seeds usually sprout to the likelihood that the stock market will fall. The time sense engenders a conception of *periodicity*—of night regularly following day, of spring evolving from winter, of old age chasing flaming youth. The expression, "it is time for such and such," harbors a tacit understanding of how events are recurrently conjoined or causally linked.

> For everything there is a season, and a time for
> every matter under heaven:
> a time to be born, and a time to die;
> a time to plant, and a time to pluck up what is planted;
> a time to kill, and a time to heal;
> a time to break down, and a time to build up;
> a time to weep, and a time to laugh;
> a time to mourn, and a time to dance;
> a time to cast away stones, and a time to gather stones
> together;
> a time to embrace, and a time to refrain from embracing;
> a time to seek, and a time to lose;
> a time to keep, and a time to cast away;
> a time to rend, and a time to sew;
> a time to keep silence, and a time to speak;
> a time to love, and a time to hate;
> a time for war, and a time for peace.
> What gain has the worker from his toil?   (Eccles. 3:1-9)

Of course, all clocks can be stopped or disrupted. Biological clocks can be thrown out of whack, as when nocturnal animals are placed indoors in artificially lighted terrariums. Likewise, the viability of the human time sense hinges largely on the opportunity to act and make calculations according to a meaningful model of cause and effect. Time, in one respect, cannot be separated from a consistent path of motion. If household clocks did not have evenly spaced numerals to which the whirling hands pointed, or if the hands only rotated about the face once and then ceased forever, there could be no "time" in any intelligible sense of the word for them to tell. However, because the measurement of time by household clocks is constant and, generally, unbroken, we can structure our lives in some purposeful routine. We know when it is not too early to cook supper, to visit the supermarket, and so on. Regardless of whether we are "slaves" to civilized time pieces, or appraise the order of the day, like the Navajos, according to the height of the sun or the rumblings in our stomachs, we still have developed a system of temporal "cues" which signify a consistent relationship between the necessary conditions of our experience (i.e., "what time it is") and the experience itself (i.e., "what usually happens at that time"). By the same token, if these cues are missing, or if what we believe the cues signify turns out to be erroneous (for example, suppose that in Miami at seven in the morning the sun came up and minutes later went right down again), both our notion of causality and our very perception of time are upset. It would no longer be possible in the modern scientific view to maintain that an overloaded truck "caused" the pavement of a highway to crack, if the fissure first appeared and *then* the truck passed over. As David Hume noted many generations ago, causes "must" be prior in time to their effects. The interruption of normal cognitive schema which make events in the world "fit" together leads to a distortion in the time sense. An alteration in the time sense may precipitate mental confusion and even madness. When the live experiences of, say, a Hamlet no longer hang together in a meaningful way, time literally is "out of joint." Recent psychological investigations have shown, for instance, that the baffling syndrome known as "schizophrenia," which involves a severe disintegration of the normal image of self and its continuity in the field of experience, also is attended by a complete scrambling of conventional time perception. Past and future may hypertrophy so much that the patient can no longer apprehend the present, or by the same token, he may find himself able to react only to momentary stimuli without recording them as memories, or interpreting them according to verbal symbols which would empower him to project thoughts beyond immediate impressions.[13] In schizophrenia the ordinary rules of causal understanding dissolve along with the faculty for distinguishing between what is "prior" and what is "antecedent."

Drugs too are chemical devices for warping the time sense. Different substances yield different types of distortion, from the quickening of time with amphetamines to the dampening, if not the complete abolition, of temporal awareness with such psychedelics as LSD, Psilocybin, and mescaline.[14] Psychedelics, in particular, distort the familiar channels of time experience by suspending all conscious habits of explanation and understanding so that things merely *appear* in their naked, sensuous immediacy. Alan Watts describes such an experience after having ingested some LSD in the early 1960s:

> To begin with, this world has a different kind of time. . . . There is no hurry. Our sense of time is notoriously subjective and thus dependent upon the quality of our attention, whether of interest or boredom, and upon the alignment of our behavior in terms of routines, goals, and deadlines. Here the present is self-sufficient, but it is not a static present. It is a dancing present—the unfolding of a pattern which has no specific destination in the future but is simply its own point. It leaves and arrives simultaneously, and the seed is as much the goal as the flower. There is therefore time to perceive every detail of the movement with infinitely greater richness of articulation . . . here the depth of light and structure in a bursting bud go on forever. There is time to see them, time for the whole intricacy of veins and capillaries to develop in consciousness, time to see down into the shape of greenness. . . .[15]

Events seem chaotic and directionless. Shapes and forms keep crystallizing and fading away without rhyme or reason. Time itself loses all coherency and, for all practical purposes, has been dispelled.

The evolution of conscious life proceeds along with the establishment of temporal rhythms derived from man's symbolic interchanges with his environment. However, there may be lapses or snaps in these rhythms due to many factors. It is this phenomenon of "broken" time which may compel man to resist time in its familiar form. The desire to resist time emerges when certain conscious patterns of experience dependent on rational models of how the world should fit together no longer can be maintained. The journey into madness, the yearning for "alternative realities," all have their origin and justification in the collapse of the everyday time sense. Broken time may be healed by a drastic reorientation of temporal attention. Very often the confusion of the time sense ensues in a new and higher perspective on the significance of temporality itself. Consciousness finds a new temporal reference point, its "center of gravity," so to speak. Consciousness becomes infused with the expansive light of the timeless instant—with the glow of eternity.

THE ETERNAL NOW

The "eternal now" of the mystical vision has often been characterized by the transcendence of time. In the words of W. T. Stace, "There are two orders, the natural order which is the order of time, and the divine order, the order of eternity."[16] The eternal is the supreme meaning and value of time, the aim of all striving and suffering. Employing a traditional Eastern metaphor, T. S. Eliot in his poem "Burnt Norton" represents eternity as a motionless point at the hub of the revolving wheel of life:

> At the still point of the turning world, Neither flesh nor
>   fleshless;
> Neither from nor towards; at the still point, there the dance is,
> But neither arrest nor movement. And do not call it fixity,
> Where past and future are gathered. Neither movement from nor
>   towards,
> Neither ascent nor decline. Except for the point, the still point,
> There would be no dance, and there is only the dance.
> I can only say, *there* we have been: but I cannot say where.
> And I cannot say, how long, for that is to place it in time.[17]

Life is like a watch that runs down and goes awry unless we are able to discover the mainspring which keeps it ticking. The source of the sense of the eternal, as opposed to the indigenous sense of time in general, may possibly have to do with an attempt to secure once and for all an order of meaning which does not corrode from the vicissitudes of continuing experience. It is the effort to find a set of temporal moorings which do not break apart in the surf and gales of changed circumstances or frustrated wishes.

The patterns of temporal significance which man imposes on his world are contingent by and large on his sensory apparatus. As Kant noted, our experience of the universe ultimately begins with the selection and organization of sensory inputs. Even certain beliefs or speculations about the "supersensible" (e.g., the notions of God) have their genesis in the contradictions of sense experiences, in the recognition that happiness, or sustained sensory satisfaction, very often escapes us, no matter how pure and blameless our moral character. Moreover, it is our very drive for sensory satisfaction which gives rise to the problem of time and frames the need for eternity. "Sensation is the function which is concerned primarily with that which is current and immediate."[18] But, as Kierkegaard pointed out, the immediate is that which, by definition, must be drowned in the relentless surge of events. Sensations never last. A satisfaction pursued must lapse as soon as it is attained. Devoid of time awareness, the consciousness of pain and suffering is not so acute, for the passing of a pleasant sensation is not necessarily followed by the feeling of regret, by a nostalgia for what has been lost, nor by a desire for a repetition of the experience. In the absence of any view to past or future, each sensory instant becomes sufficient unto itself. Alan Watts has poignantly written that "consciousness [of time] seems to be nature's ingenious mode of self-torture."[19] On the other hand, animals who do not possess the time sense in the measure that man does, are not afflicted by thwarted ambition or vanished satisfactions.

> They suffer and die, but they do not seem to make a "problem" of it. Their lives seem to have so few complications. They eat when they are hungry and sleep when they are tired, and instinct rather than anxiety seems to govern their few preparations for the future . . . every animal is so busy with what he is doing at the moment that it never enters his head to ask whether life has a meaning or a future. For the animal, happiness consists in enjoying life in the immediate present—not in the assurance that there is a whole future of joys ahead of him.[20]

The imperative for the life of pure sensation entails the *carpe diem* of Horace: "Even as we speak, Time, the churl, will have been running. Snatch the 'today,' and trust as little as possible to the 'tomorrow.'"[21] For every revel there is the sad awakening in the "morning after." Lovers at the crest of passion wistfully plead that "this moment will last forever." In order to preserve his peak sensations, man seeks to arrest time and thereby forestall the endless lapse into pain, to break the circle of desire, reward, and disenchantment.

Eternity manifests itself as the complete rupture of time, because all ultimate delights are gathered into it and there no longer lingers the threat of suffering and anguish. Traditionally, eternity has been associated with ecstasy—a profound rapture and magnification of sensation. In the ecstatic mode of consciousness the tenses of time melt into an undifferentiated present; a timeless mood which goes by the name of "joy" or "bliss" replaces the search for ever new delights.

Indeed, joy does want eternity, for it is the closure of time which makes true joy possible.

Every person's patterning of time reflects the rhythms of his sensory gratifications. His world has coherence so long as his projects now and then are realized, his thirsts quenched, his anticipated pleasures requited. "Sensory gratification," of course, includes not only the fulfillment of physical appetites, but the tangible satisfaction of one's artistic tastes, moral intentions, social goals, and so on. "Broken time" issues from lesions in a person's familiar pattern of gratification, when the expectation of rewards based on remembered successes is contradicted by certain experiences. The idea of eternity thus emerges as time repaired, as the limitations and impediments of sensory life transposed into the elation of steady enjoyment.

A number of cross-cultural studies by sociologists and anthropologists have revealed that the experience of time grows directly out of the social context in which work and opportunities for gratification are distributed. Researches concerning Jordanian and French children, for example, have demonstrated that teaching youngsters between the ages of five and ten how to defer immediate gratification for the sake of more distant rewards eventuated in a clearer concept of the future.[22] These findings recall the discoveries of Piaget that preschoolers, who are only beginning to learn how to restrain momentary wants, have little understanding of the meaning of "later." In comparison, investigations of perceptual habits among lower-class and underprivileged groups, who conspicuously are *not* achievement-oriented or career-minded, have suggested that such people are chronically incapable of imagining an open future.[23] These individuals seek only immediate gratification. The caricature of the blue-collar father who lavishes whatever income remains from his paycheck, once he has paid for food and rent, on a round of drinks at Paddy's Tavern may be overdrawn in many instances, but it does illustrate the lack of precaution or foreplanning which heavily colors the temporal orientation of men in such a situation.

At the religious level the class difference between those who put off the pleasure of today in anticipation of greater rewards tomorrow and those who rarely make provisions for a "rainy day" has been described in terms of their respective symbols of the divine. The sociologist Max Weber noted several generations ago that the poor and disinherited generally adhere to religious faiths which promise immediate, palpable benefits, rather than "deferred" salvation in the afterlife. Traditions such as Calvinism, which stress the eventual fruits of "election" on the other hand, appeal to upwardly mobile elements of the middle classes who cleave to belief in progress and personal self-improvement.[24] In a more recent analysis Gary Schwarz has explored the manner in which Pentecostalism, which slights the orthodox doctrine of a Last Judgement in its preoccupation with the immediate "gifts" of the Holy Spirit, draws its clientele primarily from the culture of poverty. But Seventh-Day Adventism, a sect which stresses the need for a secular "vocation" as well as the duty to "earn" redemption, is supported mainly by members of the middle class with upward ambitions.[25]

In all the above cases the sense of time seems to be generated by the culminative effect of the quest for gratification. Those who have a personal legacy of consistent achievement and fulfillment of their needs in proportion to their own efforts obtain a perspective on the future. A causal rhythm for one's actions, a sense of *quid pro quo,* is laid down and therefore can be projected into the future as a sequence of experiences likely to recur. In other words, one can expect to accomplish his ends by the evidence of past performances. An examination of the time-orientation among French peasants in the 1950s helps to corroborate this thesis. Two French sociologists contrasted the image of the future among city-dwellers with that of farmers in Normandy who participated in a vital *tradition* of collective memories and folk wisdom. The deracinated urbanites, having no living sense of a meaningful past continuous with their present lot, were unable to display a cohesive idea of a future over which they personally had control; while the peasant subjects were more confident about the shape of what lay beyond the temporal horizon by virtue of their rich memory of the history of their community.[26]

The modern industrial working classes, like other marginal groups displaced from both traditional agrarian culture and the success options of the affluent majorities (e.g., the unassimilated American ethnics in the big city slums), have never really acquired a viable image of the future and thereby are prone to a stifling mentality of "present-mindedness" or "catch as catch can." For such people, the time sense is constructed out of a chaotic consciousness of occasional gratifications interrupted for the most part by painful setbacks, fractured dreams, or unrelenting misery. Both past and future have little value and meaning for them, because there is nothing in their former lives to cherish, nothing about the tomorrow which appears promising. John Mander in his book *The Unrevolutionary Society* has given a profile of the *campesino,* the oppressed, landless, semi-colonialized rural worker of South America, who inhabits a precarious universe of malignant, unseen forces which can neither be prejudged or appeased (unlike the secure, magic-ritualistic world of his Indian forbear) and thus survives only by resort to a capricious hedonism and a refusal to look either to the mythical past of his native religion or the sanguine future revered by the high priests of modernization.[27] These "invisible" people who have not benefitted from either the substance or rhetoric of modern, technological progress are telling examples of how the disruption of man's search for sensory gratification telescopes the time sense into a narrow obsession with things current. Thomas Cottle and Stephen Klineberg have stated:

> Images of the future will motivate behavior when they generate feelings of anticipatory pleasure or discomfort. To the extent that people avoid painful experiences as best they can, they are likely to be oriented toward future events primarily when their anticipations are pleasurable.[28]

Underprivileged and sensorially deprived human beings must become fixed on the present because they have no precedent for putting off pleasures or even experiencing pleasure itself. "If emotional energies are absorbed in present experience, or deadened by fatigue, the future largely disappears from consciousness."[29] On the other hand, consistent sensory stimulation can broaden the time sense and allow man to live in various modes of experience. The image of eternity becomes a cipher for absent or lost forms of gratification. The eternal serves as a symbolic mode of gratification insofar as it entails a paradigm of temporal consistency unavailable within the sphere of mundane experience. The image of eternity varies according to the needs of an individual or culture.

THE ETERNITY OF BEGINNINGS

Mircea Eliade has called attention to the myth of sacred beginnings, common to archaic societies, which enshrines the theme of a vast eternity stretching backward and forward from the present time. Such an eternity embraces the timeless abode of the gods. It betokens a never changing pattern of events which becomes the paradigm for the conduct of all human affairs, the ultimate compass and ballast for "profane" existence. Religious man "refuses to live solely in what, in modern terms, is called the historical present; he attempts to regain a sacred time that, from one point of view, can be homologized to eternity."[30] Furthermore, Eliade discusses the ways in which the presence of eternity is felt by archaic humanity not only as a primeval abyss of "dream" time beyond the rim of memory but also as a perennial source of spiritual renewal and creativity.

> We here have collective rituals . . . [for which] the beneficiary is the whole community, including both the living and the dead. On the occasion of the representation of the myths the entire community is renewed; it rediscovers its "sources," relives its "origins."[31]

The symbol of the eternal in archaic societies thus performs two manifest functions. First, it gives structure and direction to the inchoate sense of temporal flow which passes beyond the frontiers of recorded experience. The lack of written documents, such as annals or chronicles, in preliterate cultures severely constricts the time continuum. The relative brevity of collective memory produces what Stephen Toulmin has called a natural "time barrier" beyond which events cannot be recollected, but only speculated about in myth.[32] Rifts in man's knowledge of the past or future are overcome through the vision of an undivided, timeless eon which extends in all directions toward infinity and thereby diminishes the fitful tempo of everyday occurrences by comparison.

Secondly, the immanence of an eternal order of life symbolized in the myth of the gods' great deeds "once upon a time" and made visible through ritual celebrations gives coherence to the shaky sense of time in agrarian societies where the life-bestowing forces of nature are quite often unreliable and the war for survival continues unabated. The "empirical" world furnishes no guarantees against precipitous calamities or sudden death. Drought, flood, or pestilence may prove the only compensation for the labors of the day. Gratification of man's most elemental aspirations may turn out to be as elusive as the spring rains which fail to arrive from one season to the next. The natural rhythms of time, therefore, even for those pre-technological peoples blessed with a temperate climate and protected from tribal enemies by favorable geography, are not necessarily as regular as the romantic idylls of their civilized counterparts may presume. The stories of the "eternal return" of the gods to earth during feast times become social and psychological necessities for archaic man who constantly lives in an aura of unseen forces and mysterious influences. The appearance of the *kachina* during the *shalako* festival at the Zuni Pueblo in New Mexico during late autumn serves to affirm symbolically the integrity and continuity of Pueblo culture. The fact that these guardian spirits appear at the "right" time annually in order to consecrate the villages and invigorate the plantings for the new year supplies "proof" to those who are perhaps anxious subconsciously about what tomorrow may have in store that the cosmos is congenial for its human denizens.[33]

Similarly, archeological and historical data on the Maya of the Yucatan Peninsula have revealed how this deceased culture contrived a marvelous and labyrinthine calendar designed, ironically, not to "tell time" in some disinterested and scientific fashion so much as to peer into the future, to estimate the prospects of good or ill fortune. For example, the Mayans envisaged time as a sort of "relay race" between divinities who were, in essence, cosmic "time bearers," each deity carrying on his shoulders the concrete character of the time interval which would affect human affairs at some point. One time-bearer would be responsible for a plentiful harvest, another for a devastating war, and so on. The "period" belonging to the time-bearer denoted the qualitative divisions of the Mayan calendar.[34] These cycles of time imagined in terms of the weal or woes of the ancient society were thought to have a "real" existence as manifestations of the eternal order of gods and men. In one important respect, the "eternity" of the Mayans was much more complicated than the simple mythical timelessness of other antique cultures, since it constituted a template for collective experience which took into account all socially relevant happenings rather than merely those events touching on the community's economic welfare. Yet it also epitomizes the groping of an early civilization for a way out of the bedevilling maze of sensory life. The procession of omens and divine augurs made time explicable and thus guarded against false expectations about the future, while making the past seem significant and repeatable.

Through the image of an eternal and immutable pattern for the universe (whether it be the *rita* of the ancient Vedic sages, the *moira* of the Greeks, or the mythical dramas of the birth and death of vegetation deities, such as Ishtar or Osiris), archaic man found a means to "stop" time in its meandering stream and to bring his temporal experience into alignment with his sensory requirements. The myth of the eternal return, however, could not suffice for all experiences, particularly when the onslaught of civilization gradually tore certain peoples from their simple, agricultural setting. A new image of eternity was mandatory for such a shift in conditions.

THE ETERNITY OF ENDINGS

The ascent of the great world civilizations, combined with the growth of urban centers during the first millennium before Christ, engendered a vastly different form of culture which left man less sensitive to the systole and diastole of the seasons and more conscious of the syncopated beat of his social history. Cities and empires rose and fell for reasons that had little to do with the sweep of the sun through the heavens or other diurnal changes. The triumphs and defeats of armies along with the expansion of commerce and culture established the rhythms of day-to-day experience.

Astrology, which tried to compute human events by fluctuations in the positions of the stars and planets, provides an example of how urban man was able to ascertain a new and more sophisticated basis for gauging time. Astrology took as its reference standard not the solar year, but the hypothetical "Great Year" which encompassed the duration it would take for all the heavenly bodies to return to their original locations in the sky. The Greek philosopher Plato in his *Republic* wrote of the cycles of decline in society from the golden age of peace and harmony to the iron age of anarchy which was based on astrological considerations. The same was true of the Stoic conception which allowed for a long process of composition and dissolution in the social and political life of the Roman Empire according to an intricate numerical formula derived from stellar observations. The idea of eternal recurrence was now elaborated as a kind of inalterable process which worked in the marrow of human civilization. The end of time would come when man had played out his noble part in the drama of world history.

Concomitantly, there developed in the Near East a conception of the eternal which paralleled, at least superficially, the cosmic fatalism of astrological speculation, yet which grounded the circle of time not in impersonal influences from above, but in the conflict between competing tendencies of the human soul. Such a conception added a radically new dimension to man's imagination of time, for it coupled the time sense with a set of moral presuppositions, with certain transcendent values. The origins of this image of the eternal are found in Persian Zoroastrianism, in the myth of the cosmic battle between the principle of good (Ahura-mazda) and the principle of evil (Ahriman) which will last until the end of the world when the former will emerge victorious and an everlasting age of peace and justice will arrive. Fused with the Hebrew prophecies of the "day of Yahweh," the judgement of the wicked, and the restoration of the fortunes of the righteous, is the image formed at the nucleus of Jewish and Christian messianism and apocalypticism. Time was represented as a contest between God's holy will and the demonic forces of the universe. The travail of men, whose immersion in time was viewed as the consequence of sin and corruption, whether by mortal or supernatural hands, would reach a climax and time itself would be abolished in the new heaven and new earth which God would inaugurate for the enjoyment of the saints.[35] The "eternity" of endings, therefore, is commensurate with the restitution of sacred beginnings, the "last' (*eschatos*) would mark the return of the "first" (*protos*) [Rev. 1:17]. The "first things," however, specifically connoted God's primordial relationship with man via an ethical compact or covenant. Whereas astral fatalism involved a highly sophisticated effort to unravel the mysteries of historical time and change with reference to natural phenomena, the messianic and apocalyptic cast of mind framed the meaning of temporality in terms of a quest for the humane society. The collective nostalgia for a lost paradise, for a moral order which had somehow slipped away because of man's shortcomings, became the foundation of a historical hope. The rupture of the traditional time sense fostered by the malaise of the new civilization was relieved through the dazzling notion of a divine purpose for human events.

In an important respect, the symbol of an eternity as the *fruition* of a moral struggle rested on the unique experiences of the Hebrew people dating back to Abraham, Moses, the Exodus, and the incorporating motifs of a chosen elite piloted by God's "promise."[36] All along the tortured "way" of their triumphs and tragedies since the close of the Second Millennium, the children of Israel had repeatedly been given signs or assurances of God's concern for them. The flight from Egypt, the subjugation of Canaan, the ascendancy of the Davidic monarchy, the liberation from Babylon—all these incidents served as beacons of confidence in the dark night of historical adversity. The endurance of God's people through time was comprehended as part of His master plan for their redemption. A pattern of meaningful temporal experience had been laid down, and the successive crises of the Israelite nation (for example, the Assyrian assaults, the fall of Jerusalem, the foreign occupations) were construed as historical interludes in which baneful elements were purged and the moral heart of the Hebrew faith reaffirmed. Once Israel fell victim to foreign invaders during the eighth century B.C. and the prospects of political independence appeared more and more out of grasp, the saga of salvation history was universalized to embrace the nature and destiny of the entire human race. The anonymous prophet named the Second Isaiah saw Israel's trials as a "light to the nations" which would be viewed with wonder by all the Gentiles. But the conviction of an imminent era of righteousness—the "kingdom of God" as it came to be called in later Christian theology—in which the time would come to a standstill persevered as the unique Hebraic contribution to man's endless pursuit of eternity.

There is, of course, in this connection a perspicuous difference between the image of eternity as the eschatological consummation of the moral struggle and the unilinear progressivism of modern thought. While the latter was born of the rational and technological spirit of middle class revolutions during the eighteenth and nineteenth centuries, which engendered a view of time contingent on the experience of rising affluence and cumulative scientific invention, the former implied a demand for the realization of certain absolute ethical norms. Modern progressivism had little need for the mood of eternity, because the value of material improvement required no strict definition, and the patent advances in man's sensible surroundings during the heyday of such an ideology were widespread enough to make the course of time seem even and unproblematic. On the other hand, the prophets and religious seers of the Ancient Near East perceived a deep contradiction between the everyday disposition of historical change and the divinely revealed goal of creation. Although they did not devalue history, they felt a great tension that persisted within it. Ordinary time—time in the sense of the regular meter of human intention and act—became unsatisfying to their uncompromising consciences and thus appeared "broken," punctuated by the power of evil. The eternity of endings furnished a form and structure to ordinary time that could not be easily described by the man of "flesh," the fallen creature entangled in his senses. The eternal appeared to lie beyond history, yet by the very fact that history was leading toward its arrival gave the experience of social time a coherence lacking in other world pictures. Astrology proved unsuitable to its task, since it ultimately could not explain the lawlessness and moral conflicts inherent in civilization. Nonetheless, there were many in the ancient world as well as today who yet did not find any meaning in history, including the Hebraic moral vision, adequate to the complexities of finite existence. The notion of an eternity at the conclusion of time, as the victory of God's holy will, required some immanent proof, some testament that the righteous would be rewarded in due course. The failure of both progressivism and apocalypticism very often emboldens a retreat from religious or philosophical interest in history. The order of eternity is believed to exist over and above the fearful ambiguities of time altogether.

THE ETERNITY OF ESCAPE

"Time," wrote the German mystic Meister Eckhart, "is what keeps the light from reaching us. There is no greater obstacle to God than time."[37] Indeed, the various forms of mystical rapture reported throughout religious traditions of mankind all share an abhorrence for temporal consciousness and an enchantment with the "eternal now" of ecstatic union with the divine center of the universe. The theologian Paul Tillich has written, "there is *one* power that surpasses the all-consuming power of time—the eternal."[38]

The Hindu sacred book, the *Bhagavad-Gita,* talks of "all-powerful time which destroys all things" and "slays" men,[39] as an illusion which must pale through right knowledge into the rapture of the timeless. In a similar vein Kierkegaard stressed "the infinite qualitative difference between time and eternity" and extolled the "moment" when religious man takes the leap of faith out of his temporal condition into an eternal encounter with his Maker. "Must not this also be taken into account, this little moment, brief as it may be—it need not be long, for it is a leap. However brief this momentum, if only an instantaneous now, this 'now' must be included in the reckoning."[40] For much of human religion time has no worth or significance. The antitemporal sentiment is entrenched not only in the Vedic spirituality of India, which denigrates the perceptible realm of change and becoming as *maya* or "illusion," but also in the Gnostic strands of Western thought and culture.

Gnosticism, originally a philosophy of radical world-denial emanating from Pythagorean metaphysics, Neo-Platonism and various occult schools, looked upon the empirical universe as the abode of pain, darkness, and wretchedness into which the human soul, a fragment of the divine *pleroma*, had fallen inadvertently. Imprisoned in time and bodily circumstances, the soul was enjoined by Gnostic teaching to flee the world of sense and return to its celestial "home." Henri-Charles Puech has analyzed Gnosticism as a "revolt" against all myths and belief systems which purport to give time some indwelling meaning. The Gnostics consider that "our temporal state is a monstrous amalgam of spirit and matter, of light and darkness, of the divine and the diabolical, a mixture which threatens our soul with infection and assails it with suffering and sin."[41] Since Gnosticism condemns the activity of the senses as the context of spiritual pollution, it finds no value in tangible life experiences and therefore sees time as a snare to salvation. Gnosticism is, of course, typical of both the ascetic and ahistorical mentality of certain "perfectionist" movements. The Gnostic imagination and its kindred world is among such religious groups as the Cathari of the Middle Ages, the Rosicrucians, the Theosophists, and the Christian Scientists, and flourishes whenever the eschatological orientation of traditional piety is either lacking or has faltered. For instance, Marcion, a well-known Gnostic of the early Christian era, ridiculed the historical God of the Old Testament as a perverse demiurge. The "mighty acts" of Yahweh vaunted by the ancient Hebrew writers were stripped of their historical significance and dismissed as sheer mischief and bungling. The same was true of the spiritualists, New Thought School, and Western Vedantists in the modern era who sought either to ignore or to allegorize the temporal language of the Bible and systematic theology. On this score, the Gnostic attitude had its *raison d'etre* in the experience of time's utter incoherence by those alienated from traditional modes of temporal symbolism. Periods of heavy social stress which render obsolete much conventional wisdom have commonly bred Gnostic speculation. In such periods time is disparaged as a ruthless, fickle despot who suppresses man's dignity and brings all his handiwork to ruin. Aldous Huxley's comments on the nature of time and eternity, set against the background of the jaded cynicism of the European intelligentsia between the two world wars, are illustrative of the Gnostic temper. In the last section of his novel *Time Must Have a Stop* Huxley calls for a rediscovery of the eternal in man:

> True religion concerns itself with the givenness of the timeless. An idolatrous religion is one in which time is substituted for eternity— either past time, in the form of a rigid tradition, or future time, in the form of Progress towards Utopia. And both are Molochs, both demand human sacrifice on an enormous scale.[42]

Man must forsake his preoccupation with temporal experience and rivet his sights on what lies on the far shore of life. For "it is only by deliberately paying our attention and our primary allegiance to eternity that we can prevent time from turning our lives into a pointless or diabolical foolery."[43]

The Gnostic complains that time in any form cannot satisfy man's most authentic desires. Eternity offers a sanctuary for those who wish to flee time altogether. Time winds up shattered irreparably. Man's sense-experience is incapable of salvage. Thus the Gnostic eternity of escape entails the recognition that only the erasure of time in its totality will yield happiness. The Gnostic admits no past or future; he lives solely in a coruscating present of his own desperate musings.

The Gnostic attitude has implanted itself in Western culture, and has survived, if not sharpened, well beyond the ancient world into the modern. We shall examine in the rest of this book the forms and variation of Gnosticism in its rebellion against life in time from beginnings through the current cultural tremors. Gnosticism's frantic wish to destroy time altogether and to secure a private and privileged eternity walled off from the contingencies of human existence represents a perennial challenge to civilization. While more a symptom of underlying malaise than an active contagion itself, Gnosticism remains formidable because of its power to capture the minds of intellectuals and other standard bearers of culture. The search for the eternal in one sense constitutes the natural metabolism of the human mind's interaction with the world. But when the search becomes an obsession, when it centers on the eternity of escape, then it begins to gnaw at the corporate bonds and institutions of human society. In the endeavor to stop time, man runs the risk of undercutting his relations with others; indeed, he threatens to stab to death his very humanity.

Chapter 2

Gnosticism and the Terror of History

History is a nightmare from which we struggle to awaken.
                                        —James Joyce

THE REVOLT AGAINST PROGRESS

Perhaps the greatest irony of the modern age is that its savants have alternately celebrated and trembled at the prospects of historical change. The idea of historical progress has been an article of faith for Western man at least since the Industrial Revolution. The historian J. B. Bury, who published his well-known book *The Idea of Progress* over a generation ago, wrote that "we now take [the idea of progress] for granted."[1] In the midst of the modern infatuation with progress there has slowly grown a counter-tradition, however, which most historians tend to overlook. Such a tradition denies the truth of progress and looks over and above human history for meaning and salvation. It is a tradition that the historian of religions Mircea Eliade has traced in the last chapter of his book *The Myth of the Eternal Return*, one that he designates as "archetypal" and "anhistorical."[2] The legacy of anhistorical thinking rejects the conventional wisdom that the present age is better than the past one and that future generations have ever cumulative blessings to enjoy. Instead, such thinking recoils from what Eliade terms the "terror of history." It cannot bear to stay with the course which human events seem to be taking.

Eliade has described the orthodoxy of the modern progressivist era as "historicism"—the doctrine that human happenings conform to a logic of their own which displaces the magnificent theodicies of the ancients,

23

the Judeo-Christian forms of "sacred history." Eliade writes that "from Hegel on, every effort is directed toward saving and conferring value on the historical event as such, the event in and for itself."[3] Over against the historicist mentality, however, can be posed the theme of *revolt against history,* a quest for metahistorical meaning which can be classified generally as "Gnosticism." The Gnosticism of modern culture, of course, must be construed in a wider context than the second century Christian heresy which bedevilled the Church fathers. For the Gnostics of the new age have set their face not against a moribund ecclesiastical establishment, but against the entire *saeculum,* against the triumphant pragmatism and egalitarianism which reckons time as linear function of social improvement.

The new Gnostics do, however, share a variety of religious and metaphysical presuppositions with their classical kin. Most important, as we have already mentioned, is their systematic aversion to the idea of progress. Integral to this break with a cohesive scheme of historical time, moreover, are (1) a preference for "cosmic insight" over empirical caution and scrutiny (2) a rejection of all providential myths of redemption, together with a recourse to elitist notions of self-salvation (3) an unabashed antiquarianism which looks to the occult wisdom of the past for inspiration and disparages the "modern" climate of opinion (4) a prepossession with the evil of the existing order, with the fatality of life in the present.[4]

We shall explore the Gnostic profile of man in the universe with respect to these key features. By and large the student of modern thought strands may quickly discover that Gnosticism has not faded with the passing of the centuries, but has attained an increased vitality. Many of us may discover that we are really Gnostics at heart, though the rhetoric has been modified and the earlier symbolism transmuted into a skein of images more congenial to the epoch of science and precise knowledge.

A. *Ecstasy and Secret Illumination.* The traditional Gnostic myth is built upon the motif of esoteric wisdom accessible only to the privileged or initiated few. This wisdom, or *gnosis,* entails an agonistic struggle with the ruling powers of the material world, a journey into forbidden territory in order to snatch away the elixir of eternal life. We find this theme conspicuous in the anonymous *Hymn of the Pearl.* The legendary apostle Judas Thomas, son of the mysterious "Queen of the East," lives in matchless wealth and splendor within an Indian royal family. For some unknown reason, however, the child is "sent away" by his parents from his sumptuous house and kingdom and forced to surrender his "glittering robe" and "purple toga" which were the signal marks of his former estate. But the parents leave him with a tempting promise:

> Should thou go down to the Land of Egypt
> And bring back the pearl centered in the sea
> Now surrounded by the hissing serpent,
> Then thou mayst put on thy glittering robe
> And thy toga again, laid over it,
> And with thy brother, who is our Second,
> Become Heir Presumptive in our Kingdom.[5]

The quest for the magical pearl, guarded by a snake at the bottom of the ocean, echoes the very ancient Babylonian epic of Gilgamesh. Yet, while the Gilgamesh epic harbors the lesson of man's inescapable finitude, the *Hymn of the Pearl* comprises a message of transcendence, the secret gateway to eternal knowledge. Judas locates the serpent, now described as a "dragon," and while waiting for the monster to fall asleep, he is joined by a stranger, another member of his "noble" clan "from the East," who admonishes him against giving himself away by his stately appearance to the Egyptians, the "Unclean ones," and allies of the serpent. Nonetheless, the Egyptians find out who the young prince is and foil his strategy. They give him some of their "own" food to eat, sinking him into a "coma of deep sleep" and making him forget his royal origin and mission. A pitiful amnesiac, Judas now adopts the vulgar manners of his captors, having finally traded his beautiful aristocratic raiments for the "filthy, unclean garb" of the Egyptians. But his parents endeavor to rescue him from his plight, and send an eagle courier carrying a "letter" to remind him of his previous commitment. On hearing the mysterious "voice" in the letter, Judas is roused from his stupor, and succeeds at last in obtaining the pearl by casting a spell on the dragon and putting it to sleep through the recitation of his "Father's name." Once in possession of the mysterious pearl, he returns to his homeland where he is given a hero's return and invested again with the superb clothing.

A rich complex of Gnostic elements are present here. The primary component, of course, is the pearl, the alluring gem of knowledge, which inexplicably has fallen into the custody of impure beings, but which rightfully belongs to the noble and illuminated ones. In the Gospels the pearl signifies the personal treasure which is the Kingdom of God (Matt. 13:46), but in Gnostic mythology and in other extra-Biblical literature it comes to represent a kind of magical talisman, an object suffused with great transformative power. Eliade, for example, has argued that the pearl is the "supreme Iranian symbol of the savior."[6] The "savior," however, in this instance, as in much Gnostic speculation, consists for the most part not in an historical messianic figure, but in an archetypal principle of enlightenment. The method of salvation for Gnosticism, therefore, does not involve struggle and suffering through time, the stance of faith as an act of trust in God's power to recover his fallen creation. The Gnostic instead demands an immediate glimpse of the inner workings of the cosmos, a decisive clue that deciphers the riddles of heaven and earth.

By the same token, we detect in the Gnostic myth revaluation of the Hebraic story of the first man's temptation, the desire of mere men to "be as gods" by partaking of the tree of the "knowledge of good and evil." In *The Hypostasis of the Archons,* an Egyptian Gnostic document, we read how the traditional story of man's disobedience toward God is reinterpreted as a universal conflict between "knowl-edge" *(gnosis)* and the dark "powers" *(exousia)* of the world, which bind the human soul in ignorance. The *Hypostasis* describes man as a stepchild of *Sophia* ("Wisdom") created according to the "model" of *aion,* the "imperishable" realm of eternity. On the other hand, it is neither God the Imperishable nor Sophia who actually is responsible in the making of man. On the contrary, the task is undertaken by the archons, the demonic powers who, because of their "weakness," entrap man in a material body and thus cut him off from his blessed origin. They place him in paradise and enjoin him against eating of the tree of knowledge. The prohibition, however, is viewed by the author of the text not as a holy command but as a malignant effort on the part of the inferior spirits to prevent Adam from having true communion with the High God, from gaining authentic *gnosis.*

Throughout the narrative there recurs the theme of the High God (the Imperishable) seeking to make Adam aware of His presence and the archons trying to thwart His aims. In order to make Adam deaf to the High God's call, the archons bring a "forgetfulness" over him and fashion a woman out of his body (as in the Biblical version) to distract him from spiritual pursuits. Nevertheless, the woman turns out to be a sort of "undercover" agent for the High God, who is charged with divulging to Adam the truth that has been withheld from him. The archons, undaunted, undertake to foul the woman's spiritual nature by having sexual intercourse with her body. But now the principle of feminine wisdom reappears in the form of the serpent, called the "Instructor," who tells the mortal pair to defy the prohibition of the archons and eat of the tree of knowledge. Alas, the woman, who by virtue of her bodily defilement has become wholly "fleshly," eats of the tree without understanding the real purpose of the deed, as is also the case with Adam. The man and woman thus fall victim irretrievably to the "curse" of the archons. "Their evil," the text says, "arose from their ignorance, and they recognized that they were naked of the spiritual,"[7] the implication being that the orthodox theological view of the violation of the command as "sin" must be regarded anew as the mindless failure to commit the act rightly in the first place. The serpent is not the Devil in disguise, but is actually an *incognito* savior. The serpent, like the human race, "has been under the curse of the powers until the perfect man should come."[8] The perfect man, of course, will be the Gnostic adept who cannot be tricked by the archons, unlike poor Adam, and will ultimately advance to the knowledge of good and evil. God, in truth, does not require man to defer to him all wisdom and power. The belief in divine inaccessibility is foisted on man perniciously by God's enemies. The God of *Genesis,* who comes to reprimand Adam and Eve after their transgression, is rudely caricatured in this tale as the "Arrogant archon" who opposes the will of the authentic heavenly father. The "terror of history," the woeful condition of man after having been driven from the garden, is not a trial that demands faith, but a diabolical hoax, an illusion which has ensnared the human creature and which can be overcome by recapturing the knowledge Adam forsook.

The genuine *pneumatic* ("Spirit-filled") personality, in his sorrow and distress, need only be reminded:

> Your soul came from the Above, from the Imperishable Light. Because of this, the powers will not be able to approach them, because of the spirit of truth which lives in them.[9]

Christian Gnosticism saw in Jesus the "type" of pneumatic man who came as a teacher and an exemplar, to show others the path to illumination.

The marvelous knowledge which Gnosticism proffered in ancient times bears a close affinity to the recondite revelation given to those who took part in the Hellenistic mystery cults. Saint Paul sets *gnosis* in apposition to *mysteria* (see I Cor. 13:2), the conventional term for the secret rites and teachings peculiar to numerous religious groups in the Roman empire. The genesis of Gnosticism in the pagan mystery religions remains a subject for scholarly dispute.[10] But it is probably safe to say that there exists a formal similarity between the ritual symbols of ecstasy incorporated into the mysteries and the more philosophically refined statements of Gnostic lore and learning. As C. K. Barrett has noted, "the object of the mystery cults was to secure salvation for men who were subject to moral and physical evil, dominated by Destiny, and unable by themselves to escape from the corruption that beset the material side of their nature."[11] The same sort of psychic therapy was available through Gnostic esotericism. Moreover, the mystery cults afforded their devotees the opportunity to erase the curse of mortality by direct encounter with the patron deity, or in many instances by actually undergoing an *apotheosis,* a transfiguration of human into divine.

The process of "initiation" in the mystery religions, therefore, had as its objective the liberation of the soul from its earthly and historical chains. Most likely the mystery rituals grew out of the fertility ceremonies of agricultural peoples who inhabited the lands around the Mediterranean. The emphasis on the dying and rising god, whose resurrection avails eternal life to the celebrant, would naturally have its proper beginning in certain vegetation rites.[12] However, the mystery cultists differed significantly from their primitive forbears, inasmuch as they gave exclusive attention to the personal experience of salvation. Myths and practices which in an earlier period had been intended as tokens of public, sympathetic magic were redesigned for private consumption, for inducing what in contemporary parlance has come to be known as "altered states of consciousness." Self-mutilation, trances, and the warping of ordinary sensory awareness all figured in the mysteries of Dionysus, Isis and Cybele. Yet the chief appeal of the mystery ceremony was probably its grant of clandestine entry into the divine presence. This entry in itself offered redemption. Thus the notion of *gnosis* as the primary mode of regeneration is ingredient as much in the mystery religions as in the major Gnostic schools.[13]

A characteristic Gnostic movement which points up the link with the mystery religions was Hermeticism. There is a fair quantity of evidence that Hermeticism had its beginnings in certain Egyptian cult practices and gradually was elevated to a more intellectual level. The cult passed from a simple mystery liturgy to a sophisticated world view. Hallucinogenic techniques mingled with Platonic and neo-Pythagorean philosophy to engender a highly elaborate syncretism that generated emotional excitement as well as obscure tangles of symbols and concepts. Cult observances, nonetheless, were downgraded with most of the activity concentrated on "personal religious experience."[14] The religious experience which the Hermetic participant underwent very probably comprised the stilling of sensory impressions, thereby fostering the illusion of having eliminated the vagaries of sense-knowledge for the sake of a dazzling and ecstatic vision of the whole, the semblance of the lowly being raised to God. "Stop the working of the bodily senses, and then will deity be born in you," the divine Hermes counsels his son Thoth in the *Corpus Hermeticum.*[15] *Gnosis* transcends mere *pistis,* the Platonic term for sense-awareness which in Christianity came to be understood as "mere faith." Faith preserves the distance between finite minds and their makers. However, it does not "ensure the happy end of those who have acquired [*gnosis*], namely to become God," as the *Poimandres* asserts.[16] Having become God through infinite knowledge, the Gnostic neutralizes the horror of time and change, the dread of constant mutability which Hermes laments:

> For [activity's] the name, O son, for just the thing that's going on,—
> that is becoming. And many things needs must forever be becoming;
> nay, rather, all things [must].[17]

Birth, death, and rebirth—all these are moments of all-devouring "time . . . [which] brings man to an end."[18]

Yet one can wash away the stain of time by the consciousness of "truth" that is to be discovered "in the eternal bodies only."[19] To become the most sublime of these "eternal bodies" is the vocation of *homo sapiens* who can no longer rest satisfied with a fleeting grasp of things in their ordinary forms. The highest, most unshakable knowledge saves, because thought and reality *sub specie aeternitatis* appear inseparable. As in the mystery cults, the effect in the devotee's mind of the theophany, his private audience with the deity, was to liberate the time-laden soul from brute destiny, from the arbitrary and seemingly insuperable rush of events. "I overcome fate; fate harkens to me," the profound Isis and mythical protégé of Hermes proclaims.[20] The mystical rapport of the believer with his blessed lord, whether it be the fabled Orpheus or the remote Ogdoad in Gnostic lore, carried with it spiritual transport that dissipated the terror of history. The individual himself through right intuition could actually transcend the plane of matter, bodily existence and suffering. The Gnostic and the follower of the mysteries refused to defer their lot to the inscrutable will of the Creator. Rather, creation and redemption were severed, the responsibility for the latter having been usurped by man himself. *Gnosis*, therefore, was always something more than simple wisdom; it amounted to a magical feat of the imagination whereby the individual achieved through privileged knowledge not only broader vistas of cognition but a new state of being.

B. *Aristocratic Shamanism*. The strata of magic in Gnostic thinking run deep and are numerous. Simon Magus, whom the Church has customarily identified with the Gnostic underground, was reputed far and wide in his time as a wonder worker and thaumaturge. The Hermetic tradition heavily appropriated magical beliefs and instruction. Hence, it is hardly surprising that medieval alchemy and Renaissance occultism harked back to this most venerable and versatile strain of Gnostic learning. Mesopotamian magical practice fused with Hellenistic speculation to generate the Mandaean school of Gnosticism. For example, in the Mandaean universe the "Word of God" passes from the spoken promise of the Almighty, as it is represented in the canonical Biblical material, to a palpable substance, a written character that can be sued for conjuration.[21]

The significance of magic in Gnosticism, of course, comes to light in reference to the classical anthropological distinction between magic and religion. Modern anthropology has defined magic as the control and manipulation of the unseen forces in nature by the omnicompetent primitive expert, whereas religion is the renunciation of human mastery in surrendering power to the superior gods, who now govern earthly affairs and must be *supplicated* for favors. In connection with the conflict between the early Church and its antagonists, we can see how the Gnostics bespeak a reassertion of the primitive thirst for autonomy in confronting the "principalities and powers," just as Christianity exhibits the tendency to dismiss magical knowledge as mere *hubris* and to preserve the assumption of man's absolute dependence on a supreme will and purpose. The *hubris* of Gnosticism, nevertheless, rested on an ethic of self-salvation which gave it a character divorced from the ritual magic central to many primitive agrarian communities. A comparison of Gnostic magic with kindred forms, therefore, draws us toward the shamanism of early hunting and gathering societies. The shaman type bears certain affinities with the lonely adept and power-seeker who fits the Gnostic syndrome.

Eliade has provided the most complete inventory of shamanism. The shaman *inter alia* can be designated by his obsessions and propensities for exotic experiences and "out of body" flights, by his unique gifts of acquiring direct access to the spirit world and rescuing helpless souls from the torments of demons, and finally by his ability to achieve emancipation from the horrors and impediments of life brought about because of human weakness.[22] As adjuncts to his otherworldly sojourning, the shaman was reputed to be able to work magic both in the upper and lower realms. His secret understanding of animals, plants, and even human behavior gave rise immediately to his capacity for managing the world around him, and he was usually awarded exalted status in the group for his talents and accomplishments.

The heroic individualism of shamanic magic crops up in the urban religious climate of Greece and Rome. Stucco reliefs found at the site of the Eleusinian mysteries depict the archetypal mystagogue Heracles rescuing Herione from the evil dragon of death. Another image has Ganymede, who represents the soul, being swept away to heaven on the wings of a divine eagle.[23] The eagle, of course, is a stock symbol in shamanistic lore; it signifies majestic power and the ability to soar far above the sublunary sphere, even to the distant abode of the divinities and spirits. In a sense, the eagle incarnates both the strength and wisdom of the shaman himself. The mysterious chanting and dancing of the shaman frequently is accompanied by donning the mask of a large bird, into which he is transformed in his own vision, a necessary preparation for becoming magically airborne.[24] Another hint of the shamanistic heritage is found in the old Aztec symbol of the eagle with a snake in its beak—again, the alliance of power and marvelous knowledge. Great bird figures recur in Gnostic mythology, an instance of which has already been mentioned with regard to the eagle messenger who carries the letter of enlightenment in the *Hymn of the Pearl*. One may also cite the following "monologue of the Soul" contained in a Mandaean text:

> Naked I was brought into the World,
>   and empty was I taken out of it.
> Empty was I taken out of it,
>   like a bird, which nothing accompanies.[25]

The magical power inherent in "soul travel" not only allows the shaman to reach the inaccessible regions of the spiritual, it also girds him for doing battle with the enemies of mankind, particularly death. Primitive shamans wrestle with, and finally vanquish, the forces of darkness that imperil the welfare of their brethren, as well as freeing deceased relatives from the toils of wicked supernatural beings.[26] Quite frequently the combat takes place in the underworld, as echoed in the Heracles-Herione motif and, no less remotely, in the saga of Orpheus and Eurydice. The descent of the neophyte into hell as part of the rites of the mystery cults, again, betrays this enduring theme. The shaman may also ascend to heaven to contend with malignant spirits of the air. Thus the Patristic theologian Irenaeus reported of Simon Magus: "Through the magic taught by him, he transmits knowledge of how to overcome the angels who created the world."[27]

The terror of history, for the Gnostic, is so overwhelming that only extreme self-reliance and self-transcendence are acknowledged as methods of redemption. The Gnostic has lost trust in what he terms the "alien God" who created the world to banish evil and break the cycle of time and change. Thus he fashions himself the monomaniacal magician who can outwit and outstrip even the lordly rulers of the upper universe. For this reason the Gnostic displays a prideful, patrician contempt for the unwashed and benighted commoners who possess neither his *gnosis* nor his mighty stature. They have acquiesced to time and fate. He, however, has learned to parry the blows of time's misfortunes and become sole arbiter of his own destiny.

The Gnostic, of course, cannot be classified straightaway as a descendant of primitive shamanism. Originally, shamanism, before it emerged as a general type in religious studies, was a very precise term indicating a particular technique of mind-control[28] developed among the aboriginal peoples of Siberia and the close vicinity. On the other hand, shamanistic symbolism and usage tends to find its way in varying degrees into the religious life of civilized man, and thus one can discern significant cultural and cognitive parallels between the different instances of the phenomenon. The object of the shaman's machinations is largely to secure personal power over all the elements of the cosmos without any assistance from higher agencies. For the shaman essentially can rely on no master but himself, since all the other spirits and beings are either impotent, indifferent, or mischievous. In a contemporary vein, one can detect many remnants of the age-old shamanic life-style in the utterances and escapades of Carlos Castaneda's Don Juan, the Yaqui Indian *brujo* or sorcerer. Don Juan testifies as to what is required of a "warrior," a mysterious expert in visions and the obscure arts who constantly contends, like traditional shamans, with the multifarious aspects and energies of the invisible world. By the same token, Don Juan urges the utter independence of the shaman, as he rebukes Castaneda for requesting "help" in his apprenticeship.[29] At the same time, the Gnostic "warrior" cannot solicit help against the forces of darkness, particularly death, which threaten him. These forces will consume him, as they will the shaman, if he fails to take measured and discreet steps. Hans Jonas has described the Gnostic attitude as intrinsically acosmic wherein we see "the self emerge in its utter solitude: the self is discovered by a break with the world."[30] The shaman and the Gnostic are estranged as selves from the cosmic order; they refuse to be consoled by the idea that things are in their right place. Instead they insist on control over all events, above and below.

The parallels between shamanism and Gnosticism notwithstanding, there still remains the plain anthropological evidence that the cultivation of the former was carried out within a prescribed framework of social institutions and traditions, whereas the latter may be implicated with the precarious world view of the alienated intelligentsia in the higher stages of civilization. The perpetuation of shamanistic behavior depends on the needs of certain prehistorical peoples for a resourceful leader with access to magical lore more reliable than the fund of conventional knowledge. The shaman's role is a socially legitimate and useful one in safeguarding the tribe against untoward disasters and uncalculated assaults of evil forces, such as plagues, famine, drought, floods, or enemy ambushes. The shaman may also use his magic to enchant animals for the hunt, or to invigorate the growth of food plants. The shaman's adversary stance against the invisible proprietors of the natural environment, therefore, is intended to mitigate the insecurity of his clansmen, much in the same way that scientific and technical experts today are charged with procuring "knowledge" for the sake of national survival. His office is sanctioned by the values of the collective, and the "mantle of power" which he wears can be transferred for the most part only with the consent of those whom he serves.

The Gnostic, though, has no ascribed social obligation. His "power" is mainly self-serving, and is usually set in opposition to the established definitions of right and privilege within his community, if he has a community at all which he can call his own. It is for this reason that one scholar has appropriately labeled Gnosticism a "religion of revolt."[31] Gnosticism consists in a rebellion not only against an oppressive and increasingly irrelevant structure of religious meaning, but also against an intolerable social and political system which the Gnostic, perhaps unconsciously, regards as the source of his spiritual discomfort. This relationship between Gnostic heterodoxy and social disenfranchisement may be confirmed not only by the fact that his religion finds its greatest appeal during periods of political corruption and the loss of coherent authority, as in the anarchy of Hellenistic times and the later phases of Rome's decline, but also by the tendency of Gnostic morality to be deviant and frequently antinomian. St. Paul, for example, writes to the Corinthians that "it is actually reported that there is immorality among you, and of a kind that is not found even among pagans . . ." (I Cor. 5:1, RSV). There is a link between this alleged immorality and Gnostic attitudes in the apostle's condemnation of *gnosis* (8:1). Thus the Gnostic attempts to execute through self-will a truly Nietzschean "transvaluation of all values," to realize for himself a set of moral standards which expresses his craving for absolute power over the gods and over his fellow men, lest they should distract him from his purpose.

In substance, Gnosticism reflects the claims of the lonely aristocrat *manqué*. He is the person who "knows" what he feels others are too ignorant to comprehend, what affords him singular opportunity for mastery and for sovereignty otherwise denied to him. One finds the basic Gnostic attitude, for example, in the ravings of the Marquis de Sade, who excused his license to dominate and torture on grounds that he alone understood the "awful" secret about nature requiring blood sacrifices. De Sade's *gnosis* constituted a furious protest against the "reason" and "sensibility" of the Enlightenment which gave rise to the French Revolution and stripped him of his social power in the name of liberty, equality, and fraternity. We uncover a similar sentiment, albeit slightly less malevolent, in the maxims of that arch-Gnostic of the nineteenth century, Nietzsche himself:

> Let everyone . . . talk about generalities, concern for others and for society, out of his mind! . . . I want more; I am no seeker. I want to create my own sun for myself.[32]

Indeed, the Gnostic does "want more." He is the aristocratic shaman weaving with his erudite symbols and fantastic *arcana* a magic spell of words which lends him power over his ill-defined combatants. His "sun" is the ganglion of radiant energy, his inflated self. That is why we find at the hub of all Gnostic speculation the irrepressible mythologem —the unrecognized messiah who is one's own will power.

Scholarly investigations of ancient Gnosticism have focused on the presence of an underlying myth of the "Redeemed Redeemer," the Primal Man who rescues himself through right knowledge from his abased, worldly condition and who returns surreptitiously time and time again to illuminate by his teaching the identical path for each soul to traverse. Regardless of the source of this myth, or whether it can be demonstrated to exist at all apart from later Gnostic efforts to cast the figure of Jesus in such a light,[33] the kernel of such a motif consists in the idea of the soul as its own liberator. Walter Schmithals argues that such an idea is tantamount to the "philosophical" distillation of whatever mythical trappings may have become attached to the Gnostic message. The *real* Gnostic gospel turns on the radical concept that the highest "power" *(dynamis)* of the universe is "placed in *every* man as potentiality,"[34] and that the goal of life is to actualize this potentiality with commitment and passion. The knowledge of God, therefore, becomes at once the power of God, for every man has God within him. Every man *is* God, but often fails to apprehend this formidable truth. Once a person seizes hold of this truth, he will become like the serpent, the incarnation of divine wisdom and *might*. The Gnostic disavows the way of faith, for faith implies the renunciation of power, the abdication of magical self-mastery in compliance with the awesome design of Providence. But Providence decrees an order and meaning to life which the Gnostic cannot reconcile with his own magnified wishes. Thus he turns against all gods who are "wholly Other." The Gnostic narcissistically bends the claims of the Other to his own desires.

C. *Contempt for "Modernity"*. The Gnostic's metaphysical allergy to Providence and to history, which in his mind is nothing more than a tyranny of indifferent actions and forces, shows up in his deep-felt disdain for all things current and "modern." The nostalgia of the Gnostic for paradise lost, for a felicitous and unperturbed state of human existence in which man had the chance for "perfect knowledge" but unfortunately let it slip beyond him, underscored his unease with the world as it has developed into the present. We can ascertain this doubt, if not cynicism, concerning the meaning of time in its perceived course by comparing the Gnostic interpretation of the Fall with the normative Judeo-Christian version. For the Gnostic, Creation itself was a mischance on the part of some incompetent demiurge, and the exile of man from the garden came about only through the intervention of inferior spirits who mischievously seduced the new innocent creature away from consciousness of his sublime origin. Time and exile, therefore, are merely the result of a grand hoax or delusion which can be suspended at any moment that fallen humanity awakes to his more noble calling; for man's predicament is essentially an unhappy and unjust incarceration in matter, not punishment for some fatal infirmity or sin. From the Jewish and Christian vantage point, however, the loss of paradise somehow fits mysteriously into God's plan for history. The past cannot be recovered, if indeed that was ever God's intention. Rather, the lessons of the past give hint ultimately of God's future scheme for salvation. The cherubim guard the gates of Eden with flaming swords for perpetuity, yet the portals to the new heaven and new earth are not closed. Admission through them awaits the fullness of time at God's behest.

The Gnostic glories in man's primordial estate and condemns all that has befallen him since then as absurd misery and folly. The Gnostic's engrossment with elaborate descriptions of the heavenly hierarchies and with complex cosmogonies reveals his primary interest in what has been real from the very beginning and untouched by the terror of history. His antiquarianism, his feeling that the authentic meaning of life was somehow forgotten long ago, manifests itself in his lack of concern with the concrete experiences of his contemporaries, who have little to gain by trusting in God's promise of eventual salvation. As H. C. Puech puts it, the acquisition of *gnosis* "shatters history into bits."[35] The anachronistic attitude of the Gnostic may be due, in part, to his thorough disillusionment with theologies of redemption in history as prescribed within the ideology of the social and religious community to which he at least nominally belongs. Robert Grant has proposed that Gnosticism gained currency in Jewish and Christian quarters with the failure of apocalyptic expectations as to the imminent justice of God, when the social upheavals and defeats of the second and third centuries led many to discard their "faith in a genuine historical future."[36] The apocalyptic writers themselves had shared with the Gnostics the sense of gloom concerning the prospects for better days. Like the Gnostics they believed the universe had become so corrupt and man so refractory that no hope for progress in time was any longer plausible. Only the dramatic interruption of time by a divinely wrought disaster could possibly turn the torrent of events around. In other words, apocalypticism gambled all its stakes on an end to the world which seemed close at hand. When the end did not materialize, the apocalyptic imagination was forced to confront the dreadful specter of history without any redemptive significance. The Judeo-Christian mind, in this case, turned to the timeless mysteries of Greece or to the Oriental theosophy that filtered through Alexandria. The antihistorical temper, regardless of its cultic origins, came to the fore with an immersion in the romantic and mystical eternity of beginnings.

The retrospective reach of Gnostic theory passes beyond mere anachronistic or antiquarian worship of dead peoples and cultures, and becomes in the long run a flight from time altogether. The wish of the Gnostic to annihilate time and history reveals itself boldly in his proclivity for ornate mythologies and metaphysical systems which suggest the vastness of space. For the Gnostic, the horizontal time dimension of human experience is rendered trivial, and in its place is substituted the spatial metaphor of the "ladder to heaven," the vertical route of the soul's escape from the mire of mundane existence through intermediate spheres to the *unio mystica* with the Godhead. The saga of salvation, which for the ancient Hebraic as well as modern progressivist mind is played out over time as part of the social and moral biography of the human race, translates in the Gnostic scheme into an ahistorical ascension of the individual, stripped of his generic and material limitations, from one cosmic level of reality to the higher. The upward path of redemption, traversing myriad planes and tiers of the great palladium of heaven, constitutes a caricature of Christian "sacred history." Gnosticism converts temporal categories into spatial ones. The Judaic Genesis myth commemorates the conquest of the primeval chaos by the word of God, the dispersion of darkness by light as the first stage in the temporal formation of the world. "And God said, 'Let there be light'; and there was light."(Gen. 1:3, RSV). Gnosticism, though, draws the boundary between the divine and the created orders in terms of their location in space. The darkness has not been dispelled, but eternally envelops the inferior realms of being, the layers of flesh and matter. The "moments" of creation do not represent points of transition from the "old" world to the "new," but rather signify grades of spiritual perfection. Theologically, these degrees of perfection are pictured as "emanations" of the mysterious High God, the hierarchy of elements in the universe according to their distance from, and reflection of, the transcendent source of life. The principal emanations are what the ancient Gnostics called *aeons* (literally "ages" or "eternities"). The *aeons* are reified as entities in space, as the chief features of the great cosmic map for which events in time are only pale and illusory likenesses.

The transposition of temporal categories into spatial metaphors is seen in the following passage from the Hermetic literature:

> Of Aeons, Powers, Intelligences, Gods, Angels, Spirits Delegate, Existing Non-existences, Generated Ingenerables . . . Years, Months, Days, Hours,—of [the] Boundless Point, from which the most minute begins to increase by parts.[37]

The Gnostic regards the cosmos as a fixed structure in which aggregate change is impossible. He incorporates into his system the doctrine of astral fatalism. The planets govern the destinies of men; the "powers" and "intelligences" are the impassible directors of what occurs below. Time on earth merely manifests the rigid pattern and rhythms of life which ultimately derive from the motions of the stars and the unfathomable decrees of supernal beings. The only occasion for the soul to unsnarl itself from the tight warp and woof of fortune is to rise above the labyrinthine universe entirely, by wending its way through the cosmic labyrinth of "principalities and powers" and relying on deceit and subterfuge when necessary. In some Gnostic schools the soul is portrayed as having to outwit the agents of fate, who stand as sentinels before the highest heavens, through the utterance of a magic password.[38] The Gnostic cannot trust in the God of history to aid him in his contest with his demonic foes. He cannot await the restoration of all things in time. The Gnostic must abolish history himself in order to assert his own dominion over the forces of destiny.

D. *The Stain of Evil*. A leading factor in the Gnostic's eschewal of the idea of temporal progress was perhaps his conviction that man cannot improve himself morally or physically. Life in the flesh is irremediably corrupt. The creation of corporeal beings was a fetid mistake, an "abortion," as some Gnostic literature indecorously describes the origin of the visible universe. God does not lay a code of strict moral precepts on man, nor does he guarantee eternal bliss for those who obey his commandments. For the Gnostic understands it is not virtue, but proficiency in magic, which bears the promise of reward. The terror of history is laid bare in the very randomness and *amorality* of historical events. Christian theologians and apologists such as Augustine and Clement of Alexandria affirmed, in contrast with Gnosticism, a moral meaning to history, wherein the fact of evil could be interpreted as having teleological significance, as God's "scourge" for those who transgressed his order, or as a "goad" for the faithful to redouble their devotion to the divine will. Consent to such an interpretation, however, required a virtual sacrifice of the intellect, a surrender of certainty along with the privileged knowledge of the whys and wherefores of suffering, which the Gnostic was disinclined to do. Since the Gnostic refused to place his life in the hands of another, he could scarcely accede to the view that evil had a higher significance than he might care to admit. Faced with the conflict between his own moral preferences and the stark realities of his world, the Gnostic fell back upon the kind of maxim exemplified in the motto of the trolls of Henrik Ibsen's *Peer Gynt:* "To your own self be enough." Outward constraints of morality limit the hegemony of the self. That is why perhaps the Gnostics tended to revile all moral authority as inherently evil, as shown in their preoccupation with extremes of conduct, including both rigid asceticism and sexual license, together with the worship in some circles of certain "disreputable" or demonic figures. For example, many Gnostic sects rehabilitated the serpent, satanized by Christianity as the Tempter, and made him into a cult object. There was also a band of Gnostics called the Cainites who claimed fealty to the mythical first murderer as their proud minion of the "transvaluation of values." The Gnostic theme of the veneration of Cain crops up in the twentieth century, interestingly enough, in Herman Hesse's popular novel *Demian*. Demian, the shadowy *Doppelgänger* of the novel's central character Sinclair, carries "marks of Cain" and represents, in essence, throughout the book the unconscious will in man to defy polite society and to practice an alternative morality, which may even involve the "crime" of killing. It is therefore quite significant that Demian's own tutelary deity turns out to be the obscure Gnostic god Abraxas, the worker of magic and dispenser of personal power which admits no customary distinction between good and evil.

Because of their distaste for conventional morality, the Gnostics harbored a fascination with evil, even though their garish metaphysics demanded that the "wicked" world into which the soul has been cast be renounced for the sake of a higher calling. It is this ambivalence toward evil—a perennial attitude embodied in what might be called the "culture of decadence"—which lies behind the two faces of Gnosticism, its insistence on spiritual purity alongside its indifference to an ethical regimen. In the same camp with philosophically sophisticated adepts there dwell rakes and wastrels, some of whom dabbled in the black arts. As W. E. G. Floyd has remarked in his excellent study of the conflict between Gnosticism and the Christian moral theology of Clement, "the concepts of a pact with the Devil, of night-riding to the Sabbath, of *incubi* and *succubi* and the other details of popular witchcraft . . . were not without their counterparts in second-century Alexandria,"[39] the holy city of ancient Gnosticism.

From a psychological standpoint Gnosticism's obsession with evil, at once leaning toward a self-conscious profligacy as well as a radical world-denial, may arise from its utter depreciation of the experience of the senses. The ancient Gnostic's dualistic cosmology drawn from Persian and Greek sources conduced to the notion that the material universe, to which man is tragically bound by his body, submerges the soul in a quagmire of confusion and spiritual darkness. By the same token, the Gnostic's antipathy toward "nature"—all that encompasses man's external environment—can be understood in light of his utter disillusionment and finite existence and the pursuit of limited goals in time and space. The Gnostic is fundamentally a "nihilist," an individual who fails to perceive any coherent scheme of values in the world where he lives and who behaves, therefore, as if he were constrained by no final moral obligations. Void of any inner moral significance, the empirical universe appears to the Gnostic as a gloomy cavern in which lurk menacing and powerful forces. Thus "a world degraded to a power system can only be overcome through power."[40] It is the mystique of raw power, of the lone hero struggling by whatever means are at his disposal against terrifying odds, that informs the Gnostic vision. The "irrationality" of Gnostic mythology and ethics derives from its abandonment of all canons of common sense, of temporal wisdom fortified by practical experience. For to compromise with the ways of the world is only a pitfall that will lead to destruction.

Although one may detect a superficial parallel between the Gnostic attitude and the transcendental perspective of many of the world's great religions, the bald fact is that Gnosticism does not reject the existing order of things in the name of a universal evangel of salvation. Only *some,* according to Gnostic writings, are gifted with the knowledge and power to control their destinies. The remainder of mankind who do not belong to "the tribe of souls" (as the Mandaeans dubbed the elect) are damned as inferior creatures who pose hidden, but profound threats to the anointed ones. The difference between the major religious traditions and Gnosticism hence lies in the latter's consignment of the human multitudes to the status of contemptible underlings, not so much by virtue of their moral knavery as because of their participation in inferior matter. The Manicheans, for example, taught that the world is an arena of combat between "good" and "evil" souls who can be esteemed only in accord with their given "natures." The "purification" of the good souls involved the suppression of the unsound elements in the human race.[41] Thus, in a world where the conflict between good and evil takes place at a purely physical, rather than moral level, there can be no genuine historical progress in the sense of a complete transformation of human personality and society, only the necessary elimination of the enemies of the elite. For this reason it is tempting to see an echo of what might be called the "paranoid" mind-set of Gnosticism in the Nazi theories of racial superiority, especially in the latter's belief that the redemption of man requires a purging of "subhuman" species. The fierce anti-Jewish polemics of ancient Gnosticism cannot be divorced altogether from the systematic anti-Semitism of the Third Reich. Despite the fact that the Nazis, unlike their early Gnostic forbears, conjured up pseudoscientific racist principles as the mainstay of their program of extermination, the inexorable division of humanity into "clean" and "unclean" generic types served as a common point of departure. The "superman" motif, evident in both mythologies, underscores the Gnostic's adamant resistance to the idea of historical progress. Such resistance rests largely on his belief that human beings have only the talents they are born with to salvage themselves as they drift along willy-nilly in an evil cosmos.

THE SOCIAL ROOTS OF THE GNOSTIC ATTITUDE

Gnostic individualism and aristocratic *hauteur* supply a few meagre clues to the social origins of the movement. While little firm evidence has been adduced to date concerning the relationship between the Gnostic world view and changes in the social system throughout Western history, we may assume that Gnosticism found its greatest appeal among the upper ranks of society, particularly within the conventicles of the disinherited nobility.[42] The aristocratic symbolism of the Gnostic cultus has already been noted. The Gnostic's segregation of mankind at the "spiritual" level into the thoroughbred or highborn on the one hand and the vulgar horde on the other betrays not only an intellectual exclusivity, but also an undercurrent of social prejudice for the proper peerage. The attitude of fear and contempt for "ordinary" humanity may be taken, therefore, as a lightly veiled ideology of a distinct class of people. The terror of history in the Gnostic systems may very well mirror the enduring anxiety among members of a ruling class in decline about the future of their positions in society, which threaten to be engulfed by the tides of the anarchical or revolutionary masses. Certainly the class conflicts in the later phase of the Roman empire's dissolution contributed to the Gnostic malaise, and it has always been during periods of widespread social ferment and upheaval throughout the evolution of European culture that the various mutations of Gnostic thinking have emerged. Gnosticism is a phenomenon that encompasses numerous collective groupings and interests, and it is for this reason perhaps that one finds it difficult to speak of a "Gnostic" social type. However, one must look first to the general condition of "decadence," the indulgence by those who have lost their socially useful or recognized functions (e.g., impoverished nobility, ruined merchants, defrocked priests, the alienated intelligentsia) in the aberrant philosophies, religious practices, and moral behavior. In short, Gnosticism would appear to draw its clientele from what might be called the *lumpen* aristocracy—persons who share the elitist pretensions of those with power and influence, yet who, perhaps because of their loss of social prestige due to economic troubles together with their high degree of learning, have set themselves at odds with the prevailing system of rule and authority.

Such a social profile of the Gnostic, of course, becomes more tentative and speculative the farther back before the modern era we go. Nonetheless, there exist certain basic clues as to this supposition, not the least of which is the very language of the Gnostic theologies. Esotericism historically has been the property neither of the toiling commoners nor the administrative classes, but rather of the free-floating intellectuals, the displaced descendants of once important rulers who now demand their prerogative in the realm of the spirit if no longer in temporal might and title. It is a consequence of the situation, described by Max Weber some time ago, wherein classes of high social privilege relinquish their political role and turn to a subtle intellectualism that forms the basis for the rise of "salvation cults." According to Weber,

> The Near Eastern salvation religions, whether of a mystagogic or prophetic type, as well as the oriental and Hellenistic salvation doctrines . . . were, insofar as they included the socially privileged classes at all, virtually without exception the consequence of the educated classes' enforced or voluntary loss of political influence and participation.[43]

The end of social and political preeminence is compensated by the rise of "illumination mysticism . . . which is associated with a distinctively intellectual qualification for salvation."[44] And it was, most notably, "in Gnosticism and its related cults [that] the intellectualist religion took the form of mystagogy, with a hierarchy of sanctifications which the unilluminated were excluded from attaining."[45]

In a word, Gnosticism represents an ideology peculiar to the latter stages in the demise of the ruling classes throughout history. A social elite gradually surrenders its leadership functions and devotes its energies to letters and learning, thus becoming enclaves of intellectual endeavors, their painful isolation from the culture of the masses leading to a self-enforced pariah mentality, expressed in both their contempt for legitimate authority and their creation of a closed symbolic universe which only those with the proper credentials can penetrate. The interest of such a group in occultism and the safekeeping of magical lore reflects a vicarious exercise of power which in reality has slipped away from them. Similarly, the radical individualism of the Gnostic betrays his profound alienation from all common life, a life which on the metaphysical plane at least he feels capable of renouncing and relegating to the abyss of spiritual depravity.

The key to the beginnings of ancient Gnosticism and its subsequent diffusion throughout the culture of the Occident probably lies in the peculiar social and historical circumstances surrounding the establishment of the earliest home of that set of traditions in Hellenistic Egypt. Researchers have long ascribed Egyptian influences, particularly in the use of the names of obscure gods and magical incantations, to ancient Gnosticism. The Hermetic literature is perhaps the most telling instance of Gnostic texts colored and inspired by Egyptian mythology and attitudes. However, the concrete mise-en-scène of the Gnostic movement has barely been explored. This omission may very well have to do with the fact that the early Gnostics themselves, as sequestered intellectuals or cultists, were markedly indifferent to temporal affairs and therefore were occupied in their writing solely with the topography of the spiritual world. They were only concerned with (to employ a recent neologism) their own "psychobiographies," which involved the attainment of diverse "altered states of consciousness," even though the Gnostic, of course, was not equipped as we moderns to distinguish between the purely psychological and the ontological, between inner and outer objects of experience. At all events, historical inquiry can provide some relatively trustworthy indicators for the social context of the rise of Gnosticism on the Eastern fringes of Graeco-Roman civilization with Egypt as a central case in point. One must look, first of all, to the city of Alexandria, site of advanced educational institutions and a cynosure for scholars throughout the Mediterranean. Within the mingling of nationalities, social classes, and philosophical and religious schools that made their way into this new city, built to honor the majesty of Alexander of Macedon himself, sprouted the crucial stalks of Gnostic speculation. The novel, syncretic, and antitraditional character of Gnostic thinking thus reflected the various cultural alloys that were poured year after year out of the great retort of peoples and customs in this part of the world.

Upper Egypt under the Ptolemaic dynasty that preceded the coming of the Romans was never a social or cultural unity, despite the ironfisted regime that oversaw state matters. The settlers who flowed into Egypt after Alexander's conquests rapidly formed the bone and sinews of a semi-colonial aristocracy, who both despised and persecuted the native population. The Ptolemies' patronage of learning in establishing a magnificent library at Alexandria and subsidizing academic careers only served to heighten irresolvable class tensions. On the whole, the fruits of education went only to the members of the foreign ruling class, and the ascendancy of Greek high culture, or what was known as "Hellenism," had meaning only for a certain ethnic group, from which the vast multitudes were excluded. In consequence, Hellenism in Egypt was, according to one historian, "little more than an upper crust imposed upon an immemorial culture fundamentally alien."[46]

The cultural and intellectual dominance of the Greek colonials, nevertheless, was ultimately buttressed by ruthless political oppression, involving the seizure of peasant lands and a crushing system of taxation. Exploitation led to resentment among the lower classes, sometimes issuing in rebellion, while the unstable political climate fostered the typical colonial ideology of the masses as unwashed and untutored barbarians who needed to be "civilized." The scornful picture of the "Egyptians" in the *Hymn of the Pearl* may very well echo the general feeling of the Alexandrian nobility.

At the same time, the chaotic social organization of Egypt gradually contributed throughout the later Greek and early Roman periods to a decline in the real power of the aristocracy. The sapping of economic wealth from the countryside through taxation and the extortion of public services by the government from the small landowners (a practice called "the liturgical system") first ruined the poor, but eventually pauperized the gentry and undermined the entire structure of social control just as a similar set of conditions brought the greater Roman empire to collapse several centuries thereafter. The forfeiture of political and economic function by the lesser nobility meant in many cases the absence of any genuine distinction between the identity of the light-skinned Hellene and the darker Egyptian. The result was much like what typically happens with the decay of a once sovereign ruling elite which finds itself engulfed by the growing presence of the peoples whom it used to keep in subjection, as occurred among the descendants of white plantation owners in the American South following Reconstruction, or among the Russian intelligentsia in the late nineteenth century. There arose a deeply rooted attitude of ambivalence toward both the new order and the social elements which had come to prevail therein, an attitude represented both in "underground" literature (in which the Gnostic tracts for the most part consisted) and, less directly, in the official cultus. On the one hand, the vitiated culture of the nobility fused with native piety and superstition, creating an Egyptianized Hellenism that combined abstruse Platonic ideas and indigenous occultism.[47] The eclectic character of Alexandrian learning itself, stemming from the fact that the educational centers of Egypt had long been an import house for all sorts of intellectual traditions, supplied a cast for this process of symbolic synthesis, and the by-products were the various unstable amalgams that have earned the broader level of Gnosticism. On the other hand, the carriers of Gnostic culture were themselves diehards in allowing the trend toward social levelling and cultural assimilation to go so far as to deny their self-convinced role of preeminence in the world they had inherited. Their practical alliance with popular lore, with magic and mystagogy, was exploited in order to assert their privileged offices as bearers of secret wisdom and power, and the shamanistic and chthonic undertones to what strangely and unmistakably appears as a faction of urban illuminati can be traced to this state of affairs. The contempt for, and exclusion of, common humanity in the Gnostic circle of the informed derives at the same time from perhaps their obsessive fear that their power will be usurped. There can be detected, for example, in the Gnostic's image of the "fall" of humanity, in his notion of an undivided spiritual substance sunk in the multiplicity and anarchy of sense experience, his concealed dread of contamination by the great unnumbered who teem outside his inner refuge.

In this respect, the Gnostic denies any moral or eschatological meaning in history. Horrified by the tempest of history itself, he seizes upon the primitive sense of evil as an impersonal material force which strikes all men regardless of their moral qualities. He looks upon his suffering, not as retribution for his own misdeeds or as a trial of faith, but as the effect of "pollution" by gross factors in his environment. This atavistic conception of evil confirms the Gnostic in his theoretical posture of nihilism, while at the same time exempts him from any conscientious concern with his role in society or his ethical obligations to humanity. History, as the ebb and flow in the fortunes of peoples, becomes irrelevant to his own singular objectives which involve a symbolic flight from responsibility to the world. The human race is conjured up in his imagination as a stupendous horde of faceless demons who must be expurgated.

Going away from ancient times and into the dawn of European civilization, we find the same psychological and sociological conditions for the growth of Gnosticism. What Norman Cohn has dubbed the "heresy of the free spirit" in the High Middle Ages fits a similar pattern. Repudiating all forms of conventional authority, especially the Roman Catholic curia, the Brethren of the Free Spirit or *cathari* ("the pure ones") were a far-spread company of mystical anarchists. Like the Gnostics of old, they believed in the perfection of their own souls as hidden vessels of divine illumination, and thus they considered public morality to have no value for them. And like the Christian Gnostics of the second and third centuries, they held doggedly to the idea that the message of salvation contained in the stories about Jesus meant specifically the call by God to each individual to redeem himself through his own inner experiences. According to Cohn, this revived Gnosticism "appealed not to the uprooted and disoriented poor but to people who had other less compelling reasons to feel disoriented and frustrated—to women, and particularly to unmarried women and widows in the upper strata of urban society." It was this culturally uprooted class of persons (who, in the medieval case, were aristocratic women, bereft of their traditional function as consort rulers in an outworn, patriarchal, and feudal society) that "often longed as intensely as the masses of the poor for some saviour, some holy man with whose help they would attain a superiority as absolute as their present abasement."[48] The same was probably true of many priests, dislodged by new social circumstances and scorned as renegades in the eyes of the ecclesiastical establishment. According to Cohn, these groups and others did not coalesce into a well-defined movement, but helped formulate a body of "quasi-religious," esoteric doctrine with roots in earlier Gnosticism passed on from generation to generation, which seems to have outlasted even the Free Spirit heresy itself, at least under its medieval guise.[49]

The rebirth of Gnosticism in the late Middle Ages at the upper echelons of society carries through into the Renaissance and ultimately the modern period. Although the course of Gnostic development in this period is difficult to trace accurately because of the paucity of sources as well as the suppression by the Church of deviant philosophies, there appear from time to time startling new examples of the ancient teachings. The Italian philosopher Marsilio Ficino, for example, practiced Hermetic magic in a tight little circle of aristocrats with the aim of developing the latent powers of the "soul." Ironically, the origins of modern science, whose empirical methods became the *bête noire* of nineteenth-century Gnostics, can be associated with the anti-traditionalism and irrationalism that flourished in Counter-Reformation Europe. One may cite, for instance, the vitalist philosophies of Campanella and Giordano Bruno, not to mention the influences of alchemical thought on the "father" of modern experimental science, Francis Bacon. Similarly, the spread of "secret societies" along with various mystical and cabbalistic cults in the sixteenth through eighteenth centuries points up the persistence of the Gnostic world vision.

In general, the Gnostic strands in late Renaissance culture bespeak a thoroughgoing revolt against Catholicism, or at least against the dogmatism and authoritarianism that came to envelop Church life after the council of Trent in 1555. The Rosicrucian movement, which spilled over into Freemasonry, embodies much of the Gnostic spirit. Rosicrucianism had its immediate genesis, according to one hypothesis, in the Bohemian resistance to Catholic oppression during the Thirty Years War. The city of Prague had become a kind of sixteenth century Alexandria, drawing within its walls students of the esoteric and abstruse. The religious and political reaction which set in under the Hapsburg Ferdinand after about 1617 served as a catalyst for the melding of these occult practices and ideas into an ongoing attack on medieval traditions.[50] Indeed, the so-called "Bohemianism" of the nineteenth and twentieth centuries out of which have sprung all sorts of experiments with the bizarre and outré in mind, manners, and morals took root in such a setting.

But it is especially in the thought of Giordano Bruno, the apostate Dominican monk and peripatetic urban intellectual, that the Gnostic shadings are most visible. Bruno, as the history books casually tell us, was burned at the stake in 1600 for his heretical doctrines, but it was not the usual theological "errors" of which the Italian philosopher was guilty. Bruno sought to implant in Christian letters an appreciation for ancient Egyptian magical lore.[51] Turning to the venerable Hermetic literature, Bruno constructed a Gnostic picture of the world which may stand as the prototype for much of non-normative and antihistorical reflection today. Bruno rejected the "closed" cosmos of the Middle Ages, in which all things have their ordained place, and opted instead for the model of an "infinite" universe into which the individual soul is tossed like a leaf on a spring torrent, much as the Gnostics of old extended in their mythology the range of space to encompass fantastic heavens and hierarchies that dwarf the minute human self. Moreover, Bruno advanced a notion of God which parallels the traditional Gnostic motif. God is the mysterious and unfathomable source of all existence (the "pleroma," in fact, though Bruno did not employ the term) out of which mortal and immortal beings proceed and to which they return. In every human creature, therefore, is contained a breath of the infinite. Bruno challenged the Church's claims to final authority and to the need of priestly mediation between man and God. For, in Bruno's vision, man gains access to the divine directly through his own inner illumination. While Catholicism required acceptance of revealed truth or "sacred doctrine" as the first principle from which understanding follows, the new Gnosticism, as represented in Bruno's writings, insisted upon *self-consciousness* as the proper window on reality. The famous *cogito ergo sum,* the basis of Cartesian rationalism and skepticism, therefore has its historical roots in the Gnostic method.

The preference of certain advanced thinkers in the 1600s and 1700s for strict knowledge over mere faith lies at the foundation of the scientific revolution and, more generally, at the heart of modernity. The well-known maxim of Bacon, *nam et ipsa scientia potestas est* ("Knowledge itself is power"), is often commemorated as the credo of the new science, but it also suits quite precisely the magico-religious mentality of Gnosticism. The methodology of early modern science was infused with certain religious considerations. The Renaissance conception of man as a bridge between the upper and lower worlds, and as a Prometheus unbound able to storm heaven with his intellect, was tied to durable Gnostic tenets long before it became the acknowledged metaphor for the scientific quest. The social context for the Gnostic entrance into the new science, however, was appreciably different from those circumstances out of which British empiricism and French materialism later developed. Whereas the triumph of experimental science was due to the energies of the rising bourgeoisie in these countries,[52] the protoscientific speculation of the sixteenth century was presided over by the *lumpen*-aristocracy, including (as in the case of Bruno) the clergy. It was this same group, whose ranks were eventually swelled by dispossessed children of the wealthy members of the middle class as well, that formed the line of resistance in the eighteenth and nineteenth century to the ethics of industrial capitalism, scientism, and advanced technology. The spiritualist, vitalist, and occult currents that circulated among the displaced public servants of the *ancien régime* in France prior to the Revolution—the Comte de Saint Germaine, Franz Mesmer, and Claude de Saint Martin, not to mention the infamous Marquis de Sade himself—all constituted facets of a broader ideology which looked to a mystical source of life's meaning beyond history and which justified the continuing prerogatives of an established elite. In contrast to the philosophes of the French Enlightenment, who esteemed "knowledge" for its practical and public uses as part of their agenda for the improvement of social life, or in comparison with orthodox Christianity which subjected any claims of supersensible insight to a normative tradition of faith, the modern adherents of Gnosticism were convinced of the private, self-authenticating, and incommunicable properties of their wisdom. Thus Gnosticism became a symbolic, rearguard protest against the revolutionary social and cultural changes that have taken place since the Reformation, while the torch of authentic, scientific inquiry gradually passed from the hands of a senescent, feudal nobility into those of the progressive classes. The linear view of history which the latter came to espouse was turned inside out by those warders of the ancient and submerged *gnosis*, who had no meaningful stake in the great transformations that were under way and who longed for fixity beyond the flow of human life itself. The next line of defense was to be the European Romantics, who were to engage themselves in a similar struggle in the late eighteenth and early nineteenth centuries.

Chapter 3

Sparks of Nature's Fire

Gie me ae spark o' Nature's fire
That's a' the learning I desire.

—*Robert Burns*

Ironically, the Gnostic insurrection against history and progress attained its modern momentum in first championing the forces which occasioned genuine historical thinking and the belief in the betterment of humanity. Whereas the Gnostic quest for eternity and the passion to arrest time persisted from ancient times through the Middle Ages as an expression of an aristocratic will to power, the modern metamorphosis of the antihistorical temper has its beginnings in an identification with the cause of the downtrodden. The context of such an identification was, of course, the French Revolution, and the cultural movement which encompasses the modern Gnostic advance is what has generally come to be known as Romanticism. The setting in which a movement originates, however, should not mislead us as to its underlying intentions. In the progressive circles of England and Germany the men who razed the Bastille and overthrew the *ancien régime* were lauded initially as messiahs of mankind. The philosophical defense of individual liberty and the denunciation of political absolutism and tyranny which middle-class intellectuals especially had brought to a crescendo in the latter part of the eighteenth century seemed to have flowered in the events of 1789 and afterwards. A stormy, but eminently hopeful phase of history appeared to have been ushered in, an epoch which even the bloody thud of the guillotine could not quell. History has left the picture of the French philosopher Condorcet, awaiting

execution in his Paris cell, yet writing down his ideas on the progress of
the future generations of Europe, which attests to the luminous and
tenacious quality of the new historical optimism. The historian Carl
Becker, for instance, has described the larger vision of that age as that
of a "new heaven" which would comprise "the perfected temporal life
of man" to be realized by posterity.[1]

But the ghoulish excesses of the Revolution rapidly turned such
musings into a nightmare. Those who had once exulted in the
destruction of the old order soon wailed with Mme. Roland, a victim of
the terror: "O liberty! O liberty! What crimes are committed in thy
name." Romantics such as Wordsworth in England and the Schlegel
brothers in Germany, who had formerly welcomed the French upheaval,
now shrunk in horror at the carnage. The promise of history became the
terror of history. The idols of progress were torn down. In their place
enthroned the mystical idea of a consoling nature, an abandoned epoch
of piety and innocence symbolized in the Middle Ages. Such notions
were promulgated by Romanticism which sought to create its own
magical universe undisturbed by the din and thunder of historical
happenings.

Traditionally, Romanticism has been regarded as an esthetic protest
against the Industrial Revolution and the soulless landscape of the new
bourgeois culture. Certainly as an historical phenomenon Romanticism
resists digestion to such a simple formula. However, the rearguard
probings of the Romantic mind cannot be denied, and the visible face of
later Romanticism can be seen to have the mien of anxiety about what
history has accomplished. Though politically many of the Romantics
were republicans and rebels against convention and authority, their
conceptions of the aims of life squared appropriately, not so much with
the nascent claims of universal democracy and the aspirations of the
"common man," as with the prerogatives of "genius," the affirmation
of individual will and power. In this respect Romanticism charted a
system of symbols proper to the Gnostic legacy of self-assertion. It
became an ideology for the disinherited privileged classes of modern
Western society who could no longer self-consciously cast their
fortunes with the decadent nobility, yet who could neither embrace
wholeheartedly the trends which history had set in motion. Instead of
subscribing to the new doctrines of reason and collective progress, the
Romantics retreated into the purely private and esoteric spirituality

which yearned through the medium of imagination for the "infinite" or "eternal." The Jacobin became what Nietzsche was later to lionize as the *Übermensch,* the "superman," who defied all the ruling powers of the world as the godlike sovereign of his own cosmos.

Such a cosmos transcended the contingencies of history; it enveloped purely poetical worlds outside of real time—the world of the heroic Greeks, of the Arthurian knights, of the primitive German *Volk,* of Islamic harems. It crystallized in the dreams, feelings, and "inspirations" of men who took themselves as the exclusive arbiters of reality. Finally, there was the Romantic yearning for "alternative reality" to the reality of the everyday. The Romantics looked for mental healing in the bower of "nature" to which the refugee from history could flee. For the Romantics, nature was no longer the mirror of man's sober intelligence and common sense, as it had been for the thinkers of the eighteenth century. No more was it a field of "natural laws" that could be discovered by the scientist or the political philosopher for the purpose of new technical inventions or wise social legislation. Nature was now a reservoir of the creative spirit to inspire the individual seer, the poet, the dreamer, who in his volcanic soul harbored glowing sparks from its subterranean fires. Nature offered profound possibilities of secret *gnosis* accessible to the unbridled imagination. The Gnostic religion took root again in the "religion of sensibility" of the 1700s. It finally flared as the Romantic cult of the "beautiful soul" consumed by the flame of inwardness.

The Eruption of Feeling

The cult of feeling of "sensibility," which gushed forth at the popular level in German pietism and English Methodism, represented an early democratic resistance to manners and tastes of the established orders, who during the early years of the European Enlightenment preserved the ideal of rationality in philosophy, classicism in art, and moralism in theology. For the most part the cult of feeling was hardly revolutionary in its initial impact. It encouraged a gentle and introspective kind of religion in Germany, known as pietism, and evangelical enthusiasm among British sectarians who became inflamed by the perfectionist preachings of John Wesley, the founder of Methodism. It was tame enough for English gentlemen such as Lord Shaftesbury to rhapsodize about the sweet, benevolent emotion, which bound all classes and races together. German noble ladies made an idyll of the landed peasant living in rapport with nature and built elegant little cottages on their estates where they made believe they were simple shepherdesses. The French philosopher Jean-Jacques Rousseau became the brooding apostle of the religion of sensibility. In *The Social Contract* he spoke of the divinity of pure human feeling, of man's primal innocence which had been violated by the corruptions and artifices of polite civilization. In Rousseau's reveries and impassioned polemics the politics of bourgeois revolution against feudal society took shape, but his thinking was also the seedbed for the broader and deeper Romantic thrust away from all older forms of authority. The celebration of feeling passed into the Romantic cult of subjectivity. Delicate truths of the "heart," which reason could not dispute, grew into an undisciplined rage of the Romantic genius to "define the world" in his own way, as the German poet Novalis put it. Subjectivism turned cancerous. By the beginning of the nineteenth century it had been transformed into the age-old Gnostic mania of exalting the self at the expense of society, of defying not only men but the gods themselves.

The metastasis of the cult of feeling has its beginnings in the Germany of the 1770s. It can be detected in the literary and philosophical movement now remembered as the *Sturm und Drang* or "Storm and Stress." While shortlived, the Storm and Stress had far-ranging historical consequences which surpassed its immediate impact. In the murky gropings and outpourings of the Storm and Stress writers surfaced a distinct defiance of the archaic class structure and its values which had wielded together German society for generations. The revolutionary leanings of Rousseau and the general restlessness of the European intelligentsia of this period were pronounced in the mood of these young Germans. Yet, in contrast with the political explosion which was about to break forth in the American War of Independence and the French Revolution, the Storm and Stress was chiefly a cultural revolt. It laid up its barricades not against the king's armies, but against the intangible norms of education, manners, and taste.

The reason for this diversion of the impulse to insurrection lies in the unique set of social conditions in eighteenth century Germany. Such conditions hewed the character of later Teutonic Romanticism and secured the Gnostic option of occultism instead of political reform. Unlike England, which had set the course of bourgeois revolution already by 1689, or France where the feudal nobility was considerably weakened already, Germany remained a politically backward country with a docile middle class and an entrenched aristocracy. The German ruling classes accepted the principles of Enlightenment, but only so far as to rationalize the machinery of state control and to organize bureaucracies which regulated commerce, stifled individual freedom and expression, and ensured loyalty to the princes. Frederick the Great's advocacy of "enlightened despotism" in Prussia was a prototype of the new form of political absolutism in an age when the free hands of kings were becoming increasingly bound by parliaments and estates general elsewhere in Western Europe. The fragmentation of Germany into myriad petty principalities, each with its own laws, army, and coinage, had been an enduring effect of the Thirty Years War over a century before which retarded the development of German institutions and quieted the kind of nationalism that from 1789 to 1848 went along with the spread of liberal doctrines.

Because of the torpor of German politics, social protest could only be directed toward symbols, not structures. The latent fury aimed at monarchs was sublimated into an assault on literary styles, moral beliefs, and cultural habits. Social criticism itself found a secret outlet in artistic theories which were culturally radical, but not necessarily politically offensive. The suppression of civic freedoms for the individual was compensated by the tendency to judge "society against the measure of personal life and inner need."[2] The power of the emotions sufficed where having a voice in government was denied to all but the traditional elite.

Significantly, however, the protagonists of the Storm and Stress did not identify with the historical interests of the middle class, even though the majority of them came from bourgeois families. J. G. Hamann was the son of a physician in Königsberg; J. G. Herder's father was a schoolmaster in Mohrungen; the great Goethe was born of wealthy *Bürger* parents in Frankfurt am Main. By and large the Storm and Stress reviled the German middle class for its venal preoccupations and philistine tastes with the same vehemence that it disdained the effete princely courtiers with their foppish manners and slavish imitation of French culture. It was the unmistakable *déclassé* character of the Storm and Stress intellectuals which accounted for their ambivalence toward their own social role. Unattached to any of the particular ruling groups of society, distrustful of the new commercial and industrial order, they indulged themselves in lofty sentiments and colorful myths of the past. The *Stürmer und Dränger* venerated the legend of the heroic nobleman (unlike the mean little aristocratic functionaries whom they saw all around him) who spurned convention and struck out with all soul and pathos against ignorance and petty tyranny. Whether such nobility ever existed was irrelevant to the critical and imaginative validity of the legend. Goethe's Egmont exemplified such a sterling, seigneurial personage. Schiller's play *The Robbers,* which tells the story of the son of an elderly count who becomes a kind of German Robin Hood, etches one of the most durable themes of the Storm and Stress—the willingness to resort to brave deeds, which society regards as criminal, but which from a higher viewpoint are *virtues*. The typical hero of the movement proves himself not so much by success in his ventures as by his bold and unflappable assertion of his own dignity. He is a Prometheus, sneering at every spiteful Zeus, as illustrated, for instance, in the soliloquy of the condemned Egmont just before the guards of the nefarious Alba escort him off to his doom:

> . . . I die for freedom, for which I lived and fought and to which I now offer myself in passive sacrifice . ... Yes, bring them on, as many as you will! Close your ranks, you frighten me not. I am accustomed to standing with spears behind me and spears before me and, surrounded by menacing death, only to feel the courage that is life with doubled intensity.[3]

Bearding the pale furies and wicked spells of fate, he summons in his own breast the force which Herder called "the profound, irrecoverable feeling of existence." He is more than a nobleman of blood esteemed for his chivalry; he is an aristocrat without peers whose regalia is not that of family or society, but of the universe. The dim, termagant forces of nature are revealed in this knight of feeling's own precious personality, and they reach vital expression in his solitary joust with every agency which hampers freedom.

In nature resided the source of true strength for the godlike mortal pitted against history and fate. Opposition to society was changed into the free expression of seething moods and natural drives. The idealized nobility, more supermen than real warriors, had their counterpart in the mysterious and pious common people, the *Volk*. Happily insensitive to the workaday world of peasants and lowly craftsmen, the partisans of the Storm and Stress made a collective myth of them. They envisaged themselves as disciples of the *Volk*'s wordless wisdom, who articulated their spirituality in their poetry and embodied their occult power in manly aspirations. Such a myth, which bordered on wild fantasy, lingered in the underground of German romanticism and was destined over a hundred years later to become the grist for Nazi lunatics.[4]

The ideal of the Storm and Stress was to be gloriously alive and creative, to relish the raw spontaneity of one's own personal being, and to express such voluptuousness in a manner which suited one's own quest for uniqueness. To drink in all experiences and appropriate them in an individual life-style was the imperative laid upon the would-be "genius." From this imperative derives the successful vacation of Faust, and the tragic burden of Goethe's youthful hero Werther, whose life ends in suicide. The passionate wish to intensify every life experience is announced by Faust to the devil Mephistopheles:

> I vow myself to frenzy, agonies of gratification,
> Enamored hatred, quickening frustration.
> Cured of the will to knowledge now, my mind
> And heart shall be closed to no sorrow any more
> And all that is the lot of human kind
> I want to feel down to my senses' core,
> Grasp with my mind their worst things and their best,
> Heap all their joys and troubles on my breast,
> And thus my self to their selves' limits to extend,
> And like them perish foundering at the end.[5]

To which Mephistopheles replies quite gamely:

> No man digests this ancient sourdough.
> This whole, believe the likes of us,
> For deity alone was made.[6]

Faust further counters that he would become like God. For what is God if not the grand artificer and creator, an occupation which man himself in song and deed can confidently essay? It is the same hubris on which Herder takes wing: "Gods in human form! Creators! Destroyers! Revealers of the mysteries of God and men! Interpreters of nature! Speakers of unspeakable things!"[7] The devil Mephistopheles is not Christianity's hateful adversary, but a shrewd counsel to Faust, for he supplies the ring of knowledge concerning nature's secrets—a knowledge which goes beyond scholarly trifles to guarantee mastery over the universe.

Faust suggests the Gnostic yearning to penetrate beyond the veil of conventional thought forms and metaphysical subtleties to the inner essence of all living entities. Such divination captures the magical vibrations in nature and harnesses them in the creative forgoing of one's own personality. In order to accomplish this task the genius must go to the wellspring of creativity forgotten by civilization and the whole of human history. In Hamann, dubbed by his cronies "The Magus of the North," we find an extreme tendency toward the uncovering of dark feelings and insights. For Hamann, the poetic genius articulates the aboriginal language of the human race, which has somehow been lost to modern man. This language is the pure grammar of feeling and precedes abstract concepts. It is immediate and sensuous, devoid of the falsifying logic of philosophical argument. It springs forth as a unity of natural rhythms, sounds, and tones: it constitutes the forgotten voice of primitive sensibility. Poetic language is "the mother tongue of the human race."

In glorifying man's primitive origins, Hamann like others of the Storm and Stress attributed a rare innocence to the person who feels and speaks as nature once intended. The poet-visionary seizes the world with a fresh vision, reenacting Adam's naming of the animals in the Garden of Eden, like the child's first achievement of language. The seer enjoys a naiveté and pristine ambition which renders his words the veritable Word of God, declaring himself in nature's sensuous harmonies. All language is "speech to the creature through the creation," the sibylline utterances of the infinite Deity transmitted through the sayings of natural humanity. The word becomes a magical talisman loaded with supernatural power. Downgraded from its communicative function, it comes to serve as pure revelation.

It is no wonder then that Herder seems to have admired the teachings of the Hindu Brahmins. Their wisdom draws man back behind time and change to the eternal source of illumination in nature.[8] In Indian speculation the soul struggles to unite with the creative Godhead immanent in the sensible universe, gleaming with purity and goodness despite its inevitable marring by the wicked world.

> Just as the blaze of light radiates forth,
>   though refracted;
> So the Good, bent by fate, strives upward.[9]

The spark of nature's fire bursts into a holy conflagration. The poet's

genius apprehends the objects of the senses, melts them down, and
remolds them into images of eternity. It is eternity alone which gives
significance to what the genius perceives. The sense of eternity, familiar
to former ages, has been dulled by the lack of deep feeling and must be
gained again in wonder and ecstatic reunion. Consider Schiller's poem
on "Genius":

> Equally clear to every breast was the precept eternal,
> Equally hidden the source whence it to gladden us spring;
> But that happy period has vanish'd! And self-will'd
> presumption
> Nature's godlike repose now has forever destroy'd.
> Feelings polluted the voice of the deities echo no longer,
> In the dishonored breast now is the oracle dumb.
> Save in the silenter self, the listening soul cannot
> find it,
> *There* does the mystical word watch o'er the meaning
> divine;
> There does the searcher conjure it, descending with
> bosom unsullied;
> There does the nature long-lost give him back wisdom
> again.[10]

The "searcher" must "conjure" the dormant truths of nature as a
magical-poetic act, thereby overcoming the ignorance which life in time
and history has thrown over the human psyche. The *Stürmer und
Dränger* for the most part turned away from real history and proclaimed
their salvation in a mystical return to the infancy of the race, when
human consciousness was not divided against itself and when feeling
disclosed the eminently real. That was even true of Herder who took an
interest in history as the abode of the infinite spirit dwelling in all
peoples. Ultimately, Herder announced, "feeling is everything."

It has sometimes been claimed that the Storm and Stress movement,
as well as the romantics themselves, succeeded in abolishing the
Gnostic dualism of spirit and matter, soul and nature. But the very
concept of "nature" in the Storm and Stress had Gnostic overtones.
While they saw man as a supreme unity of all sentient faculties, as part
of an organic totality, they held that the true nature to which he belongs
cannot be discerned by the average, mediocre mind. True nature was
covert and mysterious, engaged only with the privileged passions of the
soul. The ancient Gnostic hatred of the "cosmos" therefore corresponds to the Storm and Stress's repugnance for the rationally ordered

universe of the Enlightenment, with the conception of natural "law" and social equality. The Gnostic, with his ardor for self-transcendence and individual uniqueness, could not comfortably fit in a rational cosmos. Likewise, the rebellion of the Storm and Stress pointed toward an occult "supernature" which was the spiritual home of those alienated from the pedestrian world they knew and was not accessible to new ruling classes with their paltry concerns and smug certainties. Just as Gnosticism denies the reality of the phenomenal world, so the Storm and Stress rejected the claims of common sense. They sought a vanished unity of life known only in inward pathos, and which could be attained by flight from the kind of social existence which had been reached at that particular phase of history. Like the Gnostics of old, they endeavored to exorcize the horror of history by a magical master stroke.

THE SPELL OF THE IMAGINATION

While the Storm and Stress believed in the miraculous efficacy of feeling, the generation of the 1790s who are often called "Romantics" clarified this sentiment into an all-embracing doctrine of the "imagination." The imagination came to be regarded as a faculty of mind which actually configures the world as living forms, rather than merely apprehending its depths and mysteries as is the case with feeling. The Storm and Stress demanded the ecstatic liberation of the individual self-feeling. In mature Romanticism there developed the idea of the self as a creative agent which transforms and actually reconstitutes ordinary reality with images and symbols. The Germans talked of imagination as *Einbildungskraft* (translatable loosely as the power of unifying experience through "pictures"). The English poet and philosopher Coleridge defined imagination as the "esemplastic" power of the mind, the aptitude for raising experience to a higher level of meaning and form. Through the poetic imagination the given features of everyday experience are reordered, transmuted, and pieced together in a new harmonious design of things. Nature may be entirely *made over* by the imagination. Imagination was Novalis's "magic idealism" whereby fleeting impressions of the mind are lent solidity and substance. Imagination is a sophisticated kind of conjuring of unrealized objects and shapes. The entire universe becomes "poeticized," in Novalis's words.

In Novalis's view the vocation of the poet is to "create" the cosmos anew by the activity of the imagination, to weave around prosaic beliefs and conventional prejudices a magical spell of images. "We are on a mission; we are called upon to form the earth through images."[11] In the inner life of imagination the "eternal" is stamped indelibly on the flux of sensations emanating from the external world, thus dispelling the illusion of time. "In ourselves, or nowhere else, is eternity joined with its world, with past and future."[12] Friedrich Schlegel, a contemporary of Novalis, affirmed in a similar fashion the link between the poetic consciousness and the undraping of eternity in the imagination. "The spirit comes equipped with an eternal proof of its own existence."[13] Such a proof resides in German Romanticism's love ballad of the solitary self to itself, in the denial of time and change over which the mere individual without poetic talents has no control. "Every poet is really Narcissus," Schlegel wrote.[14] He refurbishes the world completely with his own sheaf of images, and in doing so stills the anxiety which arises from taking things in their outward appearances for granted. Rather than taking things for granted, or surrendering to time and fate, the poet redeems himself by manifesting the eternal in the very artistic production of symbols. He is saved from his own mortality by the imagination. We find the same daring claim in the poetry of William Blake:

> The world of Imagination is the world of
> Eternity; it is the divine bosom into which we
> shall go after the death of the Vegetated body.
> The World of Imagination is Infinite and Eternal,
> whereas the world of Generation, or Vegetation,
> is finite and temporal. There Exist in that
> Eternal world the Permanent Realities of Every
> Thing which we see reflected in the Vegetable
> Glass of Nature.

Similarly, Blake says, "Vision or Imagination is a Representation of what Eternally Exists, Really & Unchangeably."

Notwithstanding Blake's prophetic effusions, English Romanticism did not always take the license of its sister movement in Germany. Whereas Blake's narcissism is evident in his avowal that "Mental Things Alone are Real," the other English Romantics sought to strike a careful balance between the creative drive of the ego and an awareness of the natural limits to which it could push. That was especially true of Wordsworth for whom the imagination was a tender suitor of its mistress, nature, instead of her seducer. Still, English and German Romantics alike held that poetry is much more than an exuberant foray. Imagination issues out of the creative energy found in all nature. This energy the Romantics denoted on the one hand as God, on the other as the eternal Self of which individual selves are outward masks. Coleridge in a famous passage described the "primary IMAGINATION" (which might be construed loosely as the imaginative power of the divine) as "a repetition in the finite mind of the eternal act of creation in the infinite I AM." The poet enjoys a direct insight into nature's mysteries, and in the "magic castle of art" (in the words of the German Wackenroder) he labors to materialize a mode of reality that has not been recognized before. He materializes divinity; he is, according to Schlegel, "progressively becoming God."

One important authority on Romanticism has observed that the employment of the imagination, so far as the Germans were concerned, was "an esoteric activity" bent more on attaining elaborate metaphysical truths than serving as a "method of perception."[15] The mingling of Romanticism of art, religion, and philosophy in German Romanticism made subjectivity and imagination the key ingredients in a doctrine of salvation by individual effort alone. The German Romantic's "yearning for the infinite" *(Sehnsucht nach das Unendliche),* for the "eternal" unity of life beyond time, for the rescue of the free spirit from dreary and unrelieved monotony of his conventional affairs, makes him a compelling case of Gnostic psychology. The Gnostic turns to his own subconscious impulses and thirst for mastery in order to achieve his liberation.[16] He fails to distinguish between wish-fulfillment and the way things are in themselves and vaunts the former as his special knowledge.

We find in Novalis full-blown the Gnostic fetish of inwardness. According to Novalis, the orgin of poetic truth (the highest sort of truth) lies in the dream state. The job of the poet is to "live" his dream, to give it such strength and beauty that at last he cares no longer to distinguish between "sleeping" and "waking." "Our life [in the beginning] is not a dream," Novalis wrote, "yet it must and will perhaps become one."[17] The conversion of life into dream is the fundamental motive of Novalis's emotion-clouded *Hymns to the Night,* in which the night itself becomes a metaphor for the dark, unconscious atmosphere of inspiration. The black, starry dome of heaven spreads forth as an invitation to reach out for the infinite, for the eternal. For "timeless is the dominion of night; eternal is the duration of sleep."[18] The eternal mysteries sequestered within the night are brought to the "light" of day in the imagination, relying upon its own skillful magic. Like the ancient Gnostics, the poetic spirit, for Novalis, lies "asleep" in the world and must be aroused by the "voice" of the far-off God which beckons it upward into the vast spaces. Poetry is the unconscious discovering itself and justifying itself as the sole measure of reality. In the tenebrous desires of the soul for something deeper than immediate experience the lure of eternity becomes overwhelming. The poet's quest extends toward a reunion with the eternal oneness of existence, which is death and life woven together in the enchantment of the dream. Such a quest marks out the plot of Novalis's novel, *Heinrich von Ofterdingen*, completed in 1800, where the young hero Heinrich renounces the confusing and sorrowful life into which he has been born and embarks on a search for the "blue flower," which symbolizes the timeless object of all worldly yearning for Romantic poetry. "Far away lies before me everything I have craved to possess, but the blue flower I long to behold. It persists in my mind, and I can imagine and think of nothing else."[19] Novalis wished to use poetic reverie to the same purpose for which Icarus crafted his wings in the Greek myth—to fly beyond the sky and be free of his encumbering mortal frame. To possess the blue flower was to leap over the chasm between fancy and fact, between aspiring and having, in a clamorous fiat of the imagination.

The dilemma of the Romantic imagination was voiced by Friedrich Schiller in his *Naive and Sentimental Poetry*. "All poetry must . . . possess an infinite content," Schiller declared.[20] Naive poetry, which Schiller ascribed to the ancient Greek bards, captures the "infinite" in a simple and stylized idiom, presenting nature in terms of concrete images. It is not unlike the poetry which Wordsworth attempted, insofar as he endeavored to suggest the calm mystery lurking behind sylvan scenes, crystal lakes, verdant hills, and stolid peasants. Sentimental poetry, however, struggles to bare the infinite as its very subject matter, to uncloak the "Absolute." The sentimental poet, similar in kind to just about all the German Romantics, encounters the awful disparity between the infinite and his restricted means. He responds to the gap between ideal and real with a tempestuous assault of the imagination on the mind's limitations, and the challenge of representing the infinite adequately becomes in itself a strenuous, and perhaps tragic pursuit.

Friedrich Schlegel later dismissed the tragic note in poetry in his own refinement of Schiller's theory. The rift between finite and infinite is closed to the extent that the divine life progressively discloses itself in poetic activity. The eternal can never be grasped at once, yet comes more definitely into view with each imaginative act of creation. The human ego gradually fills itself out with the richness of poetic intuition. God "comes into being" via the imagination. The infinite incrementally takes the form of the finite.[21] The Romantic notion that the deepening of personal consciousness through spontaneous imagery could secure eternity step by step echoes, in a psychological sense, the Gnostic metaphysics of the soul's ascent across numberless planes of reality until it reaches the "plenum." The soul contends with successive mythical adversaries as a matter of gaining "experience" whereupon it can finally acquire knowledge of the highest realm.

The airy speculation of Romanticism was prompted by a profound disillusionment with ordinary philosophy and traditional art. The contrary "realities" it reached for were in conception remote and obscure, yet their very obscurity proved a symptom of the Romantic's inability to find meaning in the common life that surrounded them. The Romantics carried through the program of the Storm and Stress to its tumultuous conclusion. The world that "ought" to be became blurred with the world that "is." The dream of nature became nature itself. No wonder that the German Romantics perfected the *Märchen* or fairy tale. In the timeless "once upon a time" of the fairy tale which can be lived only in the imagination, an ideal world magically takes on the semblance of the real. Heroism and enchantment replace the actual historical milieu where coarseness, timidity and the paralysis of politics are the rule.

THE SPECTRE OF MODERNITY

The Romantic inclination to invest all hope of self-transcendence in the imagination can be understood against the backdrop of historical events in the period from 1789 to 1815. The first throb of Romantic ardor came with equal strength in both Germany and England. It arose as a flushed response to the French Revolution and its prospects of liberty. Nearly all the young romantics endorsed the Jacobin cause until the Reign of Terror. They welcomed the deposing of Louis XIV and the creation of a constitutional assembly as auguries of a new universal epoch in which the individual would at long last be freed from the yoke of tyranny.

They had no firm idea as to where the Revolution might be going, nor did they comprehend its real historical implications. From their standpoint the Revolution meant the unshackling of the individual from authority and expressed the triumph of creative élan in the social arena, of a momentous thrust toward freedom and novelty. The intent of the Revolutionaries to make all men "citizens" was not appreciated, however, as much as the fact of rebellion itself. But the bloom of liberty faded into the violence of the Paris commune, the savage rule of the Committee of Public Safety, the heavy-handed dictatorship of the Directory, and finally the wars of Napoleon Bonaparte. The grisly spectacle of history heaving in anarchy and blood frightened the Romantic mind into cowering conservatism in politics and an ethereal bemusement in philosophy and art.

In Britain, in Austria, and in those German states menaced by Napoleon, a political reaction set in that would last for several decades. The upper middle classes forgot for a time their historical quarrels with the aristocracy and united with them to suppress insurgency. On the main the intellectuals sided too with the established orders of society, at least so far as to stand against any revolutionary challenge from the common people whom Napoleon expected to applaud him in his attempts to uproot the remnants of feudalism and privilege. Nevertheless, revolution and its Napoleonic aftermath split the seams of traditional European society beyond mending. The breakdown of social life affected the sturdiest sense of plausibility and propriety. The Romantics themselves reflected the general feeling of social disloca-tion. They leapt at mystical sureties when confounded by the strife of their age, while at the same time they reveled in the chaos of experience. They despised the ruling classes, yet favored them for their role in upholding tranquillity and order. They were infatuated with the opportunities for individual expression in modern culture, but they still pined for the unadorned piety of the medieval period. Many like Novalis and Schlegel ultimately embraced Catholic orthodoxy and cheered the Hapsburg autocrats.

A generation thereafter the liberal Jew Heinrich Heine was to make light of the "Romantic school." "There is no race more devoted to its princes than ours," he said, speaking of the Germans.[22] Heine went on to observe how the German Romantics blanched at Napoleon's humiliation of the German nobility and hence sacrificed whatever liberal precepts they might have had to the idol of nationalism. In nationalism they hit upon the solution to the problem of anomie and their own disillusionment with present social trends. The values of deep feeling and imagination could be preserved in the adulation of the *Volk*, in the cult of Germany's might and in fanaticism for all forms of Teutonic "culture." The salvation of the individual could be accomplished by mystical identification with the spirit of the people and with its native religions.

Catholicism was revered, not because it offered sound dogma, but because it served as a paradigm of an ancient, organic faith rooted in the very soil of "nature." A nostalgia for the folkish happiness of long ago inflamed the Romantic passion for a "new" Germany free of liberalism, rationalism, and everything that smacked of modernity. For this reason Germany's so-called "Wars of Liberation" against Napoleon, which were supported wholeheartedly by the Romantics, proved to be the antithesis of revolution. The Romantics hoped by war to expel the foreign invader and to re-establish the principle of monarchy along with the ethic of duty to one's social class.

In the reactionary politics of Romanticism the appetite for the infinite and the eternal reveals itself. The ego expands itself beyond the normal boundaries of social involvement and takes refuge in cosmic certainties, in a realm of mystical abstractions which constitute what Peter Vierick has described as "metapolitics."[23] The political allegiances of the Romantics, therefore, rested on more recondite concerns. One swore fidelity to the state not because it was right and proper of a citizen, but because such a commitment could be reckoned as an initiation into the mysteries of the universe *per se*. The fact that Romantic political theory was tenuous, breezy, and muddled without a clear conception of how actual social institutions might be formed attests to its ulterior motives. It was not the sort of political theory to which we are accustomed. It was a Gnostic blueprint for the emancipation of the inner light of genius instead of a practical plan for reform or the establishment of legal rights and obligations.

Novalis supported Catholicism because it brazed personal feeling and social morality together in a mystical harmony. Catholicism could be a lever of social control, as it was in the autocratic Austria of his day; but, more important, its authority was justified by its ability to sustain the ever present "Manifestations of the Supernatural," which German

Protestantism could not do, against the encroachments of modern secularity. Novalis despised the tendency of Protestantism, as was the case in Prussia, to enter into a league with rationalism and bourgeois democracy and to squelch the esthetic and mystical attitudes. In the beginning, Protestantism

> ... was briefly illumined by a fire from heaven, but the source of holy inspiration was soon seen to run dry. Secular power began to rule, the artistic sense suffers in sympathy with religion; and only rarely does a pure, eternal spark of life emerge. . . .[24]

Time and history have corroded the primitive genius of the Catholic church fathers, who were men of uncommon sensibility. Protestantism is a religion of secular change which has assimilated the bogus belief in progress. It has destroyed true feeling and knowledge.

Novalis's idyll of Catholicism is stretched further in the patently Gnostic image of religion and politics which crops up in the writings of Adam Müller. For Müller, Jesus is the perfect master whose "Oriental" enlightenment has irradiated the people of the globe, especially the Europeans. The political customs and social codes of these peoples contain fragments of the broken light beam which have been scattered from their antique source. Müller's language of "Christian" politics is reminiscent of the Gnostic myth of the separation of the soul from the "uncreated light" and its dispersion in matter, or in this case the diverse cultures of modern history.

> So now coming down from the disciples among the fathers of the Church, and the saints of the first centuries, the Divine light breaks and is broken into more and more local colours; and the great task of mediation among the pagans and the peoples of the earth spreads farther and farther. The constitution of the peoples themselves comes beneath the eternal influence of Him and His representatives, mediatory forms between the individual citizens of the earth and Him. . . .[25]

Müller recommended Medieval Catholicism as the road back to this "eternal influence" of Christ. His Gnostic Christ became a symbol of all the buried "spiritual" qualities in nature which, on the surface at least, had been blown away by the winds of modern liberal politics and thought. Müller glorified the Medieval hierarchy of social classes which he said contained spiritual substance of the body of the risen Lord. Calling for vigorous new leadership among the nobility, he at the same

time saw the mystical essence of all the German people in the tillers of
the soil.[26] Through German nationalism, which would help rehabilitate
the old Holy Roman Empire, Müller sought to recover by dint of half-
baked political schemes the privileges and special enjoyments of a
spiritual elite which modernity seemingly had snatched away.
"Catholicism" became a password for the Romantic's assertion of title
against the claims of the modern world, of the value of artistic
sensitivity against that of economic gain, of feudalism against
capitalism. It was no coincidence that some of the Romantics gratefully
learned about India and began to investigate its sacred literature. India
with its caste system was a paradigm of a stable society presided over
by contemplatives and seers, which the Romantics fancied themselves.
Would-be modern Brahmins, they wanted a serene environment where
they were guaranteed the social prestige and luxury to gaze into
eternity. Heine remarked how Goethe suspected "that the Sanskrit
studies of the Schlegels and their friends had a Roman Catholic hidden
meaning."[27] The Romantics would be the new priests of a Gnostic
Catholicism and the culture bearers of a reborn aristocracy.

DISENCHANTMENT AND THE WILL TO POWER

A rift between the Romantic ideal and the prospects of its realization,
however, bred disenchantment. The hunger for eternity could never be
satisfied on the fantastic terms the Romantics demanded. The "real"
world perpetually resisted the exorbitant claims of the imagination. The
return to the middle ages was a tantalizing pipe dream irrelevant to the
forward lurch of events. No magical memory of the Middle Ages could
suffice to set the clock back.

In one paramount respect the Romantic pathos fed upon the
contradiction between its yearning and the possibilities of fulfillment,
between eternity and time. Such pathos is uttered in Novalis's famous
lament: "We seek above all the unconditioned, and yet always find only
conditioned things."[28] It is the anguish of what in German literature
came to be called *Zerrissenheit* or "disintegration," which ensues when
the writer proves unable to adjust his longing for a misty abstraction
with the evidence of the senses. It is the kind of dichotomy that was the
stuff of the so-called Romantic irony. To erase the dichotomy would be
to dampen the emotions themselves, to remove the very obstacles which
called forth intense feeling and the exercise of the will. Romantic

pathos fed on frustration, which points up the important distinction between Gnosticism and true mysticism. While the mystic silently delights in his union with the infinite, the Gnostic agonizes over the distance between his present predicament and his transcendent goal. The world in which he finds himself is forever in danger of becoming disenchanted. Thus he itches for a rapture in the depths of his psyche whereby his alienation will cease and his longings be consummated. But the work of the Gnostic is an infinite task. He must constantly ascend the ladder of *gnosis* which stretches endlessly toward heaven. He must fortify his will incessantly in order to overcome the gravity of his ascent. Psychologically speaking, he is constrained to wrestle with all his might against despair and the imperfections of his own constitution. He is unremittingly at war with the "principalities and powers" that reign in this world.

The Gnostic pathos of having "fallen" into an alien universe and the desire to escape is enunciated in Blake's poetic fragment *Infant Sorrow*.

> My mother groan'd, my father wept,
> Into the dangerous world I leapt;
> Helpless, naked, piping loud,
> Like a fiend hid in a cloud.

The tension between a childlike joy and the horror or worldly existence achieves poignant description in his *Songs of Experience*.

> What'er is Born of Mortal Birth
> Must be consumed with the Earth
> To rise from Generation free:
> Then what have I to do with Thee?

The Songs of Experience provide the sequel to the *Songs of Innocence* which celebrate the wonder of human imagination, the yen for the fullness and simplicity of life. *Songs of Innocence* hallows the child before he has embarked on a voyage of time, maturation, and suffering. They express the elation of living in touch with nature without the pain of *becoming conscious*.

> 'I have no name:
> 'I am but two days old.'
> What shall I call thee?
> 'I happy am,
> 'Joy is my name.'
> Sweet joy befall thee!

But the innocence of childhood is cruelly cut off by the process of growth and learning. Man is expelled from Eden by time itself and discovers himself as a "little boy lost," weeping in the dark. In *Songs of Experience* the desperate moan of the human spirit, now sundered from nature, is heard. The imaginative vision pales; the original enchantment is spoiled. The soul of man scans the heavens for the eternal light of redemption, as Blake suggests in *Ah! Sunflower.*

> Ah, Sunflower! weary of time,
> Who contest the steps of the Sun,
> Seeking after that sweet golden clime
> Where the traveller's journey is done:
> Where the Youth pined away with desire,
> And the pale Virgin shrouded in snow
> Arise from their graves, and aspire
> Where my Sunflower wishes to go.

But the sunflower is bound to the soil; it can only watch with heartache the blazing object of its aspiration make the daily rounds of the sky. It is "weary of time" yet tragically weighted down by its own temporality. It can merely "wish" to go where the sun that is knowledge and happiness journeys far up in the firmament.

Blake articulates the Gnostic's wistful recollection of a marvelous prehistory of the race when poetry kept man in sensuous harmony with nature. Thus in *Proverbs of Hell* Blake declares: "The ancient Poets animated all sensible objects with Gods or Geniuses, calling them by the names and adorning them with the properties of woods, rivers, mountains, lakes, cities, nations, and whatever their enlarged & numerous senses could perceive." Yet society, law, and rationalism brutally disrupted this concord, and "men forgot that all deities reside in the human breast." The original oneness of soul and divinity was fractured, and now man hankers after its retrieval. The lost unity, so far as Blake is concerned, can be gained back by the power of will, by raising to the highest expressive pitch man's untrained emotions which are themselves a melody of the sublime and violent in nature. In the dark and turbulent will the timeless meaning of life becomes evident. "The roaring of lions, the howling of wolves, the raging of the stormy sea, and the destructive sword, are portions of eternity, too great for the eye of man." The poet annihilates all conventional forms and signs of order by giving free rein to his natural impulses, and in doing so pushes himself closer to the infinite goal which seems to elude him in time.

The Romantic accent on will as the gateway to eternity, especially in the German literature, is foreshadowed in the mystical or "theosophical" writings of the sixteenth-century shoemaker Jacob Böhme, who in turn drew on Neo-Platonic and Gnostic sources. In Böhme's writings, which heavily influenced seventeenth-century English mysticism and later German Romanticism, we see an attempt of the mortal mind to delve into the secrets of the absolute God, to "know" the unknowable. Knowledge of God comes preeminently through knowledge of the self, which is created as a mirror of the divine and contains the inner light or divine spark of its Maker. This divine reality is the ground of all nature, and its very essence is pure Will—will without any cause or intention. God is the "Will of the Abyss," the "eternal chaos, within all whatsoever Eternity and time hath, is contained."[29] Similarly, in man's own will the creative energy of the divine has an outlet. The mysterious Will in all things is unveiled. Böhme exhorts man to lend complete expression to the dynamic will, to magnify the "little spark" of vitality and wisdom within him.[30]

The fixation with the will came to the fore in the German philosophy of the Romantic period. Johann Gottlieb Fichte (1762–1814) taught that the world as known to man is constructed by the ego, which at bottom is nothing but will. The human will becomes involved in, and acts constantly upon, the world, struggling to realize its purposes in time. The individual or finite will, however, is simply an outworking of the infinite will. Man's ego is a limited instance of the transcendental Ego behind all life and thought. The supreme will objectifies itself in the incessant striving of an individual consciousness to create a universe. The solitary "I" that wills the world into being points back behind itself to a metaphysical principle of volition which Fichte identified with God.

In Fichte, though, both man's will and the divine will are not purely arbitrary. They work together to bring into existence a "moral" order of things. Fichte was indebted to the thought of Immanuel Kant, who regarded the highest end of man as consisting in obedience to the "moral law" which unites all rational beings together on the basis of their duty toward each other. While Fichte's philosophy was predominantly ethical in scope and therefore lacked something of the Romantic enthusiasm for pure self-expression, the writings of Joseph von Schelling (1775–1854) tumble into the great mysteries of the unconditioned Will as a kind of raw creativity and spontaneity taking shape in imagination and art. Fichte used the Romantic conception of will to forge a theory of man's moral obligation to treat his fellows humanely and of his service to society. Schelling, on the other hand, looked upon the will as a divining rod to see through nature, as a form of *gnosis*. Schelling's Gnostic leanings are indicated in his tortured prose and Delphic utterances, which make him one of the most difficult German thinkers to understand.

The background of Schelling's ideas and those occurring in much of the Romantic "science" of nature can be traced in the influence of the Austrian physician and occultist Franz Anton Mesmer (1734–1815). Mesmer is familiar to history as a pioneer in the method of hypnotism, but his impact on his age has largely to do with his view of the universe which undergirded his successful therapies. Mesmer believed that the clue to hypnotism was the presence of a mysterious force, which he called "animal magnetism," evident in all organic life and suffusing the entire universe. This magnetism or *fluidum universale* is what accounts for both natural and psychic phenomena, and becomes concentrated in the spirit of man. It affords miraculous powers to the soul, and defines man as a creature attuned in his inward life to eternal mysteries. In the words of Heinrich Jung-Stilling:

> Animal magnetism proves beyond a doubt that we have an inner man, i.e., a soul which consists of the divine spark, of the eternal spirit which has reason and will, and a covering of light which is inseparable from it.[31]

Novalis, for example, was apparently moved by such airy notions. He saw in Mesmer's speculations a warrant for his own "magic idealism." Just as Mesmer thought animal magnetism could be utilized for superhuman accomplishments in harnessing the hidden energies of nature, so Novalis claimed that "magic is the art of using the world of phenomena at will."[32] Through magic "man becomes as powerful as the stars."[33] The attitude of magic comprehends the vital totality to which all acts and events are connected, and the assertion of the wonder worker's will makes manifest the various virtues and potencies that nature harbors.

Schelling was a theosophist of sorts who, like Böhme, lighted on the solution to the problem of time and eternity, as the way in which will and creativity unfold temporally, gradually laying open the timeless ground of all existence. The Gnostic myth of the cycle of redemption whereby the soul is loosed from its eternal anchorage, plies through time and accumulates experience until it returns to its point of origin, shows up in Schelling's later thinking. Schelling explained the creation of the finite world and visible nature as a mysterious "breaking apart" (*Abbrechen*) from God who is eternally identical with himself. But the creation is not an incident in time. It reflects an enduring split in the "Will" of God. In his *Philosophical Inquiry into the Nature of Human Freedom* Schelling echoed Böhme, referring to God as essentially Will. Yet the divine will also contains a division. It is composed of a dark, "unconscious" and indeterminate power of creativity and a principle of knowledge or light. The conflict within the Will is mirrored in the soul of man, who embodies within the finite realm the timeless contradiction in God. Man's personality develops as the will to insight rises to dominance over the unconscious will, and the destiny of the finite, "fallen" creature is precisely to return to the heights of knowledge in which God as the one behind the multiplicity of life and nature is reclaimed. The given condition of man is a profound alienation brought about through the primeval separation from the Godhead. Man may be estranged, but he still enjoys freedom of the will, the freedom which is *au fond* perfected in God alone. In asserting the unconscious will man gradually overcomes this alienation and ascends toward the state of perfection and unity once abandoned. Schelling's doctrine of human salvation parallels the ancient Gnostic tale of the generation of the universe by a capricious demiurge. The world comes into existence by an accidental rupture of time from eternity, and the "fallen" spark of divinity in man seeks to escape this predicament by the inner will to illumination. The infinite endeavors to divest itself of its finite form and become a unity again. For Schelling, religion is the process by which the human will merges with the totality of nature. The irrational will impels man toward a supreme consciousness of the Self or Oneness underlying all phenomena. It is the dynamism of God himself raising man back to Oneness with Deity. Salvation is a series of episodes in time. But viewed as a movement of the divine Will in itself, it ultimately has significance only as an aspect of the eternal drama of spirit which has virtually no bearing on lived history and change.

The Promethean Rebel

If the German Romantic philosophers gave voice to a sense of disillusionment and the drive to recapture lost innocence through an elaborate and opaque metaphysics, the younger breed of English Romantic poets made the same gestures in the cult of the Promethean hero. The figure of Prometheus, who flouted Zeus in the Greek myth by giving fire to man and suffered unceasing torment for his willfulness, became an archetype of the poetic rebel who fought against conformity and authority. Of course, most poets have a touch of the rebel within them. But what distinguished such bards as Lord Byron and Percy Bysshe Shelley was their *cosmic defiance*. The poet steels his will against not just flesh and blood, but the legions of powers in the universe. He appears as a titanic and superhuman martyr who suffers incalculable anguish for the sake of eternal calling. Cut off from ordinary human intercourse, he stands tragically alone before fate, bedevilled by his own foibles and frailties.

The poetic summons to defy heaven can be understood in light of the miscarriage of political liberalism in the age of Napoleon. Shelley's passion for liberty, for example, contrasted with widespread repression of revolutionary activity in England after 1800. Britain's resistance to Napoleon came at the price of great economic misery and the loss of certain civil liberties. The lot of the average working person was abominable, reflecting the wretched social conditions of early capitalism. Agitation among reformers for a measure of justice was put down by the government because of the war emergency. Shelley could compensate for the frustration of political hopes, nevertheless, through his poetic testament concerning the soul's own strength and power. Prometheus arises as the custodian of an arcane wisdom. It is a wisdom which emboldens Prometheus to pit himself against all opposing agencies and affirm his own magnanimity of character. Thus in *Prometheus Unbound* Demogorgon sings a panegyric to the triumphant hero:

> To suffer woes which Hope thinks infinite;
> To forgive wrongs darker than death or night;
>   To defy Power, which seems omnipotent;
> To love, and bear; to hope till Hope creates
> From its own wreck the thing it contemplates;
>   Neither to change, nor falter, nor repent;
> This, like thy glory, Titan, is to be
> Good, great and joyous, beautiful and free;
> This is alone Life, Joy, Empire, and Victory.

For Shelley, it is mystical "love" which animates the struggle against universal tyranny and informs man's higher knowledge of truth and goodness. Love is a balm which can heal the leprous frame of nature. It is a power which emanates from the remote recesses of all life. Shelley's *The Witch of Atlas* depicts a strange, mythical personage who beguiles the elements of nature with such a power. The poem tells of a "lady-witch" who has practiced her trade from the beginnings of creation.

> Before those cruel Twins, whom at one birth
>   Incestuous Change bore to her father Time,
> Error and Truth, had hunted from the Earth
>   All those bright natures which adorned its prime,
> And left us nothing to believe in, worth
>   The pains of putting into learned rhyme,
> A lady-witch there lived on Atlas' mountain
>   Within a cavern, by a secret fountain.

The disenchantment of modern living in which we are left nothing to believe in and time has taken its woeful toll poses a bounteous challenge for the witch. The witch of Atlas represents the "eternal feminine" which, for the Romantics, was the cosmic impulse to creativity. She signifies the energy of love and creative will which roils in the consciousness of the artist and begets new meanings.

> And other say, that, when but three hours old,
>   The first-born Love out of his cradle lept,
> And clove dun Chaos with his wings of gold . . .

The "witch" applies the spirit of love to redeem nature.

> Then by strange art she kneaded fire and snow
>   Together, tempering the repugnant mass
> With liquid love—all things together grow
>   Through which the harmony of life can pass . . .

Shelley's apostrophes to love are an ardent protest against man's inhumanity as well as against the conservatism and icy cynicism of his age. Yet, as is true of the broader Romantic complaint, his is a purely private rebellion at the metaphysical level. Shelley had too much of an aristocratic bent to consciously endorse revolution. His notes to *Prometheus Unbound* and *Hellas* hint of his dread of genuine revolution; and thus the terror of history must be effaced by the innocent sensibilities of the individual poet. An enthusiastic outpouring of love can be the appropriate rejoinder to history's crimes and batterings. Therefore Shelley shows the profile of righteous innocence shaming the authors of brutality, which prompted Matthew Arnold to label him the "ineffectual angel." His Prometheus is the blithe, free spirit, the genius whose deeds may be inconsequential, but whose self-will and defense of the imagination count considerably more under the aspect of eternity.

Byron's poetry is strung with the same shrill notes of defiance, but it is markedly more brooding and pessimistic. The buoyant sense of what the will can authentically accomplish fades in Byron, and the hymn to love is absent. The motif of crushed innocence gives place to that of the accursed and wayward stranger in life. While Shelley's Prometheus reminds us to some degree of Christ, Byron's heroes suggest Satan.[34] The hero takes upon himself to scorn God's very laws and authority, to become a law unto himself, to display his own will not for a higher cause so much as for the expression of will itself. In Byron the lonely ego cries out for recognition. There is a restless urge to complete freedom, a spiting of all restrictive authority. Thus in *The Prisoner of Chillon:*

> Eternal Spirit of the chainless Mind!
>   Brightest in dungeons, Liberty! thou art,
> For there thy habitation is the heart . . .

In *Manfred* Byron portrays a Faustian hero who is a sort of wizard commanding from his mountain tops the pliant spirits of the earth. The spirits, however, mock Manfred because of his one fateful weakness— mortality. Weary of life, yet contemptuous of death, Manfred berates the spirits by extolling his magical aptitudes and his allegiance to the very power of creation:

> Ye mock me—but the power which brought you here
> Hath made you mine. Slaves, scoff not at my will!
> The mind, the spirit, the Promethean spark,
> The lightning of my being, is as bright,
> Pervading, and far darting as your own,
> And shall not yield to yours, though coop'd in clay!

Later in the poem Manfred is approached by an old abbot who bids him renounce his tortured will, repent, and receive the healing grace of God. But Manfred refuses, and in the end does the only "easy" thing a being of his immense, but tragic stature can do. He dies as an act of his own will! Throughout Byron's writings is the message of the

Promethean will to power which bears punishment, pain, and even death, yet renounces any surrender to an external providence or destiny. The "spiritual" slant in man is the signature of the eternal; it cannot be extinguished with the perishing of the body or by strokes of fortune. Good and evil are arbitrary values which cannot be applied in judging the "spirit," in hampering the will. God himself may enforce his order on the cosmos, but he cannot humble the rebel. Thus Byron's *Cain* lionizes the first murderer, as in one the ancient Gnostic sects. Cain comes across as a hero, not so much because of his felony, but because he has declined to acquiesce to the rule of Jehovah instead of his own. Indeed, Lucifer admonishes Cain:

> By tyrannous threats to force you into faith
> 'Gainst all external sense and inward feeling:
> Think and endure,—and form an inner world
> In your own bosom—where the outward fails;
> So shall you nearer be the spiritual
> Nature, and war triumphant with your own.

Cain yields only to the call of his "inner world," which leads him away from the feckless God of traditional piety who is falsely worshipped as the Lord of history. Bereft of "faith," he is nonetheless the man of pure spirit bound neither by society nor customary morality. Condemned to wander throughout time, he yet realizes that he is vindicated because he carries in his soul the torch of eternity.

Bertrand Russell once characterized Byron as an "aristocratic rebel." Byron did prize the patrimony of his British noble ancestry, yet his aristocratic arrogance, like that of the Gnostics, was of a cosmic dimension. He was the type which Camus dubbed the "metaphysical rebel" who wills to push his desire for personal significance to the extent it becomes *hubris,* to reject all social values to the points of nihilism. Byron's noble family had been disgraced by a wastrel of a father. And Byron grew in his youth to become merely one of the disenfranchised intellectual classes tossed about the gusts of social change. Like Manfred, he could not accept the claims that the world made upon him, and he sought a heroic immolation to demonstrate his uniqueness. His untimely death in the Greek war of liberation against the Turks while he was still only in his thirties became a telling metaphor for the Romantic *pathos* as a whole.

Chapter 4

The Apotheosis
of the Will

The all-urging will, raptly Magnipotent . . .
                              —*Thomas Hardy*

Romanticism, Jacques Barzun tells us, "is rich in successes and proportionately rich in failures. Who tries for much stands to gain or lose much."[1] Midway through the nineteenth century the Romantic torch seemed to have flickered out across Europe, suffocated by a new worldliness and realism. A subculture (and Romanticism was exactly that) can only continue for so long to build its castles in the sky. A kind of "cognitive dissonance," a jolting realization of the contrast between the vision of sublime things and workaday reality, sets in. The bemusement with eternity and the prosaic tasks of a finite creature can no longer be reconciled. The struggle against time and its disenchantments cannot be sustained with the same intensity. The post-Napoleonic age, from 1815 onwards, witnessed the slow, but unremitting spread of industrial civilization under the oversight of new masters, the wealthy bourgeoisie who, despite the momentary debacle of the French Revolution, succeeded in tearing power away from the landed aristocracy.

The waning of Romanticism signalled the final capitulation of traditional, European society to modern, industrial capitalism. Within the new order arose, at the same time, the conventional wisdom that science and technology had teamed up at this auspicious pass in history to launch European man on a new voyage of material and moral progress. The bourgeois spirit, which the Romantics roundly abhorred as philistine and soulless, had become the *Zeitgeist* of the nascent epoch. Thus Thomas Carlyle, possibly the last Romantic sage, could characterize the turnabout as early as 1829 in his essay "Signs of the Times." "Were we required to characterize this age of ours by any single epithet," Carlyle wrote, "we should be tempted to call it, not an Heroic, Devotional, Philosophical, or Moral Age, but, above all, the Mechanical Age."[2] Romanticism's distrust of mechanism and materialism, however, did not stick in the minds of the educated European public, which soon endorsed the new thinking. A revamped prestige for the experimental sciences, boosted by a succession of breakthroughs in physics, chemistry, and biology (of which the most telling was the evolutionary theory of Darwin) contributed to the new mood of practical materialism. But it was the bare economic fact of increased wealth and rising standards of living (at least for a significant minority) owing to the industrial revolution itself which fortified the social importance and eventually assured the political power of the middle classes. Such power also established the middle-class view of the world, prompting Karl Marx to observe that the "ruling ideas" of any age are the "ideas of the ruling class."

By the same token, the political utopianism and revolutionary agitation which Romanticism had formerly championed met its tragic denoument following the uprisings of 1848, which burst and then faded out like a meteor shower across the continent. The misfire of the revolution, which disgraced the social idealists, with the exception of the Marxists who had not yet had their day, precipitated not only a widespread political reaction, but fostered a spirit of accommodation, calculation, and manipulation, or what the Germans termed *Realpolitik* (the "politics of realism").

In one important respect, though, the revolution of 1848 meant that the backward gaze of Romanticism to a past era had gone blind. It was a total revolution of the new classes against the old. While in Central Europe the middle classes had presented their brief for liberty, the vanguard of the revolutionary movement was the newly aroused industrial proletariat who vied for the overthrow of capitalism. And the spectre of a true social revolution, rather than a merely political one, panicked the bourgeosie into a rearguard alliance with traditional authority, as the appeal of the Frankfurt Assembly for the Prussian army to quell left-wing riots in the countryside handily illustrates.[3] The maintenance of privilege and the suppression of socialist or anarchist agitation became the rallying point for industrial property owners and the declining aristocracy alike. Yet the new conservatism took on a conspicuously different tone from the Romantic nostalgia of the previous generation. The longing for an organic unity of the "natural" estates in society was replaced by a self-conscious and Machiavellian strategy of social control and engineering—co-opting democratic aspirations and orchestrating class antagonisms with the aim of concentrating power in the hands of the state. The dictatorship of Louis-Napoleon during the Second French Empire and the establishment of the German Reich under Bismarck in the decades after 1850 were the palpable fruits of this strategy. Likewise, the early German Romantic notion of the heroic nobility passed over into the theory of the assimilation of state and civil society, enthroning bourgeois interests, as intimated in Hegel's *Philosophy of Right*. The heart of *Realpolitik* was the obsession with "power" and its application in statecraft as well as revolution.[4]

But the pragmatic and realist drift in politics also had an underside in a new intellectual ferment. The *mal du siècle* finale of the Romantic movement in the 1820s carried over as a world-weariness and latent cynicism which gradually gained expression in a literary revolt against idealism and sentimentality of all kinds. A rough term to describe this posture is "pessimism," but the disaffection ran deeper. Rather, it can be considered a nihilistic repudiation of high-minded morality and intentions, an assault on time-honored virtues and customary assumptions. Acceptance of the irrationality and even the naked brutality of life was as the beginning of wisdom. The Romantic urge toward discovery of private, transcendental truth had slipped over into a radical and tough-minded skepticism, a denial of any hidden truth behind the appearances. The politics of power had its counterpart in a new metaphysics of strife and blind necessity, akin to Darwin's ideas about the "struggle for existence." The doctrine of historical progress, which the earlier Romantics had brushed aside, continued to be pronounced a sham. But now the alternative seemed more sinister. The Romantics yearned for a retrieval of man's innocence in nature; but the picture of nature which the new philosophy limned was anything but pristine and benign. Nature was seen as a slaughterous circus of combatants through which was manifested the insensate striving of cosmic will. In a universe driven by blind will there could be no lofty purposes, no hand of Providence, no saintly triumphs.

From a wider vantage point the intellectual fascination with power and will, particularly on the metaphysical plane, represented the revival of an unalloyed Gnosticism, quickened by the Romantic quest for an ecstasy beyond history and inured by the failure of idealism. The Gnostic hatred of ordinary humanity and its "worldly" dealings, the distaste for everyday morality and "goodness," the emphasis on self-salvation through the affirmation of the will—all these features were set in relief.

The victory of bourgeois culture over Romanticism in the nineteenth century, moreover, could only augur well for the "practical" men of affairs, the barons of industry, the sachems of finance, not to mention the shopkeepers and small property-owners. The nineteenth century brought the steady disenfranchisement of the intelligentsia. With aristocratic patronage gone forever, the fate of scholars and artists fell more and more to the mercy of the marketplace and to the uninformed whims of the "masses." Stripped of their social moorings, the once important intellectual elites distinguished themselves from mass society through the myth of the cultural rebel, the inveterate critic of bourgeois complacency and hypocrisy.

These circumstances made possible a cult of heroes, glorified for example in Carlyle's essay *On Heroes and Hero-Worship and the Heroic in History*. While Carlyle in his hero-worship echoed the Romantic obsession with "genius," he preached in the same breath the new gospel of force and cunning. Carlyle's hero was a man of action whose exercise of the will was in step with an underlying historical necessity, a necessity which was not "moral" in the usual sense of the term, but represented an irrational struggle which turned out to be intelligible only in hindsight, or what Hegel had called "the cunning of reason." The blood and violence wrought by kings and conquerors, Hegel said, may strike the contemporary observer as pointless mayhem, but from a higher perspective it can be understood as necessary for the advance of mankind. History unfolds, Carlyle argued, primarily to illumine the masterful strokes of great individuals. Progress is an illusion, insofar as history is presumed an improvement of the race as a whole. Yet history offers opportunity for the great and the noble to leave their own imprimatur upon events. History is a mandate for the great man to attain power and to realize a grander truth, *his* truth. The dearth of "spirituality" in bourgeois society only foretells the final destruction of pious illusions which have dulled the minds of the noble and ambitious and have prevented the authentic men of destiny from responding to their ultimate calling. The ignorant herd, deprived of tradition and leaders, must at least acknowledge their true authorities—the new men of might and insight. Aristocratic Gnosticism asserted itself as an alternative to the banal values of liberal democracy. Although ideas of the new Gnostics tended largely to be colored by the rational skepticism of bourgeois thinking, they still retained the Romantic enthusiasm for nobility, self-aggrandizement and hardihood. The result was a religion of the superman which blended Romantic bathos with the hunger for earthly power. While such a religion paid attention to history, it regarded historical change only as an opportunity for the self-magnification of the select few.

CARLYLE'S TAILORINGS

The figure of Thomas Carlyle (1795-1881) looms large in this milieu. The son of a Scottish stonemason, Carlyle was molded in his thinking by the harsh, gloomy Calvinism of his father. The emphasis on human sinfulness in Calvinist theology, along with the doctrine that hard work is a sign of having been chosen among God's elect, may have influenced Carlyle's view of man as saving himself through a rigid will and arduous effort. But Carlyle's "Calvinism" was tempered by the secular *Weltanschauung* of his own era. His writings display especially those of later years, a subtle mingling of individualism, Romanticism, and the new catechism of power. The Calvinist belief in predestination surfaced as a fascination with the mysterious forces guiding human history, the doctrine of the chosen ones as the insuperable destiny of great individuals.

Like those of the Romantic generation immediately preceding him, Carlyle was both awed and appalled at advancing industrialism, the new system of economic relationships which had laid feudal society to rest. It was Carlyle who described how "cash payment" had "grown to be the universal sole nexus of man to man,"[5] how confidence in eternal verities had given place to a concern with "the all-importance of physical things."[6] The station and dignity of the savant had been cut down from below by the entrepreneur, the stockbroker, the commodity trader. Later in his career Carlyle would give the devil's due to the social leadership of the business magnates, and would make his peace with the new culture. But it was out of his angry sense of being a stranger in a world made by money and capital that he turned to a metaphysics which give the lie to the common-sense viewpoint of bourgeois modernism. In Carlyle's "literary" philosophy the enigmatic and arcane vision of the Gnostic is given review. The "illusion" of this world and its moral pretenses are exploded, and what one finds on the other side is a mystical asylum for the alienated and spiritually starved. One grasps a more profound meaning to his wretched life, awash in the vortex of time and change, which has all the luster of eternity.

In his youthful, halfway satirical and maddeningly oracular work *Sartor Resartus* ("The Tailor Retailored"), Carlyle set about to articulate his own complicated and esoteric notions about the cosmos. Despite its wordy, obscure, and allusive style, *Sartor Resartus* contained the essential nuggets of Carlyle's Gnostic philosophy. Tempting the reader with word tricks, recondite symbols, and epigrams, rather than straightforward argument, the book aims perhaps at illumination more than exposition. The theme of *Sartor Resartus* is deliberately facetious; it is all about "clothes." The book is putatively a record of the "life and opinions" of one German professor named Teufelsdröckh (literally, "devil's dung") who has completed the first comprehensive treatise on sartorial problems and fashions. The topic of clothing, however, proves allegorical. Just as the wardrobe a person wears serves to express his personality as well as to cover his nakedness, so the phenomenal universe furnishes clues about the nature of God while keeping from mortal eyes the divine refulgence. Visible things, Teufelsdröckh suggests, are merely "emblems" of a deeper and less apparent truth; they are cloaks of mystery. Man's finite intelligence is challenged to disavow crude knowledge of appearances and to penetrate within the ultimate riddle of existence. The "garment maker" must retailor his apparel in order to make them disclose what lies behind them. As the foremost interpreter of German Romanticism to the English public in his day, Carlyle relied upon the Teutonic technique of employing intricate, but evocative language (what Emerson termed his "projectile style") to tease the reader into abdicating his own everyday suppositions and common sense.

Following the Romantics, Carlyle dwelt on the deception of time.

Time is a dragnet for capturing the dull-witted and waylaying pure "spirits."

> Once more I say, sweep away the illusion of Time; compress the threescore years into three minutes: what else was he, what else are we? Are we not Spirits, that are shaped into a body, into an appearance; and that fade away into air and Invisibility?[7]

Time is the "universal wonder-hider" which disguises the genuine "World of Miracles."[8] It is a shabby patch of material which shuts out an everlasting radiance. "Pierce through the Time-element, glance into the Eternal."[9] Opaque time, moreover, keeps out not only the light of eternity, but the god-like spark of transcendent knowledge trapped in the human body. "That little fire which glows star-like across the dark-growing *(nachtende)* moor . . . is it a detached separate speck, cut-off from the whole Universe; or indissolubly linked with the whole?"[10] The answer to such a rhetorical question can easily be discerned from Carlyle's own cast of mind. Matter is only "a visible Garment for that divine Me of his, cast hither, like a light-particle, down from Heaven."[11] The Gnostic motif of the plunge of the soul into matter and ignorance crops up itself in this passage. The soul divine sinks into the chaos of nature, and struggles to liberate itself through wisdom. The contemporary era, Carlyle averred, has witnessed the darkening of man's spiritual life. Authentic knowledge now avails itself only to anointed seers or initiates.

> How changed in these new days! Truly may it be said, the Divinity has withdrawn from the Earth; or veils himself in that wide-wasting Whirlwind of a departing Era, wherein the fewest can discern his goings. Not Godhead, but an iron, ignoble circle of Necessity embraces all things; binds the youth of these times into a sluggish thrall. . . .[12]

Carlyle, as was the case with the Gnostics of old, brooded over the grinding "necessity" (the ancients would have called it "fate") which crushes human freedom. Freedom, though, still lies within reach of those who have the capacity to understand that they have a destiny higher than is evident to the everyday mind. Emancipation from time and necessity is possible by exerting, in Carlyle's phrasing, one's own spiritual "force." It is the force expressed in the will of heroic personalities who have an "Original Insight" into the "primal reality of things." By this insight they have mastery over history; they no longer fear the juggernaut of events.

Carlyle depicts the Gnostic luminary as helmsman of history in *On Heroes and Hero Worship.* "His virtues," Carlyle writes, "all of them, will lie recorded in his knowledge."[13] The great man manifests "the unguided instinct of the world:" he is a work ascribable to the "aptitudes of nature." In *Heroes and Hero Worship* Carlyle distinguishes among the various kinds of heroes including the legendary demigod, the prophet, the poet (such as Dante), and the king, or "the Commander over Men." The last type, "he to whose will our wills are to be subordinated, and loyally surrender themselves, and find their welfare in doing so, may be reckoned the most important of Great Men," Carlyle proclaimed. "He is practically the summary for us of *all* the various figures of Heroism; Priest, Teacher, whatsoever of earthly or of spiritual dignity we can fancy to reside in a man, embodies itself here, to *command* over us, to furnish us with constant practical teaching, to tell us for the day and hour what we are to *do*."[14] The heroes whom Carlyle made larger than life were such august, but misty personages as Cromwell and Napoleon, not to mention certain yet unmaterialized "revolutionary" figures who smack perhaps of Louis-Napoleon, Mussolini, or (daresay) even Hitler. The king, or political hero, combines insight and determination, wisdom and practical shrewdness. Such a hero comprehends the inner imperatives of history and demands compliance from his subjects in realizing his ends. The spiritual justifies the political. Carlyle's critics have noted in his views a peculiar secular mythology: the substitution of the earthly grandee for God. Belief in God was difficult for such men as Carlyle who were infected by the spirit of both British skepticism and Romantic individualism, which could no longer accept the existence of the supernatural. The mystique of the great-souled individual, the captain of fate, supplanted the worship of God the creator, whose benevolent guidance of human dealings had evaporated into the secular belief in a bleak historical determinism.[15] Although God could no longer be invoked to make sense of historical contingency, the idea of the hero who wrests order out of the flux of happenings was beguiling. Through his spontaneous acts the hero manifests the mysterious dynamism of nature; he redeems a society wedged within the steely vice of mechanism and materialism.

The specter of violence and anarchy raised by the Revolution of 1848 seems to have soured Carlyle thoroughly on democracy and encouraged the elitist attitudes of his middle and late years. The mixture of overrefined spirituality and contempt for modern political developments (while idealizing the heroic past) symptomatic of Gnosticism became evident, particularly in his *Latter Day Pamphlets* and *Frederick the Great,* a kind of hagiography of the will to power. His mature books enlarged, according to one of his more recent interpreters, "the gap between self and society" and voiced "a lofty alienation that soon generates a vocabulary of power and contempt."[16] Like Nietzsche after him, Carlyle lashed out at the *canaille,* at socialist and democratic innovations, at utilitarian legislators who envisioned nothing more noble for man than a full belly. Democracy represents the debasement of aristocratic virtue and superiority. The "freedom" which it promises is nought but the empty liberty of the rabble to enforce their mediocrity.

> Free men,—alas, had you ever any notion who the free men were, who the not-free, the incapable of freedom! The free men, if you could have understood it, they are the wise men; the patient, self-denying, valiant; the Nobles of the World; who can discern the Law of this Universe, what it is, and piously *obey* it; these, in late sad times, having cast you loose, you are fallen captive to greedy sons of profit-and-loss; to bad and ever to worse; after at length to Beer and the Devil.[17]

Carlyle's adulation of heroes could hardly hide what LaValley sees as his desperate sense of "failure and futility."[18] Or, as Nietzsche diagnosed it, there appeared in Carlyle "a yearning for a strong belief and the feeling of his incapacity for it."[19] A haunting feeling of powerlessness, nourishing the Gnostic's mania for personal control of his situation, can be detected in Carlyle. The climate of historical optimism which marked the nineteenth century, however, left Carlyle as something of an untimely aberration. Of course, all Gnostics, like prophets for whom they are readily mistaken, have an "untimely" quality about them. But Carlyle seems woefully out of place in English letters. He belonged to a tradition of mystical antimodernism which was ironically quite modern, inasmuch as it fits in with the rebellion of the latter-day Gnostic against middle culture. It is difficult to judge what real influence Carlyle had, which is perhaps due to the fact that his message could have had more of an impact in Germany than in Victorian England. The metaphysics of the will found its most astute disciples on the Continent, where the success of democratic reform was lacking, and the clash between the new and the old resounded more stridently.

SCHOPENHAUER AND THE WILL TO LIVE

The backwash of Romanticism in Germany carried with it a pervasive climate of world denial and disillusionment. A realism, that often bordered on the cynical, reached the level of *bon ton,* and intellectual pacesetters found their minion in the philosopher Arthur Schopenhauer (1788–1860), who during the last decade of his life climbed from quiet obscurity to popular renown. Schopenhauer, however, displayed a personality and temperament which eschewed trendy thinking and facile publicity. History remembers him as a misanthrope and irascible recluse who passed a bitter sentence on the human condition.[20] The arch "philosopher of pessimism," Schopenhauer devoted himself to exposing the false ideologies and delusions of Western civilization. The young Nietzsche, himself a votary of Schopenhauer's ideas, lauded the master for his unsparing "candor" in philosophical matters.

> In this way must Schopenhauer's philosophy always be interpreted; as an individualist philosopher, starting from the single man, in his own nature, to gain an insight into personal miseries, needs, and limitations, and find the remedies that will console them. . . . He teaches us to distinguish between the true and the apparent furtherance of man's happiness: how neither the attainment of riches, nor honour, nor learning, can raise the individual from his deep despair at his unworthiness; and how the quest for these good things can only have meaning through a universal end that transcends and explains them.[21]

The human goal of "happiness" within the everyday routines of living proves to be a chimera. A deep-felt alienation from the world in all its aspects was a Gnostic note which Schopenhauer constantly struck. As in the Gnostic vision, Schopenhauer counseled redemption through personal flight. The mind must slash through the net of the senses (the veil of illusion the Hindus call *Maya*) to the coruscating truth beyond. Historical optimism of human beings toward their own accomplishments is a self-serving and self-inflicted deception. History has no rhyme or reason; it is "a European catfight," as Schopenhauer remarked in one of his conversations.[22] Man must puncture the delusion of progress in order to attain a transcendental awareness by which all striving after goals or projects are viewed as trifles. One must withdraw from historical existence and reflect eternally on the wretchedness of the human lot and the fundamental fact of suffering.

The primary datum that "life is suffering" is, of course, a key Buddhist notion which Schopenhauer mediated to the West. Schopenhauer was the first Occidental thinker to do more than pore curiously over Oriental scriptures: he incorporated the "wisdom" of the East into his own metaphysical system. And the study of Eastern philosophy and religion in Europe owes much of its impetus to Schopenhauer's own writings. Schopenhauer, however, was not some exotic and mushy-headed guru who spoke in cryptic utterances. He was a scholar tutored in the tradition of classical German philosophy which included Kant, Hegel, and Schelling. The murkiness of much of his thought was offset by methodological clarity and stylistic verve. The vanity of life, the sham of progress and the lie of history, were convictions which he derived from subjective experience. Private intuition tells us more about the whole human experience than moral idealism.

> History shows us the life of nations; but it tells us nothing but that of war. The peaceful years appear as short respites, interludes, when and if they occur. We find the life of the nation a constant battle, and it is exactly the same with the life of the individual. He goes constantly from one skirmish to the next, embroiled in ceaseless warfare, and dies with sword in hand.[23]

Historical life is a portion of the "phenomenal" world; it is exactly as it appears to us on the surfaces—a play of life forms struggling among themselves which rise into view and dissolve back into an underlying chaos. "The character of all things is transience," Schopenhauer declared.[24] One cannot rationalize the terror of history, nor find any enduring meaning within it. Instead one must understand profoundly and critically the hopelessness of the human lot, thereby quelling all desires to enjoy or confirm it, and resolve to pull oneself out of the quagmire of time and becoming while resting in eternity.

The linchpin of Schopenhauer's metaphysical doctrine was his conception of the "Will to Live" *(Wille zum Leben)*. The Will to Live, for Schopenhauer, is a blind, unconscious striving that affects all living beings. The will to live is impersonal and amoral in its many effects. It drives all organic beings to act in a way conducive to their own self-preservation and thus precipitates the battle for survival in nature. The Will to Live is the supersensible force behind what those who have read Darwin would recognize as the "red tooth-and-claw" contest for existence governing natural selection. The Will to Live avails to no obvious purpose but is "objectified" by the human mind as conscious intentions or aims. The ascription of intentions to the Will rests on a self-deception, or what Nietzsche termed a "necessary lie," which supplies a semblance of order and direction to life. The personal will, however, has no more rational or moral objectives than the cosmic Will to Live—it is simply the greater Will expressing itself as an individual life. "Will," whether it be personal or universal, furnishes man "the key to his own phenomenon, reveals to him the significance and shows him the inner mechanism of his being, his actions, his movements."[25] Will keeps all sentient creatures in constant motion, though it does not steer them toward any happy resolution of their wants, projects, and sufferings. Each particular constellation of acts of will comprises the "character" of the person and determines how he will conduct his life. But this character is not the basis of freedom. On the contrary, it signifies a kind of "script" according to which every individual will make certain kinds of decisions and demonstrate distinct preferences. The character of the individual derives ultimately from the Will to Live, which manifests itself as his own unique "fate." Schopenhauer favorably quoted the Greek philosopher Heraclitus: "Character is destiny." Personal freedom in the material world turns out in the final analysis, like all moral notions, to be a bald illusion. Caught up in the crashing wheelworks of events the individual has no other option than to suppress the Will and disengage himself from life altogether. In a universe where values and ideals have no reality other than as that which Schopenhauer termed the "representations" of the will (Freud would have spoken of unconscious "wish-fulfillments"), the sole recourse is either to take a nihilistic posture and abandon oneself to his own inclinations or to retreat from all worldly striving and aspirations. For Schopenhauer, the latter beckoned as the royal road to salvation.

In general, the web in which human existence is entangled, according to Schopenhauer, is time itself. Time consists in the objectification of the Will to Live within the succession of phenomena. Time can be regarded as the structure of cognition within which the experience of change and duration takes place, since every alteration or movement in the perceptible world issues from the striving of the Will. "Time has no beginning, but all beginning is in time,"[26] for time continues so long as the Will is forever behind the restless flow and churning of life. Moreover, time is what makes possible the recognition of causal links between phenomena. Because each event follows upon another in time, we can trace a causal connection between them. Hence we are constrained to grasp our world as determined by a scheme of mutual conditions and influences. Time and fate are interlocking concepts in Schopenhauer's philosophy. On the other hand, both time and the system of ideas about the world which are a part of workaday experience reveal themselves to be basically illusory. Schopenhauer bastardized the teachings of his philosophic predecessor, Immanuel Kant, who held that time and space are not real in themselves, but are *a priori* (i.e., "prior to experience") forms of thinking existing in the mind through which objects of perception appear. Thus, Schopenhauer reasoned, time is no doubt unreal. The only Reality is the Will to Live, which is the "thing in itself" made apparent in phenomena. To escape the tight nexus of time, change, and causality, one must acquire deep insight into the thing-in-itself lurking behind the curtain of sensory impressions. One must extirpate his own private will and desire, as elements in the phenomenal order, and unite his self with the unconditioned Will to Live which is located not in time, but in eternity.

The mystical absorption of the individual will into the Will itself constitutes a sanctuary from the horrors and torment of temporal existence. The fear of impermanence and finitude is overcome by taking refuge in the Source of life itself. In a word, the act of identifying with the Will itself amounts to a total immersion in the present, the "eternal now," which is the still point around which mortal life turns.

> We can compare time to an endlessly revolving sphere; the half that is always sinking would be the past, and the half that is always rising would be the future; but at the top, the indivisible point that touches the tangent would be the extensionless present.[27]

Eternity is "an extensionless point" that "cuts time which extends infinitely in both directions, and stands firm and immovable, like an everlasting midday without a cool evening, just as the actual sun burns without intermission, while only apparently does it sink into the bosom of night."[28] The *world* as Will embodied in phenomena grinds on toward dissolution and death, but the Will itself cannot be attenuated or destroyed. Transfigured into pure Will, man becomes one with the deathless stream of nature. But the identification with the Will to Live can only come about through a subtle *gnosis* or intuition. It comes through an "immediate knowledge" of the inner essence of one's own character and volitions. Thus the riddle of suffering, for Schopenhauer, is unravelled by insight into the subterranean recesses of life. Schopenhauer's way was the Buddhist way of esoteric enlightenment.

The renunciation of the Will to Live as a consequence of a mystical grasp of things in their totality rescues the individual from the toils of time and history. In the same leap of awareness all the illusions of history burst in the face of a more profound truth. The man of knowledge realizes that humanity's "ceaseless efforts to banish suffering achieve nothing more than a change in its form"[29]; the cure of one ailment leads to another, as the Will continues to rage in the struggle for life. In place of the idea of progress Schopenhauer substituted the Hindu view of time as an endless, cyclical process—the wheel of karma, suffering, and rebirth. Anticipating Nietzsche's theory of "eternal recurrence" which we shall discuss shortly, Schopenhauer sketched a picture of a universe in flux and always returning inexorably to the same point of departure. "The true symbol of nature is the circle . . . for recurrence is the most general form of nature, which is realized in all things from the motions of the stars to the death and birth of organic life."[30] By the same token, "our personal existence has no foundation on which to rest except the present. Thus its form is unceasing motion, without any possibility of that repose which we continually strive after."[31] The individual allays the burden of temporality by merging with the stream of time and becoming. He spreads his soul wide to an "undiminished infinity . . . always open for the return of any event or work that was nipped in the bud."[32] He conquers the Will to Live by ceasing to exist a mere moment in it, by embracing the fullness of active, restive life forms and losing his own pimping sense of particularity.

In one significant respect, Schopenhauer's "great extension" of the idea of will from the motivating principle of individual action to a metaphysical notion which he described as the "sufficient reason" for all that occurs mitigated the Gnostic *hubris*, the drive for self-assertion. To affirm all life as propelled by the Will to Live, Schopenhauer proclaimed, is tantamount to an empathetic recognition of the sorrow and anguish of all finite beings. To participate in the Will to Live is to suffer with all animate species who are inflamed by the very same Will. On this score Schopenhauer offered ethics of "compassion" similar to the Buddhist morality which he admired. Compassionate involvement in the world of suffering and affliction results in a feeling of unity with humanity, rather than an estrangement from the "unspiritual" multitudes which Gnosticism has always condemned. The compassionate soul "extends his own inner nature to embrace his countrymen, and continues to live in them; in fact, he covers the generations to come, for whom he works."[33]

Nonetheless, his worldly pessimism, resting on the metaphysical precept that ultimate reality is blind, striving Will, was a harsh hint of the bankruptcy of ethical as well as historical thought which befell the generation of the mid-nineteenth century. While he did not worship *à la* Carlyle iron men of destiny, his disparagement of egalitarian and democratic aspirations betrayed a Gnostic elitism with uncomfortable political implications. Talk about the rights of man, Schopenhauer said, is tiresome twaddle, for nature installs the rule of the most powerful, or what Schopenhauer termed *Faustrecht* (literally, the "right of fist"). Petty despots have no greater legitimacy than republicans or anarchists, since each attains his station in society through the caprices of the Will. Yet neither can there be any moral criticism of their privileges. Schopenhauer sided with monarchs against partisans of popular government, and he dismissed the Revolution of 1848 as just another noisy imbroglio. Independently well-off from an estate inherited from his *Bürger* father, Schopenhauer vehemently defended the prerogatives of wealth. Various scibblings in his adolescent diary reveal a slightly decadent obsession with macabre oddities, such as public executions and torture. In fine, the tone of his thinking reflects that of a dispossessed and solitary malcontent fearful of the social upheavals around him and yearning for peaceful release. The reduction of all phenomena to an amoral Will to Live may be seen as a sophisticated justification of a thoroughly unjust world which the melancholy seer is content to leave as it is. The terror of history can only be surmounted by discounting history itself.

NIETZSCHE AND THE WILL TO POWER

Schopenhauer perhaps made his most immediate and perhaps lasting impact on the young Friedrich Nietzsche (1844-1900). While Nietzsche's major works were published in the last two decades of the nineteenth century, and therefore postdate for the most part both the Romantic and the realistic phases of that era, they contain a startling philosophical solution to the problem of time and of the will. Nietzsche's first encounter with Schopenhauer occurred when he picked up a copy of *The World as Will and Representation* in a bookstore. This turned out to be a sort of revelation. Admiring his "perspicacity" and lack of sentimentality, Nietzsche was impressed with Schopenhauer's hard-nosed temperament and impiety. Nietzsche, of course, eventually turned against his erstwhile philosophical mentor, as he also did against his artistic docent Richard Wagner; for it is perhaps the earmark of a creative thinker that he can first derive inspiration from another's ideas and then completely make them over. Nietzsche's entire corpus of writings is so vast, labyrynthine, and fertile that we cannot do justice in this space to the nuances and development of his thought, let alone biography. Yet we can, at least, explore the process by which the concept of life as Will was incorporated into his own peculiar vision of human destiny and thereby marked a turning point in the nineteenth century valuation of history. In casting aside Schopenhauer's portrayal of life as dominated by the Will to Live, he shaped a more radically uncompromising theory of voluntarism which deflated familiar moral assumptions and ideas about God.

Nietzsche's quarrel with Schopenhauer centered mainly on the meaning of "will." Nietzsche soon came to abhor Schopenhauer's "pessimism," his "world weariness" and forswearing of life. The ascetic resignation of the saint, which Schopenhauer commended, was not at all to Nietzsche's liking. Throughout his writings Nietzsche extolled the "Dionysian" man who affirmed human existence in its most poignant and tragic dimensions, who could courageously affirm both the joys and miseries of experience, the peaks and the valleys, the successes and defeats of daily conflict. Nietzsche revered the agnostic ideal of ancient Greek culture, the delight in constant combat and suffering which had no aim other than the creative activity of confronting obstacles and surmounting them. The Greeks, Nietzsche thought, had a dark intimation of the fortuity of life; but instead of shrinking from fate, they were infatuated with it. Nietzsche glorified this disposition which he dubbed *amor fati* ("the love of fate"), and he made it the colophon of the "Dionysian" life. In his later works Nietzsche modified Schopenhauer's notion of the Will to Live into what he called the "Will to Power" *(der Wille zur Macht)*. "Life is the Will to Power,"[34] he remarked. "This world is the Will to Power, and nothing other than that."[35] Though Nietzsche never specified carefully, or enlarged on, what the Will to Power comprises, he saw it as the opposite of the mere will to exist or get by, the instinct for survival. "Above all, a living thing wants to expend its strength, for life itself is *Will to Power*: self-preservation is only one of the most oblique and most common consequences of it."[36] The Will to Power is, in essence, the will to *more* power, to a continuing conquest of life as it presents itself. Power comes through the struggle to leap over the impediments placed before man by nature as well as those obstacles inherent within himself. The Will to Power, however, involves an act of affirmation, a "yea-saying" which does not begrudge adversity or hardship, but which relishes them as stimuli to further "overcoming." Indeed, it is the Will to Power which distinguishes the supreme type of humanity which Nietzsche christened *Übermensch* or "overman" (often incorrectly translated as "superman"). The overman is one who, by cultivating and expressing his Will to Power, incessantly *overcomes* himself and reaches new plateaus of self-transcendence. For "man is the still unfinished animal"[37]; he is "that something which must be surpassed."[38]

Nietzsche regarded the expression of the Will to Power as the cipher to the puzzle of existence in a world where "God is dead" and the old systems of moral value have been shipwrecked. The death of God, which Nietzsche hailed, is an "event" that man is slowly coming to acknowledge. The death of God represents not only an enervation of belief, the collapse of the "illusion" of an "other" world, but the breakdown of all firm reference points and structures of order, shaking the very cross-beams of society and ethics. The destruction of the illusion of the other world unmasks the kaleidoscopic character of reality.

> O heaven above me! Pure! High! For me this is your purity now: that there is no eternal spider and spiderwebs of reason, that you are for me a dancing floor of divine coincidences, that you are for me a table of the gods for divine dice and dice-players.[39]

Philosophical understanding delivers the world from "bondage to purpose." No eternal plan or pattern of things can be glimpsed from within the maelstrom of forces and changes. "But it concerns time and becoming about which the best images should speak; they should be a praise and a defense of transitory things."[40] Yet the corrosion of steady moorings for human thought and hence culture makes possible the liberation of the overmen, the "free spirits" who as "lovers of knowledge" and titans of the will create new meanings within the giddly whirl of happenings. "Will brings freedom . . . in recognition also I feel nothing but my will's pleasure in generation and becoming,"[41] in shepherding new values and meanings into being through a vision of life as a great tide surging and overflowing. To affirm the chaos and then to will new meanings into existence, meanings which are nevertheless as fugitive as the ones which have expired—that is to exercise the Will to Power. The Will to Power is the creative urge toward growth and expansion of the individual self amidst the chaos of experience. By the will the "higher man" averts the peril of meaninglessness; by willing what he is to become for himself he invents new meanings, thus dispelling the ravages of fate and the loss of life's coherence. He gains authentic freedom. "Everything is freedom. You can, because you *will*!"[42]

In Nietzsche's view freedom is not a given, but something to be wrested by the will from life. The will, however, cannot reweave the tapestry of fate; it cannot conjure up a purpose to existence where purposiveness, in the metaphysical sense, is a mirage. Rather, one can strive to appropriate what is imminent for all time as one's destiny. One can "love" fate by embracing it as his own. One can "will" whatever occurs as though it were one's own sovereign choice. Thus Nietzsche's hero Zarathustra avows:

> I instructed them in all my poetry and endeavor. I taught them to compose and gather together as one everything which is fragmented and puzzling and a horrible accident in man. As a poet and puzzle-solver and one who delivers them from mischances, I taught them to create the future and everything that *was*, to redeem creatively. To redeem the past in man and to refashion all "that was," until the will speaks: "But I willed it so! So I will will it." This I named for them "redemption," this by itself I taught them to call redemption.[43]

It is in this connection that Nietzsche downplays the significance of history. In his early essay "On the Use and Abuse of History"

Nietzsche rued the advent of historicism in modern culture and the overrefinement of the "historical sense." A prepossession with history stultifies "life" in Nietzsche's words (and by "life" he meant something akin to what years thereafter he would describe as the *Will to Power*). A methodical attention of the historicist to all that has been and continues to happen leaves the mind weary of details and the will paralyzed when it comes to asserting the significance of one's own life: "(but) with the smallest and largest happiness, there is always one thing through which happiness comes into being; that is the ability to forget or, as we might say in a more erudite manner, the capacity to perceive things 'unhistorically' in their duration."[44] For "man cannot develop into man without first limiting the unhistorical element in his thinking, reflecting, distinguishing, and unifying habits. Only within that all-enveloping cloud of vapor a clear, shining light suddenly appears; only then, through the strength to use the past in order to live and to make history again out of that which has happened. . . ."[45]

The superior individual is one who climbs to a "transhistorical" standpoint for the sake of making history "minister to life." In the same vein, Nietzsche spewed his wrath at the apostles of evolutionism, and especially at the proponents of progress. The idea of progress is just another "moral prejudice" which saps the will, which prevents us from embracing the moment and attaching significance to our own personal struggles. In numerous passages from his more mature treatises Nietzsche mocks the notion that history, and Western history in particular, gives evidence of any movement toward the betterment of mankind. For instance, Nietzsche says:

> *Mankind* does not progress; it does not even exist. The total aspect is one of a monstrous, experimental workshop, where there are some successful efforts, strewn through all ages, and countless failures, in which all order, logic, unity, and obligation are missing.[46]

The few "successful efforts," the overmen, rise to power and notoriety not because of any immanent historical thrust forward by the species, but because as solitary and venturesome geniuses they have nourished their own will to power. They live within history but are not part of it; they are as gems in the offal. Their sense of "truth" transcends what can be discovered and digested from any knowledge of the historical process *per se*. Similarly, Nietzsche looked upon the belief in historical progress as a pallid, secular variation on the theological idea of Providence. Where divine purpose could no longer be fathomed, the human mind had concocted the fiction of a "goal" for the race. Darwinism was a pseudotheory which attributed stellar virtues to modern humanity simply by virtue of its having survived through natural selection. But survival is not the key to greatness. What has survived in history on the main has been the average and mediocre, the democratic "herd man," who prizes not nobility but *equality*. What the evolutionists vaunt as "progress" is a lapsing "measure by measure further into decadence."[47] By "decadence" Nietzsche meant the weakening of the Will to Power and the ascendancy of the communal animal over the self-made herd-type, a propensity which becomes obvious in liberal democracy and socialism. True "progress" consists in "the reinforcing of the type, the capacity for great willing."[48] Authentic evolution is "to win power over nature and a power over oneself as well"; it is "Will to Power, which is self-exaltation and self-fortification."[49] The overman thus evokes in his own time and because of his own will a definite admiration. No one can account for his appearance with regard to any indwelling "purpose" in nature, since nature has no purpose. Nature is nought but the ongoing generation of the Will to Power, and through the will the exemplary individual constructs his own purposes and meaning for existence.

The absence of God, or any abstract canon of meaning in history, is the hard truth the overman realizes, even though this truth menaces the stability of the collective, the endurance of species as a whole. But of greater consequence is the fact that the death of God must bestir the great individual to forge a higher aim for himself, to discipline his will and become the master of circumstance. God, that most "tenacious lie," must be replaced by the courage to face the universe starkly and honestly, by "saying *yes* to life even in the teeth of its unknown and most difficult problems," in "the eternal desire of becoming oneself without terror and pity."[50] While there can be no "eternal life" in store for the pious, no "beyond," no cosmic caretaker, there yet remains the opportunity for *self-salvation* through the Will to Power. In this regard Nietzsche, even though abjuring the great satisfaction of "eternity" outside mortal life, stumbled upon a solution to the problem of time and becoming which pointed beyond time and becoming. It was not a religious doctrine which he formulated, but a very "scientific hypothesis," that of "eternal recurrence."

Nietzsche introduced the idea of "eternal recurrence" in *Thus Spoke Zarathustra*. Given that the universe is an unremitting flux of events, a pageant of force and energy, in which no transparent pattern or direction can be described, Nietzsche asked, how can an individual life acquire meaning? To what avail is the cultivation of the Will to Power? The answer lies, according to Nietzsche, in the nature of the flux itself. Though the world exists to no climactic purpose, there is still great import in the fact that it is finite and that a finite world must come into being and pass away repeatedly. The "scientific" or logical argument for the cyclical character of the world process was enunciated by Nietzsche in *The Will to Power*.

> If the world *may* be conceived as a specific magnitude of force and as a specific number of certain centers of force, and every other image remains indefinite and hence of no use, then in the dice game of its existence, the world must complete a calculable number of combinations. All possible combinations in an infinite span of time would at some point have been achieved . . . Since between each combination and its subsequent repetition, all yet unrealized combinations at all times must have run off, and since each combination determines the entire succession of combinations in the same sequence, therefore a circuit of purely identical sequences would have been prover. As a circuit the world, having already reiterated itself without end, thus goes on playing its game *in infinitum*.[51]

Nietzsche's claims notwithstanding, the foregoing has never really been considered an exercise in scientific cosmology, and it is open to question how seriously Nietzsche took what he was doing as amounting to "science." The argument in favor of "eternal recurrence" does not constitute a theoretical account of matter in motion so much as an exhortation to alter the perspective on one's own thoughts and actions. "Everything eternally recurs, and we ourselves with everything . . . we have already been here an eternal number of moments, and everything has also been with us for the same."[52] The fact that every incident in our lives recurs eternally poses a redoubtable challenge: we can meekly acquiesce, perhaps with silent rancor, to the torque of fate, or we can affirm the majesty and bounty of life by the Will to Power. Again, we can *will our destiny as eternally meaningful*. We are heartened in "the eternal desire to create, so that the will to life asserts itself on and on forever. . . ."[53] It is the ecstasy of this realization that Nietzsche labels "the gay science" *(Fröhliche Wissenschaft)*, the deepmost knowledge or *gnosis* of the "higher things;" thus "joy wants eternity." It is the infinite act of will which says "yes" to the infinite complexity of existence, and to one's place within it. Even fatality is celebrated. "All things are chained, trapped, infatuated. If you ever wanted one thing twice, and each time you said, 'you are pleasing to me, happiness! ah, moment!' and you wanted *everything* back! Everything renewed! Everything eternal!"[54]

Awareness of eternal recurrence comprises a fusion of insight and Will to Power, an affirmation by which the overman compresses all history into his own action, his own volition. It permits him to "feel the history of man in its immensity *as his own history*."[55] It stands as the "Moment," the "Great Noon" which divides past from future, and the lower men from the overmen; it is the occasion for the final manifestation of the "higher type." "One lives *before* him; one lives *after* him."[56] The epiphany of the overman snips the thread of continuity in history. History does not bring him to fruition; he is above all a happenstance of history who nevertheless incarnates the meaning of all history[57] through his wisdom and will. The overman overleaps history in the avowal of eternal recurrence. By banishing all value from history, he becomes the paramount value in himself. He outlasts history in a triumph of the will.

The Gnostic side of Nietzsche's thinking is fairly noticeable. Man is redeemed from history by the knowledge of eternal recurrence. The assertion of the Will to Power extricates the "free spirit" from the chain of causality and gives a uniquely personal and unconditioned meaning to his life as seen in the "moment." The spell of time is shattered in the acceptance of "eternal recurrence," of the endless repetition of all lives, including his own. There is too a reminiscence of the shamanic vision flight in Nietzsche's symbolism. Nietzsche contrasts the "lightness" of Zarathustra's joy with the "spirit of gravity" weighting down the mind. "[He is] Zarathustra the dancer, Zarathustra the light, waving with wings, one who is ready to fly, waving to all birds, prepared and ready, blissfully light-headed."[58] Just as the Gnostic dreams of flying beyond the sublunary spheres through the magic of unconscious projection, so the overman wings upward across the innumerable planes of inward reality.

Let us suppose that somebody in his dreams had ofttimes taken flight and at last became conscious, as soon dreamt, of a strength and art of flying that can be regarded as his prerogative and his own peculiar, enviable happiness. A person who believes to be able to negotiate

every sort of curve and angle with the most delicate of impulses, who
has the feeling of a divine light-headedness, an "on the way up"
without tension and pressure, an "on the way down" without
patronizing or humiliating, that is, without being *heavy*."[59]

In flight the free spirit suffers no encumberments of his surroundings,
displaying the Will to Power in its purest expression. He fashions his
own destiny; he writes his own life-script; he creates his own universe
of meaning. Like Zarathustra, he is a lonely, but mighty artificer, a man
aspiring above mere mortals, and belonging to the undefiled aristocracy
of the spirit.

Nietzsche's theories, indeed, have been dubbed an "artistocratic
radicalism." The image of the high-bred, aloof, and puissant noble
"type" suffuses Nietzsche's comments about the overman. Historically
speaking, Nietzsche seems to have idolized the blue-blooded masters of
bygone feudal cultures: the warriors of Homeric Greece, the dukes of
Renaissance Italy, the Brahminic caste of India. The figure of nobility
appears as a stylized exemplar of strength, self-possession, and finesse.
In his *Genealogy of Morals* Nietzsche sought to trace the development
of all moral values from the dictates of the ancient aristocracy.
"Goodness" originally signified nothing more, according to Nietzsche,
than that which is willed by the mighty and subsequently imposed on
the weaker. The Will to Power represents the touchstone of aristocratic
ethics. The overman stands in relief atop the pyramid of talents in
feudal culture. "Heretofore every elevation of the type 'man' has
actually been the contribution of an aristocratic social order . . . a social
order that believes in a lengthy ladder of rank-ordering and variations in
value from man to man, a society that requires slavery in some
sense."[60] The slave is necessary as a foil and as a slate for the
nobleman's stamp of his Will to Power. For this reason Nietzsche had
the utmost repugnance for the middle classes and for their democratic
"sentimentalism" which makes sham merits of pettiness, meanness,
the commonplace, the "average," and which esteems the herd instead
of the individual—the "moral charlatanry" which is implicit in "a very
ordinary, common, bourgeois life of mediocrity."[61] Bourgeois civilization has been responsible for a thorough levelling of the traditional
orders and has made an opprobrium of aristocratic virtues. The moral
duties of the nobleman, though, are distinctive in that they are not
"duties for everybody."

In keeping with Gnostic mythology, however, Nietzsche aimed to "spiritualize" the image of the nobleman. One is not noble by birth, but by the will and intellect, not by "function" nor simple "rank" but by "passion." His insignia is a "spiritual haughtiness," a "reverence" for himself, an alacrity for doing "evil" in the customary sense of the word if it augments his will to power. He *becomes* noble by constantly overcoming himself and mounting to ever new heights of sensibility and grandeur.

The "philosopher king" may be considered an illustration of the sort of individual Nietzsche had in mind, but many passages indicate that the overman stands for a more imposing and mythical ideal. Certainly Nietzsche refused to pinpoint any specific historical personalities who might correspond to his paragon. Great men of state such as Napoleon and Caesar Borgia came close, but each one Nietzsche found flawed in particular ways. Goethe was perhaps in Nietzsche's mind most deserving of the designation of overman because of his aplomb, his critical intelligence, combined with majesty of vision.[62] However, the idea of the overman as literally one who consistently "surpasses" himself, or is always raising himself to higher levels of fitness and excellence, rules out the possibility that he could reside among mere mortals. The overman is a limit, an asymptope forever to be approached but not reached.

In lieu of the Gnostic image of the soul ascending the infinite ladder of perception, Nietzsche composed the secular myth of the free spirit ever traversing and overcoming his own humanity. The superhuman ideal which Nietzsche dangled before men, together with his imperious attitude toward common humanity, constituted a colossal revolt against the entrenchment of middle-class culture and mores. Nietzsche's writings, therefore, can be seen against the backdrop of the growth of the bourgeois German state under Bismarck in the decades after the Franco-Prussian war of 1870. Nietzsche exhibits in a certain degree the *Junker,* or German aristocratic mentality, horrified at the spread of parliamentary democracy and social liberalism. Like Bismarck, Nietzsche inveighed against the "nihilism" of modern social democracy and bourgeois values which had edged out the old traditions and statues.[63] But, in contrast to Bismarck, Nietzsche was unwilling to accept the victory of the middle class as a *fait accompli*. Instead of making an accommodation with the modern world, he fell back on a lavish mythology which exalted strength and heroism. The "decadence" which he perceived all around him, ruining the manly virtues of the ancient castes, became a shibboleth in the Gnostic anathema of the new order, and which continued to have sharp resonances into the next century. In the end (as history is well aware) Nietzsche's personal struggle with the universe gave way to a madness which removed him from the public eye and reduced him to occasional outbursts of monomaniacal blather during the final ten years of life (he died in 1900 just as the new century he had fore-glimpsed with Cassandra-like fury was dawning). If it is the cosmic aim of the Gnostic to attain an ultimate transfiguration to divine, so Nietzsche in his dementia seems to have granted himself such an achievement. In a letter to his former confidant, the great Renaissance historian Jacob Burckhardt, Nietzsche wrote: "Dear Professor, when it comes right down to it I'd much rather have been a Basel Professor than God; but I didn't dare be selfish enough to forgo the creation of the world."[64] "From time to time we practice magic," Nietzsche went on, "Wilhelm Bismarck and all anti-Semites," the tokens of the German Reich and all of middle-class society, "are done away with."[65] To his own gleeful satisfaction Nietzsche had halted time and wished away the modern era.

Chapter 5

Intimations of Other Worlds: The Flowering of Occultism

I have come to hold sacred the disorder of my mind.
—Arthur Rimbaud

In February 1871 there appeared in Paris a penniless, adolescent boy of seventeen, who could be found wandering the city, scavenging for food scraps, and sleeping in the streets and under bridges. The times were quite grim. The army of the Second Republic had just capitulated to the Germans in the Franco-Prussian War, and Parisians were smarting over the humiliation of defeat. In three months the Paris Commune would stage a revolt against not only the German occupation and the quisling-government at Versailles which had arranged the surrender, but also the whole of bourgeois society and morality. The boy, named Arthur Rimbaud, who came from the provincial city of Charleville, had been a brilliant student who had fled from home in order to join up with the patriotic militia in Paris. But Rimbaud's urge to insurrection was directed more toward the Catholic piety and moralism of his family than against visible political adversaries. His running away to Paris seemed the typical, romantic whimsy of a restless, stiff-necked youth chafing at the psychological confinements of a small town and a domineering mother. His subsequent accounts of those days disclose little about the actual political situation, but they throw in relief the thrashings of his own mind. An obscure but traumatic sexual experience as part of his vagrant escapades affected him in such a way that his life was changed. Returning to the staid haven of home, he was transformed from a quiet and conscientious student into a brash eccentric, a debauchee, a perverse visionary who would eventually be remembered as one of the world's most celebrated poetic geniuses.

Rimbaud's fateful experience in Paris, although only happenstance, can be taken as a sort of metaphor for the outcome of the revolutionary spirit among the middle classes in late nineteenth-century Europe. Like Nietzsche in Germany, Rimbaud was a cultural and artistic rebel against bourgeois hypocrisy and philistine values. Born into a "good" family, he grew up to condemn as well as scandalize the mores and habits of French polite society. But his verve for rebellion could not truly be sustained in political activities. Narcissism and self-indulgence led him into a metaphysical war of personal symbols, an agonistic struggle with the phantoms of his dark consciousness. Both Rimbaud and Nietzsche wound up in combat with the Christian God, whom they sought to dethrone from his place in the heavens and replace with the inwardly divine and illumined self. For Rimbaud the plunge into his own private universe was a desperate gambit. Rimbaud was obsessed with the chaos of the everyday world and the depravity of his own mind. The squalid contradictions of life could only be smoothed out by an inventive and seemingly omnipotent imagination, which sought to make over completely the content of ordinary perception and "purify" the individual's own debased self-awareness.

Wanting to be more than a mere poet, Rimbaud styled himself a *voyant*, a "seer," who devotes his art to supernatural anomalies. In the hands of the poet as seer, language becomes something much more than a vehicle of communication or even entertainment. Language is a magic wand which metamorphoses the features of ordinary reality and opens wide man's consciousness to an altogether different and utterly bewitching universe. Each word in itself harbors a secret code; it belongs to an occult index of feelings, tones, and moods which bespeak an uncommon dimension of life. Words have sorcerous *power* not only to disarrange the individual's senses, but to hasten a mutation of his character. Through words one gains cosmic knowledge. The poet-seer becomes a god himself. And through such a translation he rids himself of the false beliefs, self-loathing, and baggage of guilt with which society, traditional religion, and moral education encumber him. He blanks out the misery of existence with the glaring light of inner certitude. He has the capacity to rejudge and reconstruct the world with the hocus-pocus of his own vital symbols.

The subject matter and technique of Rimbaud's poetry, not to mention his conduct, was intended to outrage his audience. Rimbaud caused a literary sensation by renouncing his own literary career almost as soon as he had declared his radical agenda for the art. Upon completion of *A Season in Hell*, which has soulful echoes of the inner turmoil brought on by the Paris experience, Rimbaud abruptly retired from the poetic profession before the age of twenty. He sought to have the manuscripts burned, then fell silent, and went off for the rest of his brief life to be a merchant in the African colonies. The bewildering, outré manner of Rimbaud's poetic craft and personal demeanor only testified to what was his fundamental conception of how man may attain spiritual liberation and wisdom. One must prostitute himself in the lowest fashion. One must mock and torture all conventional expectations— social, ethical, and linguistic—in order to set free the spark of knowledge which is buried in the banal and the workaday. One must use all poetic metaphors and emotional impressions as means to a higher end: the transcendence of life in its given circumstances.

In effect, Rimbaud aimed, like Nietzsche, to warp and violate the customary sense of "truth" to acquire deeper insight, to go beyond good and evil with a Dionysian dash. He struggled to unlock, as his biographer Enid Starkie says, the essential "core of his being" which was "purity and innocence with a yearning for absolute perfection."[1] But such perfection, he thought, was only possible through denigration. The world as he knew it would have to be consumed with the fire of passion. Words and objects would have to be stripped of their usual meaning or moral implications. The artificial structures of the bourgeois mind would have to be shaken down and dismantled by a kind of shock therapy and supplanted with a pristine and undefiled new consciousness. Everything would be permitted so that everything heretofore cherished could now be seen as snares and impediments to genuine knowledge, as dusty knickknacks to be tossed away because they had lost all value.

The rise of Rimbaud's star coincided with a tide of occultism that washed over Europe in the late 1800s. Satanism, divination, necromancy, and assorted forms of black magic came into vogue, particularly among the urban intellectuals who adopted as their watchword *épater le bourgeoisie*. Paris became a holy city for this "occult underground." In the 1880s and 1890s Paris crawled with

Bohemians and malcontents of many stripes. Notable within its cenacles were such names as Marquis Stanislas de Gauita and Joséphine Péladan who smoked hashish, cultivated decadence, and endeavored to revive the Rosicrucian Brotherhood.[2] But de Gauita and Péladan were also esthetically inclined, and they combined their interest in secret doctrines and practices with a new and unprecedented theory of art. Authentic art was to be a kind of occult happening superintended by a caste of priest-estheticians. Not merely would inspired art unsettle and ultimately undercut the confidence of the bourgeoisie, it would also ennoble the outcasts of society as high spiritual beings. In Péladan's words, "Artist you are a magus: Art is the great miracle."[3] The artist could accomplish his miracle by revealing the eternal sublimity and significance in the ugly and commonplace, by exhuming jewels from the filth and mire. He would make himself deliberately a rake, for among the Paris avant-garde occultism was basically a sophisticated way of expressing one's contempt for all rationality and order. The joint aim of both advanced art and what must obviously be called a Gnostic spirituality was to spike all man's consoling illusions while offering a frightening presentiment of hell in the midst of life. In this respect Rimbaud mirrored his own times.

The literary movement for which history recalls Rimbaud as one of its chief proctors was known as "Symbolism." In fact, the larger Symbolist esthetic was closely interwoven with the magic and occultism which Rimbaud so prized. Symbolism sprouted out of the carrion of a dead Romanticism. The Romantic pathos spent itself, as we have seen, in its feverish longing for the god within the human self. And it finally came to ruin in its painful recognition of the cleavage between aspiration and possibility, between ideal and reality. The upshot of this failing on the one hand was the turn in *belles-lettres* (and in social attitudes as well) after the 1840s to a cool realism and rationality which steered clear of the emotional "extravagances" of the Romantics. Such a stance was evident in the method of detailed, detached description of everyday life in the prose literature known as "naturalism," among the neoclassical French poets who were called Parnassians. On the cultural level a similar trend showed up in the shift from revolutionary enthusiasm and ideology to a cynical rapprochement with power politics and the requirements of corporate capitalism. Yet, on the other hand, the great Romantic dissatisfaction with things as usual was never entirely stilled. The pressure of protest welled up once again, this time in the form of a cult of decadence and a fascination with the barbarous and bizarre. The Symbolist movement preserved the Romantic fetish of interiority, but where the later proffered the ideal of the "beautiful soul" in concord with nature and nourished by creative imagination, the former perceived sublimity in plain fantasy and perversity, in a chaos of impressions. It did not simply assault convention, probity, and "common sense," as the Romantics had done, while clarifying a noble and transcendental vision. It found a glory in disorder alone, in madness. Symbolism grasped for a deeper meaning to the world, but such a meaning could no longer be derived through Coleridge's "esemplastic" power of symbolic synthesis. Meaning could only be had on a totally different plane of reality where the "natural" references of symbols no longer make sense. Thus the ordinary tokens of experience had to be subjected to an elaborate process of decoding into their purely "spiritual" equivalents recognizable only by the initiated. Man's private consciousness was the countersign; fugitive images and dreams became esoteric ciphers for the "other" side of existence. Hence subjectivism passed into occultism. The Symbolists had no real hope of altering life through an imaginative perspective. They purported to scotch the "illusion" of this world, even the poetic world, and find a sanctuary in an unfamiliar cosmos independent of the senses. There could be no discrimination as to what was significant and valuable in experience, since all forms of experience were acknowledged, as the Mahayana Buddhists say, to be "empty." The truth lies beyond discrimination. Anything is appropriate subject matter for the poet because he no longer need be a poet at all. His objective is to become a mystical seer.

In a number of respects the Symbolist view of the arcane significance of individual consciousness was prefigured in the writings of the eighteenth century spiritualist Emanuel Swedenborg (1688-1772). Symbolism drew inspiration from the thought of the Swedish philosopher, scientist, and occultist, even though Swedenborg himself was no esthete and "considered heaven and hell and God," as William Butler Yeats put it, "as if he were sitting before a large table in a Government office putting little pieces of mineral ore into small square boxes for an assistant to pack away in drawers."[4] Symbolist poetry, through the mediation of Charles Baudelaire, adopted Swedenborg's theory of "correspondences"—the notion that each thing that exists in the visible and natural sphere "symbolizes" or "corresponds" in an oblique and mysterious way to some object or objects in the supersensory realm.[5] By the same token, poetic vision empowers the seer, according to the Symbolists, to glimpse the secret, spiritual signification of a word or object. Symbolism was not so much interested in the grammatical or even metaphorical implication of language so much as the capacity of isolated words or images (what Baudelaire called "hieroglyphs") to point completely beyond themselves to a higher, ineffable truth. Just as ancient interpretations of the Kaballa and numerological lore dwelt on the veiled and internal import of mere letters, signs, or numbers, so Symbolism strove to uncover the dazzling radiance beneath the lusterless, outward facets of the world. Even a tawdry brooch must have its transcendent mode of correspondence. To discern the subtler strata of reality requires a revelling in the grosser forms in which the very treasures of creation are contained.

That, of course, was the central message of Baudelaire's masterwork *The Flowers of Evil*. Out of the draff of human existence grow the delicate blooms of profound knowledge. Out of decadence springs beauty. Baudelaire, in essence, repudiated the traditional Romantic conception of nature as a balm for the aching spirit and thereby underlined the typical Gnostic repudiation of the apparent universe. "Nature" in itself has nothing to do with artistic or moral values. Like de Sade, Baudelaire stressed the pointless cruelty and wantonness of the "natural" man. Genuine nature must be seen as a theatre of the absurd, of incontinent lusts and violent struggles among animals and men. But such a picture of nature should not prevent the devotee of wisdom from shunning bitter reality. In vice is harbored virtue; from pain comes release. *Flowers of Evil* opens with an invitation to celebrate the horror of life as a preparation for rapture.

> Come to my breast, cruel and sullen spirit
> You idolized, indolent beast;
> For I would long plunge my trembling fingers
> Into the depths of your heavy mane;
>
> And bury my aching head
> Within your perfumed folds
> To breathe, as of a faded flower,
> The sweet, musty fragrance of my withered love.

> I long to sleep! To sleep rather than to live!
> For only within a death-like slumber
> Would I be free to kiss your opulent, glowing body.
>
> To drown my sorrows there is no cure
> But to wallow in the depths of your bed.
> The power to forget lies on your lips,
> And Lethe flows through your kisses.

The weight of suffering, as in the trance of the shaman, causes the seer to recoil back into his own consciousness. The natural world *outside of* man is annihilated by the energy of mental creation. Nature "exists" only for the sake of the ever innovative imagination[6]; its elements are exploited as symbolic counters for a purely psychic game. In "Landscape," for example, Baudelaire contemplates a pastoral scene ("the stars in the blue sky," "the lamp at the window," the moon), but converts these images "with [his] own will" into an "atmosphere of . . . burning thought." The "truth" of nature lies in the riot of sensation, in the degradation of the orderly mind, which brings about inspiration. Thus Baudelaire experimented with hallucinogenic drugs, particularly hashish, as an instrument of ecstasy. Nature does not offer its own Garden of Eden. Man must create his own "artificial paradise" in which to perfect the soul.

Concerning hashish, Baudelaire wrote:

> . . . man's endless longing to rekindle his hopes and rise to infinity, has led him, in every age and clime, to display a frantic craving for any substance—dangerous or not—that could excite his individuality, and set before his eyes, if only for an instant, the second-hand paradise that was the object of his every desire.[7]

The simmering thirst for self-transcendence drives the seer to wrest from his own perceptions of things a brilliant manifestation of the infinite. He yearns for a different field of vision.

> Behind the scenery of boundless space,
> Darker than the abyss,
> I see distinctly unique worlds

The union of the soul with the infinite, the breakthrough into eternity, induces an ecstasy which hitherto is unavailable to those trapped in time and change.

> I know how to evoke happy times
> And relive my past nestled within your thighs.

> For what is the good of searching for your languid
>   beauty elsewhere than in your dear body and soul?
> I know how to evoke happy times!

Time is, for Baudelaire, the great, cosmic enemy. "Time devours the living." Yet out of the rubble of time and temporal experience, in the embrace of the mind with nature in all its sordid garments, the poet lifts his eyes "toward heaven." In letting himself go, as if carried away by an "avalanche," he breaks his attachment to petty things and becomes one with all phenomena. He has absorbed nature into his own pure consciousness and through the magic of thinking has become a free spirit.

In Rimbaud's case the effort at magical transformation through the vision was even more deliberate. The longing for a change of state, for an escape from the meanness of his condition, resulted in his attempt to discard mere poetry and take up the practice of *conjuring*. Rimbaud refined to a consummate degree the Symbolist method of devaluing the poetic word in favor of the "correspondence." For him, as for all the Symbolists, the aim was to reveal how the poetic image "mystically partakes of the psychic reality it symbolizes."[8] The psychic reality, moreover, is *the* reality. Because the image participates in reality, it has transfigurative power. Rimbaud felt that in order to arrive at such images, the rigid and encrusted forms of common linguistic expression would have to be savaged. His goal was to devise a new, primordial, "universal language" that would light up the vast "unknown." The apparent jibberish of occultism, therefore, is not a deficit but an asset. For the strangeness of such an argot enables the occult seer to use language for more than communication. Language can be invoked as a means of mind alteration because its import resides not in its logic or grammar, but in its *effect on consciousness*. Thus seemingly verbal banter passes into what Rimbaud dubs "the alchemy of the word."

Certain lines of *Illuminations*, in fact, have a tremulous impact. Like a Zen *koan*, they shatter one's sense of appropriateness and make one expect the unexpected. They make one see that words are products of the intellect which obscure an essentially nonverbal intuition. The round contradictions in the following images are intended to make a person forget the verbal description itself and direct his attention toward the truth which lies beyond what the Buddhists have called "name and form."

> There is a clock that never strikes.
> There is a hollow with a nest of white beasts.
> There is a cathedral that goes down
>   and a lake that goes up.[9]

The "clock that never strikes" represents the stillness and immobility of a world without time; the "hollow with a nest of white beasts" perhaps signifies the void of eternity where good and evil co-exist together; the "cathedral that goes down" and "the lake that goes up" suggest the reunion of heights and depths, of holiness and humiliation.

The business of the seer is to bring about such a reconciliation, which *au fond* constitutes a magical act. The act is accomplished by the omnipotent "I" who calls itself "a wizard or an angel, free from every rule of morality."[10] Rimbaud, the shaman *qua* Gnostic of modern culture, believes himself "the author of supernatural powers." He dreams, he hallucinates. Yet under the spell of such enchantment, illuminated with the energy of "the sun, the fire god," he sets about to create a new order, to "unveil all the mysteries . . . of religion or of nature, death, birth, future, past, cosmogony, non-existence."[11]

Through the "disordering of the senses" Rimbaud attempted to emancipate the mind from the strictures of his Catholic conscience and from rational fixations. At the same time he intended to recapture the sensual immediacy and innocence of the child before the growth of self-doubt, as expressed in the Gnostic myth of the unity of opposites and the ideal of the primal man. "My wisdom is scorned as chaos," Rimbaud proclaims in *Illuminations,*[12] implying that the return to instinctual spontaneity is the key to knowledge. The darkness of passion conduces to the "primitive state of child of the sun." In such a state one's duty is to "respond to all" while remaining free of confusion and guilt. "I have never done evil," Rimbaud professes in *A Season in Hell,* because good and evil themselves, as moments in nature under the aspect of eternity, are ultimate illusions.

> My innocence would make me weep.
> Life is the farce to lead everywhere.[13]

The task of both Baudelaire and Rimbaud was to provide a "way out" for the severely alienated individual from a world of social anomie, hypocrisy, and insensitivity. The glittering idols, the moral fictions of bourgeois culture, had to be toppled. But that could only be done by a total disorganization of the self and a flight into extreme subjectivity. The summons was to descend into hell by a road which, as in *Dante's Divine Comedy,* led finally to heaven. Satanism, black magic, egomania, and libertinism—these all stood for the necessary means to freedom. The same obtains for occultism and the Symbolist imagination as well, John Senior has argued. The "way down" is at once "the way out."[14]

The "way down," of course, was not the way of civilization and progress, but a recantation of modernity. "Why a modern world at all?" Rimbaud asks. "The world has no age."[15] Such a view is "just what I have always had; no more faith in history."[16] One is left with faith only in his own fantastic consciousness. The solution is "alchemy," the transmutation of dross into gold, an estimation of wretchedness as if it were a holy grail to be won.

CRYING FOR A VISION

The Symbolists as a whole were not only virtuosos of the ethereal and obscure; they were also self-avowed elitists. The leveling of artistic taste in industrial society, they felt, had forced them to champion certain refined and aristocratic values. Their esotericism was indispensable as an antitoxin to vulgarity. In view of the darkness of the times, they saw themselves as besieged saviors of the race. They were like the Hindu avatars, spiritual heroes, who appeared among the benighted men of the mythical Dark Age to dispel ignorance and steer their brethren back to divine knowledge.

In the 1890s and in the first decade of the twentieth century, the Symbolist occultism and estheticism stretched its influence far beyond the borders of France. Likewise, the nascent reputation of Nietzsche's philosophy was also fanning out across Europe. The ideal of the *Übermensch* or overman was fast becoming a minion of self-worshiping decadents and Gnostic dreamers among the *literati*. Both these currents in art and philosophical speculation represented a defiance of the dreary scientism and materialism which identified the bourgeois mind during the high water of industrial capitalism in Europe. On the one side the period represented a furtherance of the slide into cynicism and despair begun during the post-Romantic reactions, a crystallization of so-called *fin de siècle* culture. Symbolism's repudiation of beauty and meaning in nature *per se,* along with its elevation of the purely human and factitious (as found in Baudelaire's praise of the esthete, the "dandy"), devolved onto a cult among the generation of English decadent writers of the last decade which made a scarabaeus of triviality and artificiality. As for the Symbolists, truth was to be located not in ideal verities or classical spiritual values, but amidst the private, the banal, or the everyday. "It is only the superficial qualities that last," Oscar Wilde wrote. The writers of the 1890s, instead of surrendering entirely to the beggarliness of their surroundings, tried to spiritualize and ennoble their world by finding transcendence within the very texture of the commonplace. Such transcendence could be achieved through the mediation of the sensitive soul, the lucid genius, who rises above the attachment of ignoble personalities to temporal things and becomes blissfully conscious of his higher status.

The effort to derive a supernal vision from profane life was taken up in the poetry and praise of William Butler Yeats, whose work soars as a majestic monument to the aspirations of this era. In Yeats the occultist and visionary interests of the Symbolists coalesce with the Romantic and Nietzschean morality of the superman. By consensus Yeats has been hailed as a genius in his own idiom, insofar as he worked the raw material of Irish folklore, Western esotericism and Gnosticism, and the new esthetic principles into a breathtaking mythology that he hoped would sum up reality for modern humanity. In this connection Yeats was much more than an artisan or esthete. He was a seer, and he aimed to redefine the larger Western world picture. With profound practical consequences for both politics and culture, his thought was, for all intents and purposes, the quintessence of the modern Gnostic.

Yeats's own occult posture was shaped by his studies in theosophy, hermeticism, the Kaballa, and Celtic legends and fairy tales. Taking an eclectic and synthetic approach to his subject matter, Yeats was drawn to just about everything in magical or spiritualistic lore which served to amaze and mystify, as well as to offset the philistinism which in modern society crowded out serious self-reflection. Yeats desired to bring about a spiritual renovation of human affairs.[17] By and large Yeats's wish for magical transformation was played out through his membership in a secret society called the Golden Dawn. Inspired by the famous French occultist Eliphas Levi and founded by MacGregor Mathers and Wynn Westcott, the Golden Dawn claimed many European luminaries, including the celebrated Yeats and the infamous apostle of sorcery

Aleister Crowley. Yeats can be considered the tutelary spirit of the order. The fortunes of the Golden Dawn rose and fell in keeping with Yeats's commitment and participation. Yeats used the Golden Dawn as a kind of laboratory for experimenting with his recondite philosophy. One of the purposes of the Order, according to Yeats, was to enable certain select individuals to climb a "ladder into heaven" and acquire "divine wisdom."[18] By such wisdom they would flaunt their magical power. The Golden Dawn was instituted for the practice of ritual magic, including ceremonies of purification and rebirth in the style of the ancient mystery cults.

Yeats's occultism, however, was only a refraction of his more complex Gnostic philosophy and psychology. He regarded all nature and consciousness as interpenetrating aspects of a unitary divine Mind, a spiritual substance or energy which can be harnessed or captured in mental representations. In other words, the manifestations of cosmic Mind can be "evoked by symbols" which in themselves *correspond* to the supernatural reality. The *real* association between symbol and Mind accounts for the efficacy of magical analogies, for the ability of thought to *create* something by imagining or conceptualizing it. Similarly, the contents of the poetic mind are actually "emanations" from the World Soul, the *spiritus mundi*. This relationship explains how poetry and occultism are coupled with each other. Poetry presents in a concrete, sensuous way the paradigmatic forms of Mind. Words themselves are more than lyrical contrivances. They possess a universal power insofar as they bring about the intersection of the supernatural with the natural universe. The poet skillfully employs words so as to manifest a mystical ideality, to cut through time and sense-experience with what Yeats termed the "artifice of eternity."

Yeats' philosophical mentor was Bishop Berkeley, who argued that all human perceptions or ideas are contained in the Mind of God. All authentic insights radiate from a transcendental source. The modern era, nonetheless, has let the wellhead of divinity run dry. Science, materialism, and utilitarianism have left shrivelled the faculty of inspiration and prompted men to trade "truth" for the "useful." In Gnostic fashion Yeats aimed to recapture a forgotten primal wisdom through the presentation of archetypal symbols in poetry. Yeats held up the image of medieval Byzantium as representing man's intercourse with the supernatural through magical symbols. In his poem

"Byzantium" Yeats draws a graphic contrast between eternity and flesh, limning the beauty and stillness of a world beyond time.

> The unpurged images of day recede;
> The Emperor's drunken soldiery are abed;
> Night resonance recedes, night walkers' song
> After great cathedral gong;
> A starlit or a moonlit dome disdains
> All that man is,
> All mere complexities,
> The fury and the mire of human veins.

The essence of life is conveyed in the "starlit or a moonlit dome" which rises in the stately splendor above "the fury and mire of human veins." Man is bidden to emulate the Byzantine ideal of spiritual perfection. Man must become like God in conformance with the Byzantine notion of saintliness, shedding his mortal hulk through spiritual discipline. "I hail the superhuman," Yeats hymns in "Byzantium." Humanity is itself a fragment of Deity which has dropped away from its origins. In "Leda and the Swan" Yeats utilized the Greek myth of Leda, the wife of the Spartan king Tyndareus, who is raped by Zeus in the disguise of a majestic, white bird. Humanity exists as the offspring of this union sharing God's "knowledge with his power." Man's vocation is to discover this veiled, cosmic knowledge and use it to regenerate the race.

The wand for the transformation of humanity, according to Yeats, is the imagination. The imagination grasps the universal structures and emblems of the spiritual world and stitches them into an alternative universe for man to reside in. The *elixir vitae* of such a spiritual and imaginative universe is myth. Yeats lamented the attrition of myth in modern civilization, whereby the mind is drained of feeling and deprived of passion and mystery. The imagination, however, can rescue humanity from this grievous plight. The strategy is not to refurbish the traditional and now frayed fabric of religious stories and beliefs, since history has already pronounced its rude verdict on the faith of the fathers. Instead the imagination must be massaged to create new mythologies which, in fine, turn out to be markers of an eternal and heretofore unappreciated wisdom. Yeats admired William Blake for attempting to repopulate the psyche with a swarm of imaginative figures and symbols. Blake was, Yeats wrote, "a man crying out for a mythology, and trying to make one because he could not find one to his hand."[19] Like Blake, Yeats regarded himself as in need of a "mythology [that] stood on the threshold of his meaning and on the margin of his sacred darkness."[20] The mythical imagination sorts out the farrago that is sensory knowledge and apprehends the spiritual forms which are only confusedly seen in ordinary contact with human beings and nature.

> The world of imagination is infinite and eternal, whereas the world of generation or vegetation is finite and temporal. There exist in that eternal world the eternal realities of everything which we see reflected in the vegetable glass of Nature.[21]

Thus Yeats quoted Blake.

Yeats endeavored to enact his own policy for salvation by contriving an applicable mythology. In A Vision, published in 1938, Yeats set out to delineate a totally mythical (we might even be inclined to say "fanciful") view of humanity's role in the cosmic drama as an occultist's account of historical change. While the details and nuances of Yeats's Vision are too numerous to reiterate altogether, it is fair to say that the book rides on the notion of human life as piloted by mysterious and ineluctable forces which human intelligence or intention is unable to resist. The universe, Yeats insisted, is a play of opposites, the twin powers of love and strife, as in the cosmology of the ancient Greek philosopher Empedocles. Time and civilization are hitched to a "wheel" of fate which passes through all moments of good and evil, order and chaos, creativity and destruction. This wheel, akin to the lunar cycles and containing its thetical and antithetical phases, determines the long-term course of human affairs. Its time reach is comparable to the "Great Year" in ancient Greek and Persian thought, whereby the universe rotates through various stages on a path from perfection to corruption and is finally dissolved itself in eternal fire, only to be renewed again and to repeat the cycle. Yeats described the process as the motion of interpenetrating "gyres": "concord" and "discord." "I see that the gyre of "Concord" diminishes as that of "Discord" increases, and can imagine after that the gyre of "Concord" increasing while that of "Discord" diminishes, and so on, one gyre within the other always."[22] The seed of decrepitude sprouts within the fullness of life; annihilation is the inherent goal of existence. Astral fatalism, spiced with the occult symbolism of the zodiac, is conspicuous in Yeats's often weird and labyrinthine reckoning of the forces behind history. The idea of the Great Year becomes for Yeats, the key to spiritual liberation. In the eternal and supermundane order all things have their indefeasible pattern and coherence. The vicissitudes and violence of history are merely surface phenomena which mask an underlying stability and continuity. The ongoing conflict of opposites is resolved into a metaphysical "Unity of Being" which Yeats maintained as the true state of life. But the Unity of Being is merely an ideal construct which refers not to an actual summing up of history, but the principle of order contained in the revolutions of the ages. The Unchanging manifests itself in the continual closing of the circle of change. Good and evil, composition and dissolution, progress and regress, are all necessary from the standpoint of eternity and constitute vital polarities which complement each other, like *yin* and *yang* in Chinese Taoism. The Great Year represents the balancing of these polarities within the "gyring" course of time. The poet-visionary therefore rises above the momentary disruptions and traumas of history in beholding through his symbols and imagery the indissoluble nexus of relations between all phenomena. He celebrates the eternal recurrence of things in a detached mood of personal transcendence.

Yeats thought that the volatility of twentieth-century history was a symptom of the end of a cycle. The closing of the circle is always attended by an exhaustion of human intellect and spiritual energy, combined with a slump on the social scale into disarray and barbarism. Yeats conceived his own special poetic mission as that of midwife for the dawning new era—the opening of the circle once again—following the final passage into chaos. His occultism served him as a "higher" point of view which superseded the moribund theology and myths of Christianity. "One must bear in mind," Yeats commented, "that the Christian era, like the two thousand years . . . that went before it, is an entire wheel" which has come back to its starting point.[23] In conventional Christian understanding the "two-thousand-year" period is to climax with the "Second Coming," but the Second Coming of Christ is but the terminus of the Great Year. The Second Coming is, in fact, the advent not of the New Testament Christ, but of the Antichrist, the embodiment of ascendant turmoil. As Yeats describes it in his famous poem "The Second Coming,"

> Turning and turning in the widening gyre
> The falcon cannot hear the falconer;
> Things fall apart; the centre cannot hold;

> Mere anarchy is loosed upon the world,
> The blood-dimmed tide is loosed, and everywhere
> The ceremony of innocence is drowned;
> The best lack all conviction, while the worst
> Are full of passionate intensity.

There can be no "progress" in the historical sense, for Yeats. Temporal advancement is only a gaudy illusion to be knocked down by downward swing of the historical pendulum. The man of knowledge has no interest in progress or in twentieth-century history *per se,* but only in the Unity of Being which encompasses both forward and backward motion, growth and decay. In the poem "Among School Children" Yeats gives the nugacity of temporal life a bittersweet rendering. The school children are taught to admire the "achievements" of their civilization.

> The children learn to cipher and to sing,
> To study reading-books and histories,
> To cut and sew, be neat. in everything
> In the best modern way . . .

Their "modernity," however, stands in contrast with "a sixty-year-old smiling public man" who has his mind trained on deeper and more mystical affairs. Through his consciousness float images of a transhistorical reality. He, like Plato, sees even nature as "a spume that plays upon a ghostly paradigm of things." The public man, who is Yeats, belongs to the "self-born mockers of man's enterprise," and is willing to become forgetful of all finite obsessions for the sake of an ecstatic union with what is outside of time. All motion returns to its source. Birth and death fill out the ledger of wisdom. Yeats, as Gnostic, was persuaded that nothing man does can even brake the momentum of change and fate. Though man must endure the twisting of fortune, his glory arises not in his mortal burdens, but in his sublime awareness of what is eternally the case. He escapes fate by returning through *gnosis* to his home beyond the stars.

The escape from fate, however, is a privilege bequeathed exclusively to a select class of supermen. Yeats was influenced in significant measure by Nietzsche. Nietzsche had spoken of the self-transcending genius who vanquishes fate by will and heroism, by the affirmation of all life in its eternal recurrence. Just as Nietzsche had called for a new breed of cultural aristocrats with the bearing of true "masters," so Yeats looked toward the rule of men with noble breeding. Yeats also echoed Nietzsche in his view that all genuine aristocracies prove their prowess through war and gallantry, welcoming the restless flux of existence as an individual challenge, as an occasion for self-assertion, creativity, and conquest.[24] The loss of coherence in the modern period represents an invitation for these new men of confidence and action to transvalue all values, to recreate the sense of truth and disengage themselves from a stultifying social consensus. The disarray of historical life which for common men becomes a menacing prospect turns out for the superlative personality to be a golden opportunity. "History is necessity until it takes fire in someone's head and becomes freedom or virtue."[25] Like Nietzsche, Yeats saluted the old aristocracies for supplying the opportunity to exercise the will to power and to redefine reality. Their peerage and prerogatives were the essential conditions for seeing the world in a new way. The uneconomic leisure of scholars, monks, and women gave us truth, sanctity, and manners. Free power is not the denial of that past that it can be grasped in a single thought.[26]

In political terms the dynamism of the superman entails the abolition of the modern democratic community and the reconstruction of the state "like a Chartres Cathedral for the glory of God and the soul." Society should exist for the preservation and the enrichment of spiritual life which is held in trust by the *cognoscenti*. It is the duty of the superman to organize through his own will the disintegrating democratic society with the completion of the Great Year. "History is very simple—the rule of the many, then the rule of the few, day and night, night and day forever."[27]

At least in outline, Yeats's conception of history and society went hand in hand with the justification of fascism. In his diary of 1930 Yeats uttered his sympathies with fascist authoritarianism:

> The abrogation of equality of rights and duties is because duties depend on rights, rights on duties. If I till and dig my land I should have rights because of that duty done, and if I have much land, that, according to all ancient races, should bring me still more rights. But if I have much or little land and neglect it I should have few rights. *This is the theory of Fascism* and so far as land is concerned it has the history of the earth to guide it and that is permanent history.[28]

"Permanent history" is the history of powerful men who resist the levelling process of modern social revolutions and struggle to give preeminence to the rank and distinction that comes with spiritual illumination. Permanent history, in effect, annuls all history. The import of ordinary history is disclosed in the attainment of visionary knowledge by seers and in the awesome feats of the legendary heroes. The seer realizes himself as god in the world, and the concerns and ambitions of simple worldlings cannot even hold a torch to his magnificence. He embodies "nobleness made simple as a fire," a fire which blazes forth in the dark night of time and suffices as a beacon for vagrant and disinherited minds to steer by.

THE SECRET DOCTRINE

In 1889 a young Austrian professor travelled to the celebrated city of Weimar in order to collaborate on an updated edition of Goethe's works. The new edition would among other things emphasize the scientific strides made by the father of German learning and letters. But the young Austrian was bent on doing more than simply making a name as an exegete of Goethe. He wanted to go beyond the classicism and realism of Goethe in surveying the terrain of the spirit. The year 1893 saw the publication of this young Austrian's *chef d'oeuvre,* which struck Goethe epigones as something out of its proper element. The book was entitled *The Philosophy of Spiritual Activity,* and its author was one Rudolf Steiner.

Steiner (1861-1925) was a physicist who had been tutored in positivism and scientific materialism. Yet his writing signalled a defiant uprising against such a hard-nosed *Weltanschauung.* Perhaps his opposition to materialism can be explained by his earlier flirtation with the miracles and mysteries of Catholicism. At any rate his original piety had now been transmuted into a preoccupation with esotericism and occultism, which showed up in the argument of *The Philosophy of Spiritual Activity.* Inward revelation takes the place of religious authority and collective morality. The greatest truth is to be found in the expansion and growth of "soul." "The unfolding of my soul," Steiner remarked in an autobiographical monograph, "rested upon the fact that I had stood in spirit before the Mystery of Golgotha in most inward, most earnest solemnity of knowledge."[29]

Reliant on his own special reading of Goethe's observations on biology, Steiner was attracted to Goethe's organicism and teleology, particularly the latter's ideas concerning the self-directed character of plant growth. Goethe had regarded the development of plant life, as well as that of all other organic forms, as the articulation of "primal phenomena" (archetypal models) found in nature. Each individual instance of life exemplifies a primal phenomenon, a variation on a basic theme. Steiner adapted this theory to explain the appearance and evolution of human personalities. Human life and consciousness represent the unfolding of certain spiritual patterns or tendencies independent of time and space. Man's given nature is enmeshed within a cosmic net of relationships and potentialities. It is man's calling to give form to these relationships, to realize his own spiritual aims which link him with the whole of sentient and insentient existence. Occult teachings are invaluable, because they urge man away from his terrestrial, common-sense habits of thinking and make him aware of his involvement in the spiritual world. The doctrines of *karma,* past lives, and reincarnation help to orient the individual to the farther regions of reality that are imperceptible within his own, immediate consciousness. The purpose of such doctrines is to acquaint the individual with the universe of souls that hides behind visible phenomena.

> When the soul is surrendered to the phenomena of the outer world by means of physical perception, it cannot be said—after true self-analysis—that the soul perceives these phenomena, or that it actually experiences the things of the outer world. For, during the time of surrender, in its devotion to the outer world, the soul knows in truth nothing of itself.[30]

Man, however, must draw away from his allegiance to the external world and through self-knowledge and discipline cultivate the soul substance within him. It was Steiner's conviction that the spiritual goals determining life can only be reached by a new appraisal of humanity, by a different anthropology replacing mechanistic and behavioristic philosophies which deny man's spiritual essence.

Steiner formulated this new conception of man according to a school of thought that he dubbed "anthroposophy." Anthroposophy is in itself a modification of a more familiar word—"Theosophy"—used by the followers of Madame Blavatsky (whom we shall discuss in Chapter Seven) to designate their own path for spiritual investigation. During his earlier career Steiner came profoundly under the sway of theosophical notions and practices. Throughout his life Steiner continued to refer to his own approach as "Theosophical," but in order to single out his own innovations from the tenets of the Blavatsky circles he coined the phrase "anthroposophy" (literally, "wisdom of man.") The fundamental difference between the two occult modes was one more of semblance than substance. Though both gave great weight to esoteric intuitions and used occultist language, Steiner was more willing to claim a "scientific" cast for his deductions instead of identifying them principally with religious conceptions, as did the Theosophists. Furthermore, Steiner concentrated somewhat more on the understanding of human nature as the starting point of spiritual explorations— hence the expression *anthroposophy*. The General Anthroposophical Society, as it came to be known, was established in 1923, two years prior to Steiner's death, and continued to carry on the master's program for the education of humanity for years thereafter.

Steiner's own biography is not striking, nor is the story of the General Society momentous. Anthroposophy wound up, like many kindred occult groups, to have a restricted clientele, the bulk of whom were either curious or disaffected intellectuals marshalled together by the promise of esoteric psychology and metaphysics. The social storm that struck Germany in the 1920s fostered the right circumstances for the outbreak of mystical and messianic doctrines. Steiner's disciples, who comprised the anthroposophical movement during and after the First World War, were teachers, clergymen, scientists, and other professionals bound together in the hope of rebuilding a crumbling Western civilization. At the Goethenum, Steiner's utopian and experimental institute in Dornach, Switzerland, the anthroposophists dabbled in such practical and arcane arts as eurhythmy (a form of ritual dance), "biodynamic" farming which was a kind of organic gardening, and techniques of "spiritual" healing. The intention of the various activities at the Goethenum was to create the right climate within an intimate community for inner growth and self-disclosure.

But Steiner's importance must be gauged less in terms of his blueprint for the reform of civilization, which was improvisational and ethereal, as are the schemes of many utopian dreamers, than with respect to his voluminous lectures and books on occult subjects. Indeed, Steiner may be remembered as the occult theologian *par excellence,* summing up and synthesizing after the fashion of a Gnostic Thomas Aquinas many disparate strands of hitherto secret tradition. Steiner stitched together the main fibers of hermeticism, Rosicrucianism, theosophy, and Eastern mysticism. He displayed the quintessence of the modern Gnostic attitude. Man is not a finite, historical being, but an exiled citizen of many different, ascending, unrealized "worlds." His task is to repossess step by step his patrimony in these worlds, rising by means of will and self-discipline to a state of psychic oneness with all of creation. "The real being of man lies in his interior, not his exterior" was Steiner's maxim. It is the real being of the "higher self" which "must be looked for in the universe, in the stars, in the sun and the moon as well as in stone and animal."[31] The reality of the other world of which man is in his everyday torpor remains regrettably ignorant must be made transparent. Yet only the seekers, the initiates, can ever become privy to this reality. Like his Gnostic forbears, Steiner emphasized the private and exclusive character of religious truth. The way of transcendence is narrow and steep along the winding staircase of inner consciousness, rather than wide and even along the axis of history. The spiritual worlds now and then break into time, but they are easily left unnoticed or disregarded. They are worlds that make up the infinite expanse of eternity. Though man's sojourn at the sensory or physical level may be brief, his greater voyage takes him through countless planes and universes that beggar the imagination. The terror of history subsides with the anticipation of self-perfection in an altogether different dimension. Broken time, within which all physical labors are frustrated, is repaired through the striving of the disincarnate soul upward. In doing so the soul attains *gnosis* which transcends the fulfillment of human tasks in time.

AT THE EDGE OF THE MIRACULOUS

The evolution of the soul, Steiner insisted, requires "work and devotion" as ends in themselves. It is "the love of work, and not of success," that liberates the soul from its terrestrial cravings and attachments. Such, of course, is the psychology behind many mystical and ascetical traditions. Effort and exertion become not implements for subsequent rewards, but methods of self-purification and spiritual deliverance. The doctrine of *karma-yoga* in Hinduism, for example, which lays stress on doing work without attention to its consequences, illustrates this disposition. Life in time can have no closure or purpose. One endeavors solely to forget that one is endeavoring for anything at all. Labor itself can be a species of *yoga,* a technique for extricating man from the wheel of desire.

Perhaps the most interesting episode in the spread of Gnostic occultism during the early part of the twentieth century was the Gurdjieff-Ouspensky school, whose inception coincided with the fall of the czars and the Russian Revolution. G. I. Gurdjieff and P. D. Ouspensky were both refugees from Bolshevism, who first met in Russia during the year 1915 and collaborated in the propagation of an esoteric view of man and the universe. The chief author of the esoteric system was Gurdjieff. Gurdjieff drew upon an abundance of occult lore and experience stemming from his travels about Asia and from his childhood among the peasants of the Caucasus. Endowed with a sharp, synthetic mind, Gurdjieff stuck together bits and shards of secret doctrine and engraved them with his own peculiar perspective to produce what Ouspensky referred to as "a new model of the universe." Ouspensky served as the literary mouthpiece for Gurdjieff, who imparted his ideas by direct and personal instruction instead of through pamphlets or books. Ouspensky succeeded in tabulating Gurdjieff's random reflections into a mystical philosophy. But it was Gurdjieff who was the prime mover and flamboyant genius behind the movement.

Gurdjieff's teachings are aligned with the theosophical belief in the cosmic evolution of soul. Yet, whereas theosophical (and "anthroposophical") doctrine dwelt on the advancement and transformation of the spiritual personality apart from nature, Gurdjieff sought to fashion extraordinary human beings in the visible realm. These superhuman beings, or "supermen," would be distinguished not so much by their external features as by their penetrating knowledge of themselves. "The idea of superman is directly connected with the idea of hidden knowledge," Ouspensky observed. "The expectation of superman is the expectation of some new revelation, or new knowledge."[32] Similarly, "the evolution of consciousness, the inner growth of man, is the 'ascent towards superman.'"[33] The conveyor force behind the evolution of consciousness is "esoteric thought," kept under guard by an "inner circle of humanity." Out of this circle materializes the mysterious, self-cognizant cadre of supermen, charged with inducting others into their society of *gnosis*. But the superman with his magical knowledge must remain anonymous and elusive, for he is a special instance of nature's thrust to perfection which bars the same achievements for ordinary individuals. The sufferings and deaths of those who make up the ignorant masses only provide compost for the growth of superior spiritual beings. Not the "masses," but only incomparable individuals can evolve toward higher types. Ouspensky explained this proposition as follows:

> The ordinary view of life either finds no aim in life or sees the aim in the "evolution of the masses." But the evolution of the masses is as fantastic and illogical an idea as would be, for instance, the idea of an identical evolution of all the cells of a tree or all the cells of an organism. We do not realize that the idea of the evolution of the masses is equivalent to expecting *all* the cells of a tree, that is, the cells of the roots, bark, wood-fibre and leaves, to be *transformed* into cells of flowers and fruit, that is, expecting the *whole tree* to be transformed into flowers and fruit.[34]

Thus "what is possible for individual man is impossible for the masses."[35]

Gurdjieff is reported in a conversation to have likened the development of the superman to the growth of a huge oak tree from a single acorn. Though many acorns each autumn are shed upon the ground, only a very few, fortunate ones will ever sink into the ground, take root, and become a tree.[36] Similarly, Ouspensky denied that the appearance of supermen from the inner circle can be considered historical "progress" in any precise sense. The inner circle perpetually segregates itself from the multitudes, while using their resources for its own aggrandizement. There can never be a numerical increase in supermen; nor do the supermen aid in the betterment of humanity as such. Instead the supermen must "control" the masses for their own secret purposes. The proper environment for the nurturance of rare superhuman types can be established through a caste system, as sketched out in the ancient Hindu text The Laws of Manu, which "represents an ideal social organization in accordance with esoteric systems."[37] Both Gurdjieff and Nietzsche admired the ancient Brahmin priests and mystics, who asserted their own esoteric knowledge, will, and dominance over against the leveling tendencies in history, and who commended caste privilege as a bulwark of individual status against the spurious "rights" of the majority. Nature herself allows only for the perfection of some, not many. History therefore cannot contravene what have been nature's workings since time immemorial.

While real growth in terms of numbers is restricted by the parsimony of nature, the capacity for development within the clique of nascent supermen remains enormous. Nature evolves though the self-transcending activities of select individuals, not through the transformation of the human totality. And the measure of self-transcendence for these individuals is, of course, unbounded. The essence of Gurdjieff's understanding of man is described by J. G. Bennett. "Man is not by nature an immortal soul nor is he a soulless automaton. He is a natural being with supernatural potentialities."[38] Man in his given and average condition, nevertheless, does resemble an automaton or a machine.

> Man is a machine. All his deeds, actions, words, thoughts, feelings, convictions, opinions, and habits are the results of external influences, external impressions. Out of himself a man cannot produce a single thought, a single action. Everything he says, does, thinks, feels—all this happens. Man cannot discover anything, invent anything. It all happens.[39]

Gurdjieff's remarks suggest that man as such is *unfree*. Indeed, most people are slaves of their own ingrained habits and prejudices. This lack of freedom is due, he implies, to the influence of planetary and celestial bodies, an idea that smacks of astral fatalism. In his unfinished state man does not realize his natural possibilities. He is a somnambulist sunk in a mindless "sleep," a characterization which harks back to the Gnostic picture of the natural or "fleshly" man. But through knowledge, man "awakens." "A man realizes that it is precisely because he is asleep that he lives and works in a small part of himself. It is precisely for this reason that the vast majority of his possibilities remain unrealized, the vast majority of his powers are left unused."[40] "Self-observation" stimulates the "man-machine" into exerting his will, discharging his occult powers, and thus becoming a navigator of his own destiny. No longer expending his energy through rote and undirected actions, he achieves in incremental fashion the grandeur latent within him at the outset.

Self-observation inevitably leads to self-discovery. And self-discovery is a kind of magical act whereby the mastery of mind is attained. Knowledge breeds power. Gurdjieff explained that self-mastery is tied to what he called "self-remembering." Self-remembering consists in a process of sweeping away all "masks" of the personality, all "identifications" which give an individual a false sense of significance or place. Self-remembering is cognition of one's eternal origins, of the true and timeless self unconditioned by habit or social training that is not a part of automatic *doing*. The difference between the counterfeit, outer man and the genuine *inner* man is the difference between "personality" and "essence."

> Essence is what is *born* in man. Personality is what is *acquired*. Personality is what is *not* his own. Essence cannot be lost, cannot be changed or injured as easily as personality.[41]

Personality keeps man in bondage to collective expectations and requirements. Essence is that dynamism locked within him which enables him to develop as he is in himself. Personality is what governs the "man-machine." Essence is that to which the superman must awaken.

Here Gurdjieff introduces two more terms which have critical significance: "buffers" and "conscience." "Conscience" is that aptitude in man for discerning his essence; it is the vehicle for self-remembering. "Buffers" are what cushion man against the shock of this fundamental knowledge and thus preserve false security of his everyday beliefs and perceptions. The most common buffer is the illusion of "morality." Morality supplies a convenient course of action for the unwise and unitiated; but it is a course that leaves him dependent on others, rather than himself, for guidance. Hence, Gurdjieff declares, "we do not teach morality. We teach how to find conscience."[42] Good and evil in themselves are chimeras, self-deceptions, that belie actual knowledge. The moral man is one who remains content to be asleep. The true "good" is the accomplishment of knowledge. "If a man understands that he is asleep and if he wishes to awake, then everything that helps him will be *good* and everything that hinders him, everything that prolongs his sleep, will be evil."[43] The superman rises above "good and evil" and yields only to the virtue of self-overcoming, of power. What is forbidden to the ignorant is permitted to him, because he has gone beyond the restrictions and hindrances to his own growth, including the moral rules of society. It is not what he does, but what he *knows* about himself that counts in the final balance.

The achievement of self-knowledge, for Gurdjieff, rests on disciplined and directed action, on "work." "Man acquires soul through work," Gurdjieff is quoted as saying.[44] But Gurdjieff did not mean "work" in the usual sense of the term. He was not referring to spiritless labor that has as its end certain palpable rewards. Again, the concept of *karma-yoga*—the "yoga of action"—comes to the fore. Authentic work is a method of ripening one's self-consciousness through "remembering oneself." One must become acutely conscious of the work he is performing. He must not understand it as an instrument for garnering distant rewards, but as a way to "value what he gets today without thinking of what he may get tomorrow."[45] Through *absorption* in his work a person reaches insight into his permanent self, his *essence,* his source of vitality and power. The meaning of life is immured in the everyday, if only the individual can comprehend this fact. The individual must break through the fretful rhythms of time and becoming based upon finite goal-seeking and the hunt for temporary gratifications in order to grasp the timeless and constant essence of his own existence. The purpose of work, therefore, is not a prosecution of certain projects in time, but a breakthrough into eternity.

Thus work done in a self-conscious mode lifts the individual beyond time, beyond sensory experiences and the anticipation of pain and pleasure. "Time is the boundary of our senses," Ouspensky notes.[46] Outside the senses lies the solution to the dilemma of temporality and becoming.

> The problem of time is the greatest riddle humanity has ever had to face. Religious revelation, philosophical thought, scientific investigation and occult knowledge all converge at one point, that is, on the problem of time, and all come to the'same view of it. Time does not exist! There exist no perpetual and eternal appearance and disappearance of phenomena, no ceaselessly flowing fountain of ever appearing and ever vanishing events. Everything exists always! There is only one eternal present, the Eternal Now, which the weak and limited human mind can neither grasp nor conceive.[47]

The evolution of soul transpires on a different plane, in the infinite "space" of eternity. Man is "now" what he can become, if only he seize upon this truth forthrightly. The superman lives in this world, but he is actually not of it. He is the consummate goal of nature, realized in the depths of his own consciousness. His trail of evolution lies perpendicular to the line of historical evolution, and for that reason he has nothing to contribute to history. He stands outside of history, sneering at all faith in historical "progress." Responsible for himself and himself alone, he bestows no lasting gift on "humanity," as humanity *en masse* is a misplaced value. The superman belongs to the inner circle which safeguards a wisdom that cannot be altered or vitiated by strife and confusion of the fleeting centuries.

To Gurdjieff and Ouspensky the ambiguities of historical life appear so stark that the enlightened soul can only hope to gain salvation by a leap into an alternate universe. The momentum of spiritual life is not forward in time, but an upright vertical ascent toward inward self-realization. As expatriates forced from their homeland by the revolution in Russia, both Gurdjieff and Ouspensky longed for a revitalization of the exiled aristocracy. The aristocracy they yearned to create would be a nobility founded on *gnosis,* rather than primogeniture—a marvelous compensation for those displaced forever by social upheaval and the dismembering of the old order. Such an aristocracy would constitute an unprecedented kind of "intelligentsia." Ouspensky depicts the makeup of the new intelligentsia thus:

> The formation of an "intelligentsia" is the beginning of the gathering together of people of higher castes, people who are not yet conscious of themselves and do not understand themselves, but who, nevertheless, act in accordance with the principles of their dimly felt caste. The characteristic features of the "intelligentsia" are always and everywhere the same. First there is a craving for *disinterested* activity, then a very impatient feeling of the indispensability of *personal freedom* for all and a very rebellious attitude towards everyone and everything standing in the way of freedom of thought, speech, and individual manifestation.[48]

A caste of spiritual adepts would restore for the politically dispossessed their topmost position in the ranks of the race. The ruling class is magically sublimated into the inner circle. Within the Romantic, Nietzschean, and occultist web of symbols the discredited rights of the *ancien régime* are transposed into the prerogatives of supermen. Their lapsed power over the masses becomes the secret mastery of the cosmos. No longer respected by their underlings, they glorify themselves as the illumined ones. Decadence turns into holiness; self-interest becomes a matchless destiny. Eternity holds a recompense for what historical change has robbed them of. The intimation of other worlds serves as a restitution of what has been lost with the cave-in of *this world* with all its pelf and promise.

Chapter 6

Rumblings of the Dark God

Our epoch will certainly see the end of the disease of Christianity.
—*Adolf Hitler*

The *fin de siècle* with its submerged currents of esotericism and irrationality had been less a symphony than an overture. Europe after the Franco-Prussian War of 1871, Nietzsche observed, had grown "overripe" and was poised to fall into a new barbarism. The cataclysmic events of August 1914, when the "civilized" nations of the world plunged into a war which nobody wanted, yet which lunged along its unbending course until an entire culture was in shambles, have been amply documented. The toll from the First World War encompassed not only millions of deaths on the battlefield, but also the dismembering of traditional societies and the crumbling of old beliefs and values. Empires vanished with the treaties of 1919. Monarchies, such as the Romanovs in Russia and the Hapsburgs in Austria-Hungary, which had ruled for centuries, came to an abrupt end. New international political movements like Bolshevism and Fascism made their debuts and stirred anxiety among the defenders of the established order. Artists rebelled with a mania against all conventional canons of creativity and taste, inflaming the vendetta toward middle-class life which had begun a generation earlier. Christianity itself—or, more exactly, the notion of Europe as "Christendom"—was called rudely and radically into question. And amid the wreckage of a collapsed world view many distraught and sensitive souls started to pick for shards of a new faith, a new God. The world of the past had gone forever.

The world that took the place of the old, however, proved frightening, confusing, and fragile—especially to countless young men who had cowered in the trenches on the Western front, growing cynical and disenchanted with everything they had been told they were fighting for. To these young men, too, there was one poignant lesson to be learned from the war experience. The war had exposed the utter falsity and corruption of bourgeois culture. Patriotism, self-discipline, and worship of their fathers' gods—all in all the kind of morality which had girded Europe's material and social "progress" during the previous century—showed itself nothing more than a miserable fraud. It was bourgeois civilization's own hypocritical idealism which had prevented it like a blind sentry from realizing the threat down below. The generation that came through the war was in a mood to trample upon the toppled idols. Ridiculing the unself-conscious rationality and moralism of their elders, they searched for a new meaning within the dark retreats of the human spirit. They longed for salvation from the times by penetrating a different world in what psychologists were now calling the Unconscious.

The mounting notoriety of Sigmund Freud's work, of course, seemed to scour out many of the mysteries of what lurked in the depths of man's mind. Whereas the war had pricked the pious pretenses and illusions of European society, Freud had left topsy-turvy many comfortable, rational assumptions about the individual psyche. He had trained a spotlight on the tenebrous "inside" of everyday consciousness, just as novelists, poets, and philosophers were beginning to expose the ugly overleaf of middle-class existence. Freud's own meticulous and cautious scientific attitude, though, together with his instinctive pessimism about the force of the unconscious, or what he termed the "return of the repressed," was ignored by those he inspired. Freud the conservative in many quarters became Freud the revolutionary. To liberate the Unconscious was to liberate humanity; to express one's dreams and libidinous impulses would compensate for civilization's slaughter of the innocents. Freud's materialism and rationalism was overlooked. He was regaled as the new Moses who might lead his chosen ones into the yet barely glimpsed land of the inner psyche flowing with milk and honey.

In an important sense the cult of unreason which burgeoned after the war represented a *psychologizing* of the Gnostic heritage. The

Romantics had spurred the process a century before, inasmuch as they tended to reinterpret esoteric religious symbolism in terms of hazy psychic contents. The "other world" could now be located in immense and largely unmapped regions of the mind, in the obscure layer of awareness which they metaphorically labelled "spirit." The Symbolist poets and artistic *avant-garde* of the late nineteenth century also grasped the relationship between occult realities and the depths of personal consciousness. But psychoanalysis gave this mysterious universe of the mind a "name." It was the Unconscious. One no longer need apologize for the truth of dreams or subtle revelations as having some external or strictly metaphysical significance. They were products of the recently discovered unconscious cosmic *within*. The "within" was more genuine than the "without." The visible world may have perished in flames, but the world which manifested itself in the unmediated flow of intimation and fantasy had a greater weight and significance. Unconscious reverie harbored more insights as to the nature of things than conscious deliberation and logical analysis. Redemption would come through an interior "enlightenment" which consisted in the enthusiastic appropriation of all that had previously been glossed over by rationality; it would be an affirmation of the totality of the *self* in opposition to society and conventional knowledge. It would bring an epiphany of the dark God dwelling in a holy of holies shrouded from the light of day.

The sovereignty of the Unconscious was dramatically endorsed in the artistic brouhaha that came to be known as Surrealism. For the Surrealists, the First World War "had proved that reason is less reasonable than the dream," that there was a need "to make room therefore for onenism, the search for a reality deeper than appearances," and to confirm "the omnipotence of the subconscious."[1] Fired by the findings of psychoanalysis, Surrealism aimed to employ Freud's discoveries not so much for self-understanding as for a sweeping cultural reformation. Although the Freudians regarded psychoanalysis as a weapon in civilization's fight against neurotic obsessions and the perversions of the instincts, the Surrealists viewed their mandate as a battle to the death against all forms of *repression*, particularly the repression of fantasies. Such a battle, they believed, would serve to undermine the rotten structure of twentieth century society.[2] "We really live by our fantasies," André Breton, the doyen of the movement, boasted in his first *Manifesto of Surrealism* composed in 1924.[3] The Surrealists hoped to abolish the disparity between man's spontaneous wishes and what Freud termed the "reality principle." For "reality" to them was nothing more than a pale consensus, an arbitrary definition, imposed on the individual mind in the interest of preserving bourgeois conformity and mediocrity. "I believe," Breton wrote, "in the future resolution of these two states, dream and reality, which are seemingly so contradictory, into a kind of absolute reality, a *surreality,* if one may so speak."[4] Breton spoke of "the secrets of the magical surrealist art" which would give the individual a command over his surroundings impossible for the ordinary dolt. Art would warp customary language and logic to the point of "reestablishing dialogue in its absolute truth,"[5] the truth of unabashed "madness" and the effusion of feelings. No ethical judgement could be placed upon the impulses emanating from the Unconscious; for the Unconscious contained what was most healthy and "natural," in contrast with the soul-stifling moralism of the bourgeoisie which injects into mass consciousness "the contamination of money" and the pharasaic commitment to "fatherland," "justice," and "duty." Like all Gnostics, the Surrealists summoned forth an elite corps of "seers" who would use their new self-knowledge to explode the hypocrisy of modern values. The Surrealist must become a thoroughgoing antinomian, a terrorist in unflagging combat with sentimentality and propriety. Indeed, the most authentic Surrealist gesture, Breton suggested, perhaps as a facetious jibe, would be to empty his revolver into a crowd on the street. Even death could have a wry charm about it, since the extinction of life would mean a return to the pure springs of unconscious life. "Everything remains to be done, every means must be worth trying,"[6] was the maxim for those whom Breton invited to join him in a league with the Devil.

While Surrealism betokened the most extreme and possibly most nihilistic variation on the new theme of *laissez-aller* ("let everything go") which engrossed the postwar Bohemians, the broader tenor of intellectual protest was more pacific. Except among certain German youth, for whom a kind of social mysticism of the *Volk* harking back to the Romantics combined with outrage over the lost war ultimately to beget Nazism, the recoil of the disaffected from the now dishonored culture of their parents took the form of ardent soul-searching. The drift of the times was away from politics and into the enchanted castle of the self. Psychological theories swiftly became all the rage. But, in contrast with the hard-nosed and essentially rationalistic Freudian schools, there emerged at the same time a strong concern with the spiritual dynamics of the individual, with a "cosmic" solution to the problems of anxiety and anomie. One of the chief exponents of this stance was the German author Herman Hesse, whom we shall discuss later in this chapter. The pathos of the sensitive spirit, so wounded by the war that it becomes virtually disembodied and seeks refuge in another plane of reality, was given voice by Hesse at the end of 1917 in an essay published under the pseudonym of Emil Sinclair, the hero of his influential novel *Demian* which appeared in print two years thereafter. The essay compared the brutality and dehumanization of war with the sublimity of extraterres- trial flight. "Sinclair" describes how as "a boy I have been in the habit of disappearing now and then, to restore myself by immersion in other worlds."

> So now, once again, I vanished for a time. The present has lost its charm for me after two or three years of war, and I slipped away to breathe different air. I left the plane on which we live and went to live on another plane. I spent some time in remote regions of the past, raced through nations and epochs without finding contentment, observed the usual crucifixions, intrigues, and movements of progress on earth, and then withdrew for a while into the cosmic.[7]

Sinclair returns to "this world" only to find that the war continues and the regimentation of society is total. He encounters a government official who apprehends him for taking a walk without a permit. The official questions him and upbraids him for having not observed the regulations, threatening to revoke his "existence permit." Sinclair replies that his one desire is to *die*, but the official demurs: "But dying isn't so simple. You belong to the state, my dear man, you are obliged to the state, body and soul."[8] The official informs him that all that remains of life is war itself. Sinclair lugubriously admits that he "understands," is released, and wanders off into the streets. Immediately he disappears from sight again.

> Before anyone could notice me and stop me, I inwardly recited the short astral spell, turned off my heartbeat, and made my body vanish under a clump of bushes. I pursued my cosmic wanderings and abandoned the idea of going home.[9]

Indeed, the dislocation of the mind wrought by the war left many with the sad conviction that they could never return home. It was the same sense of a gossamer and delicate state of being beyond the tragedy of human fatality and time which Nietzsche christened the "spirit of levity" and which suffused, for example, Rainer Maria Rilke's postwar poetry.

> Killing is only an aspect of the wandering grief
> we endure . . .
> To the spirit without passion
> what happens to us is pure.[10]

The introverted longings of the European mind following the war aimed toward an Archimedian point of consciousness from which all discordant passions and ideas could be traced and explained. Poets and dreamers yearned for solace from the time and becoming by immersion in the eternity of unconscious life. In the lap of a shadowy, inchoate Deity who revealed himself in reverie and whimsy would a restoration of the fragmented personality get underway.

THE PERCEPTION OF THE FLOW

Nietzsche's doctrine of eternal recurrence, though philosophical rather than psychological in scope, persuaded many intellectuals of the contingency and mutability of all existence. Einstein's views on the relativity of things in the universe, which was just starting to be understood outside the garret of scientists, influenced popular notions that no longer could there be conceded any permanent entities or enduring realities left for man to refer to. The experience of an entire way of life falling apart after the war provided an important basis for the new supposition that there might be nothing unchangeable in human affairs besides change itself. A book by the German philosopher Oswald Spengler entitled *The Decline of the West,* published in 1918 on the eve of his nation's disastrous defeat in the First World War, attained wide recognition for its thesis that history swallows up and casts into oblivion all culture, even that of the proud and progress-minded European. The postulate of Spengler's work was that all life consists in the emergence and extinction of forms, that flux and impermanence are the rule for all time.

The splintering of old values and the puncturing of once fiercely held illusions underlined the chaos present not only in social institutions, but also in the mind itself. The novels of Thomas Mann and Hesse, for example, explored the raging, inner conflicts of bourgeois man who seemed to have jettisoned not merely his social ballast, but his psychic rudder as well. The Unconscious was a roiling, swollen stream of curbed wants and inclinations which corresponded to the undulating social and political currents which were transforming his everyday relationships with his fellow beings. Though the outer world appeared to have no fixed axis of orientation, could the postwar intellect discern a constancy of some sort in his own inner states? That was the question which haunted and puzzled many of the new generation.

Whereas the time scheme of ordinary experience seemed broken and meaningless in the disarray of betrayed hopes and promises, the buried freshet of personal imagination might possibly contain hints as to the actual meaning of life. Deep behind the mask of the average person's consciousness might be concealed a timeless absolute. Self-knowledge might be the portal leading to an existence of an entirely different order. The suggestion of an "eternal life" within the Unconscious crops up before the war in the writings of the French philosopher Henri Bergson (1859-1941). Bergson, who was more provocative than influential in the long run, set the tone for the kind of speculation which posited an eternity in the midst of the flow of life. Bergson termed this eternity *la durée* ("duration") which he set in opposition to *le temps* ("time"), the measure of external or mere conscious temporality. Pervading all phenomena, Bergson claimed, is a mysterious vital force, the *élan vital*, which intertwines all living creatures.

The historian H. Stuart Hughes has remarked that Bergson's work is a "curious combination of poetic flights of fancy and a specifically French logic and clarity."[11] Indeed, Bergson employed the well-stropped scythe of philosophical reflection to thresh all rationalistic judgements and managed to harvest in the same vein a mystical slant toward ultimate reality. Bergson scrapped plain conceptual analysis for what he called "intuition." Intuition, Bergson claimed, allows us to grasp the truth of existence as an undifferentiated movement in which all things cohere. Reality can be defined as pure flow. Just as in a great river all the drops adhere as an onward, rolling mass of water, so in life the "moments" of time are actually nothing more than interpenetrating elements of the *élan vital*. The future is implicit in the past, and the past persists into the future. The "present" signifies simply a narrow and fleeting perspective on the all-encompassing flow, in exactly the same fashion as an observer standing on a bridge above a stream can see objects only one at a time as they float by. And, as the river is more than the discrete drops which coalesce together in the mass, so "duration" is more than the passing instants of time. It is a veritable *eternity of change and variation* realized by suspending the critical faculties of intellect that tend to divide up and "freeze" the rush of life. Bergson's insight as to the nature of duration, or "real" time, arose while he was pondering a famous paradox of the ancient Greek philosopher Zeno. The paradox has to do with a race between the legendary hero Achilles and a tortoise. Given a head start by the tortoise, Zeno argued, the fleet-footed Achilles could "never" catch up, since he would always have an endless number of infinitesimal intervals to traverse before reaching his goal. He would be two inches away, then one inch, then a half-inch, and so on indefinitely, but he would never surmount the very last and infinitely tiny gap. Bergson concluded that Zeno's paradox rested on an important confusion of ideas which, in fact, belied reality. Zeno mistook distance for motion. Similarly, the ordinary person is apt to misidentify time as conceived and quantified by the intellect with genuine duration which must be intuited. At bottom there is no such thing as time in the usual sense. There is only an "eternity of life" which billows forth. As Bergson put it in his key book, *Creative Evolution,* "reality is a perpetual growth, a creation pursued without end."[12]

At times, Bergson labelled the vital sources of existence as "instinct" or "pure willing." In this respect, he had a metaphysical attitude similar to Nietzsche's. Yet Bergson was not concerned with the ethics of the will to power or the self-development of the creative individual. The edge of Bergson's philosophy was toward mysticism, toward the dissolution or what he called the "reabsorption" of the conscious self in the plenitude of unconscious energy. Like a good number of his cronies of the 1890s and thereafter, Bergson set his face against the mechanistic philosophy and positivist science which had muscled its way into the academy and captured popular thinking. Bergson criticized the philosophers of his era for centering their attention predominantly on the structure and behavior of matter. The material universe, Bergson insisted, is but the hard, outer integument of the inner realm of spirit. "Mechanism" as well as those philosophies which arrange the world according to rigid, mathematical principles are "only external views of our conduct."[13] The hidden surface of existence is boundlessly variable and many-textured. In opposition to the intellect which takes cognizance only of material forms, Bergson posed the fact of unconscious "memory" which registers images of all that is experienced. "Pure memory" is the gateway to awareness of duration: it is the font of intuition. Later, the psychologist Carl Jung would talk of the "collective unconscious" that constitutes the repository of all human memory traces and symbols. Like Bergson, Jung took stern issue with mechanistic psychologies that denied the profound reality of the inner life. The collective unconscious lies beyond time and cannot be explained by any materialistic hypotheses. For Bergson especially, however, the active pulse of life should be regarded less as a psychic phenomenon than as a cosmic force. The *élan vital* is the covert drive behind biological evolution. It suffuses all life from moment to moment and makes for the freedom and spontaneity of man's will to create new things, the yearning to ride with the tide, and to reunite himself spiritually with all sentient beings. When man comes to "know" the vital origins of his existence, he can rid himself of false assumptions and futile wishes.

Bergson's thought was fundamentally dualistic, insofar as he continually laid at odds the material and the spiritual, the external and the internal, the mechanistic and the vitalistic. Indeed, he seems to have blazed a trail for the subsequent rebellion of the intelligentsia against all rationalist and materialist ideologies in the cause of sanctifying the individual psyche. The Gnostic insignia was imprinted on Bergson's ideas. In the same breath as many occult psychologies, Bergson placed the blame for man's unspiritual condition on the pressures of society. The human need to live in society stands in tension with the urge toward an expansion of consciousness. Indeed, society arises in the first place for the sake of collective survival, a purpose which bars complete self-knowledge. In society man is trained to respond as a kind of automaton to the demands of his group. He becomes overly rational and guided by his ego. He is like an ant blindly obeying chemical messages from kindred insects in the colony. Society, of course, is a "natural" outgrowth of spirit having "sedimented" in matter. Material require-ments nudge out spiritual ones, as man becomes conscious and confronts the necessity of guarding against enemies, baking his bread, building shelter, and so forth. Thus he is compelled to leave off communing with a deeper reality. "Nature asks of us only a quick glance at our inner selves."[14] Yet conformance to the survival strictures of the social order must at last contribute to a feeling of unease and thereby spur certain individuals into departing from their common routines in search of a grander wisdom. Those who release themselves from society's talons are visionaries who in the long run succeed in uplifting the human race.

In his last major writing, *The Two Sources of Morality and Religion*, composed in 1932, Bergson laid out the particulars of such an extensive theory. The bulk of this work was devoted to an exploration of the spiritual possibilities inherent in man's religious life. Bergson sorted out two types of religion: the "static" and the "dynamic." Static religion puts stress on creeds and deeds, on corporate myths and morality, on uniform beliefs which are derived not so much from personal illumination as from authority and tradition. Static religion serves to uphold the norms of society and is therefore conservative as well as collectivistic. Static religion ensures stereotyped or "mechanical" behavior from all its adherents. By static religion Bergson seems to have had in mind state churches and nationalistic faiths, which would include among others French Roman Catholicism with which he was familiar, traditional Hinduism, and Islam. Such religion "supplies strength and discipline," and is characterized by the prevalence of "rites and ceremonies."[15]

In contrast, dynamic religion transcends the use of creative energy for the sheer aim of group security. Whereas static religion is founded on the application of consciousness or "intelligence" for keeping members of society in harmony with each other, dynamic religion takes its thrust from individual intuition. It is not collective, but private. Dynamic religion stems from the development among the most spiritually gifted personages of society of a brilliant *gnosis,* a vault of insight into the essence of the world disguised by petty cares and opinions. In *The Two Sources* Bergson envisaged "a soul strong enough, noble enough" to put himself in touch with "the transcendent cause of all things." Such a soul would wrest itself from the ignorant opinions of the multitudes, from their narrow horizons of experience, and would bathe himself in the great, creative life force. His "*detachment* from each particular thing," supervening upon his sacrifice of intellect, "would become *attachment* to life in general."[16]

His mission would be that of "working back from the intellectual and social plane to a point in the soul from which there springs an imperative demand for creation."[17] The mastery of this creative power in one's own spirit Bergson denoted as "love"—not merely physical love or even altruism, but precisely the love (what Plato once called *eros*) which binds the soul with the fullness of existence. To love genuinely is to merge back into the flow of life, to abolish time and finitude, to perdure unconsciously with the entirety of unnamed Being. Naturally, Bergson saw the achievement of cosmic love through intuition as the perennial strength of the world's famed mystics. Mystics and other religious innovators, he contended, have repeatedly sustained an intimate relation with the *élan vital*. Bergson's testament was really a clarion call for modern man to redeem himself from his psychic estrangement, from his anxiety about history, by tapping anew the dynamism of the Unconscious. In retrospect Bergson turned out to be more allusive than definitive, more pioneering than momentous. He was a philosopher whose metier was mostly that of a poet or an imagist. He was a metaphysician whose impact came really in the area of psychology, though he was not, and should not, have been recognized as one. He epitomized the inward turn of European thought without directly affecting the chief representatives of that movement. *Bergson-ianism* frequently met the accusation that it was fanciful and obscurantist. But, of course, the new climate in the early twentieth century was conducive to certain excesses of premonition. In spite of the fact his reputation tapered off almost as fast as it had risen, Bergson helped to survey the complex psychological and religious terrain which more specialized investigators of the spirit would begin charting.

A Voyage into the Shadows

If the paramount metaphor for the mysteries of the mind and body was "Life" for Bergson, for Carl G. Jung (1875-1961) it was the "collective unconscious." A lion in his own era, Jung stands also as one of the major links to the present preoccupation with things occult, psychic, and spiritual. Jung, it may be said, perhaps more than any other seminal mind since Plotinus in antiquity, served to give legitimacy to esoteric and Gnostic concepts with a well-wrought theory that the famous renegade student of Freud wanted accepted as being somehow "scientific." Unlike Bergson, Jung did not have to contend with philosophers, only other psychoanalysts, who attracted wider public attention anyway by this time than those who wrangled over abstruse theories of knowledge. Jung made the murky symbols of spiritual discernment seem plausible with a flair that religious cultists lacked and philosophers would never have bothered to cultivate (with the possible exception of Bergson) because of the very language and subject matter involved. In fine, Jung was able to lend cogency to many strange claims about supersensory phenomena with one deft hypothesis—that of the collective unconscious. And he added authority to his notions by purporting to adduce them from clinical data, since Jung *always* referred even the most remote surmises back to evidence from his sessions with patients.

Poor "mechanist" that he was, Freud, who was Jung's early mentor, could never have gone as far as his student in theorizing like the latter. Freud, as Jung himself publicized, was forever suspicious of the "black tide of mud of occultism." Occult surmises and even religious sentiments would *have* to be explained according to Freud's "hydraulics" of sexual energy, in terms of repression and displacement, wish-fulfillment and sublimation, neurosis and failure to deal squarely with "reality." Despite his suggestions of "inherited" guilt and genetic memory in *Totem and Taboo,* Freud did not want to propose that the unconscious was much else besides a storage bin for personal traumas the individual had forgotten, or anything other than a closed cauldron of dangerous impulses welling up from the *id*. Jung, however, took the view that the *personal unconscious*—the glob of repressed desires which take shape from a person's painful life experiences—were relatively inconsequential when compared with the true source of dreams and fantasies. In his clinical work Jung alleged to have uncovered numerous ideas and symbols which could not possibly have been formed out of everyday experience. A patient, for example, would have a dream of heaven or hell which was something more than an imaginative distortion of concepts from earlier religious training. The dream would bear close affinity with an ancient myth buried in some obscure text or compare with a medieval woodcut that the patient had never laid eyes on. The cause of the dream, Jung reasoned, must be an unconscious disposition to symbolize experience in a fashion that was only intelligible as some impersonal psychic force. The analogy between the dream and the myth must derive from a faculty of imagination that was present in all human beings, *regardless* of the biographical or historical context in which the symbols arose. Jung dubbed this universal and ahistorical capacity for symbolization the "archetype." The term "archetype," which he borrowed from Neo-Platonic mysticism, signified an ideal form, though an unconscious form, outside time and space. The genesis of archetypes was itself independent of culture or history. Archetypes resided in a layer of the unconscious below the personal level. This plane of the unconscious was primary and common to the human race—hence its "collective" character.

At one remarkable stroke the notion of a "collective unconscious" became, for Jung, a construct which for the first time in the history of mainline thought could be cited to warrant not only the claims of mystics, but the odd and often convoluted metaphysical statements of seers, spiritualists, and Gnostics. In fact, Jung was outspokenly sympathetic to the entirety of the Gnostic tradition. Suspicious of orthodox Christianity and Western rationalism (which he tagged as intimate bedfellows), Jung thought the Gnostic perspective on the universe deserved a thorough rehabilitation. "I grant you," he wrote in a letter of 1932 to a man named Velter, "that I am on the best way to delivering up the Christian concept of the spirit to the chaos of Gnosis again."[18] The underground strand of occultism in modern Western culture, according to Jung, was a discreet manifestation of Gnostic insights. "The spiritual currents of the present have, in fact, a deep affinity with Gnosticism."[19] Moreover, the Gnostic heritage would well provide the solution to the spiritual "crisis" of the modern Occidental soul. Jung spent much of his professional career perusing seldom read arcane texts (especially those of the medieval alchemists who he felt were the latterday heirs of ancient Gnosticism).[20] Several thick volumes of his *Collected Works* are devoted to meticulous and frequently pedantic interpretation of alchemical and Gnostic symbolism.

Why was Jung preoccupied with recondite, bizarre, and antiquated cults? In one respect his obsession had to do with his studied distaste for the basic motifs of Western thought, particularly its modern permutations. Jung himself displayed much of the style of the Gnostic with his introspective bias, his esotericism, and his "aristocratic" uneasiness with contemporary "mass" society. He preferred Oriental wisdom (whether it be Vedantic Hinduism, Buddhism, or Chinese Taoism) to

Occidental logic and scientism. He insisted that the meaning of human history actually was to be found outside of history—in the collective unconscious. The time dimension was only the visible escarpment of the inner workings of man's spiritual nature.

But the nub of Jung's attitude toward the Western mind was his passion to find the unifying factor for both conscious and unconscious experience. History, and modern history in particular, is far from irrelevant, inasmuch as it constitutes the continual, but yet indeterminate process whereby conscious life struggles to attain an equilibrium with the unconscious. The peculiar dilemma of the twentieth century, or what he called "the spiritual problem of modern man," lies in the sudden rift of the developed, conscious mind (the individual, ego-consciousness) from its unconscious, mass or "collective" origins. The modern European in the name of "reason" and "progress" has sundered himself from the inchoate and dark powers within his psyche. He has turned his back on the past, not only the remembered traditions and consoling myths of his ancestors, but also the archaic and immutable psychic links with which he is bound as a human being to nature.

> The values and strivings of those past worlds no longer interest him save from the historical standpoint. Thus he has become "unhistorical" in the deepest sense and has estranged himself from the mass of men who live entirely within the bounds of tradition.[21]

Modern man has become a derelict staggering "before a void." The hypertrophy of his insular, rational consciousness has thrown him into a kind of chronic *neurosis*. In his autobiographical *Memories, Dreams, Reflections* Jung quoted approvingly a seemingly ingenuous conversation he once had with a chief of the Pueblo Indians in New Mexico. The chief's words, spoken from the heart of a primitive, depict the strange, restless, and uprooted dementia of the "advanced" European.

> "See," Ochwiay Biano said, "how cruel the whites look. Their lips are thin, their noses sharp, their faces furrowed and distorted by folds. Their eyes have a staring expression; they are always seeking something. What are they seeking? The whites always want something; they are always uneasy and restless. We do not know what they want. We do not understand them. We think that *they are all mad*."[22]

By arrogantly cutting himself off from his primeval nature, by denying and repressing his participation in the collective unconscious, modern man has "lost his soul." By "soul" Jung meant the intricate totality of all conscious and unconscious psychic energy. The loss of soul is tantamount to a fatal division in nature itself brought about by the urge in modern culture toward an abstract individuality coupled with a basic forgetfulness that the individual person is never autonomous, but always rocked and buffeted by impersonal forces surpassing his understanding. The modern person's epochal refusal to acknowledge and deal with these forces can have disastrous consequences, because "nature" will not allow itself to remain out of kilter for long. The collective unconscious will tend to reassert itself, irrespective of what the conscious mind thinks or motivates man to do.

In sum, modern man suffers from a grievous psychic one-sidedness. This one-sidedness has been fostered on the one hand by an overexertion on the part of the conscious self to break free from the dominance of the Unconscious and on the other hand by the influence of Christian morality. Jung held that Christian morality (in the context of his writings one might actually read "Protestant bourgeois *moralism*") has enjoined that man strive to be unqualifiedly "good" while eradicating what is inherently "evil" within him. But "good" and "evil" from the standpoint of the Collective Unconscious are complimentary and reciprocal elements. As archetypes they have equal worth in the economy of nature. There is no such thing as an absolute dichotomy between good and evil. Good and evil are what particular societies brand them. And, if individuals succeed only in incorporating the "good" side of their psyches into consciousness, the evil aspect will rear its ugly head.

Jung identified the attributes of "goodness" with the *persona*. The *persona* is the ideal or "social self." It is an "excerpt" of the collective *consciousness* of the group. It is "the individual's system of adaptation to, or the manner he assumes in dealing with, the world."[23] The *persona* therefore is a representation of conventional morality, or at least the moral expectations which every society has toward its members and which are internalized in the members' definitions of who they are. In contradiction to the "goodness" exemplified in the *persona*, however, stands the *shadow*. "The shadow personifies everything that the subject refuses to acknowledge about himself and yet is always thrusting itself upon him directly or indirectly—for instance, inferior traits of character and other incompatible tendencies."[24] The shadow consists in "that hidden, repressed, for the most part inferior and guilt-laden personality whose ultimate ramifications reach back into the realm of our animal ancestors and so comprise the whole historical aspect of the unconscious."[25] The sacrifice of the archetypal shadow at the expense of the *persona,* as happens in modern culture, will finally result in a colossal and most likely explosive eruption of the power. Pent-up and kept down, the shadow will burst forth in deviant symbolism and behavior; it will swell and engulf consciousness in a manner which Jung called "inflation." Jung accounted for many hysterical, fanatical, and destructive mass movements, especially Nazism, as instances of inflation. In the case of Nazism, the good, "Christian" face of the German soul was suddenly turned inside out and exposed to the brutal promptings of ancient, Teutonic barbarism. The only way to avert such historical calamities, which Jung argued were becoming ever more menacing as modern consciousness evolved, would be for persons and cultures to become aware of their own murky undersides. Thus Jung looked to occult philosophies which by his reckoning glimpsed the "natural" union of opposites, the coincidence of good and evil in a fashion which modern ideologies were wanting.

Jung, as we have indicated, was particularly enamoured with Gnosticism. "It is clear beyond a doubt," Jung declared, "that many of the Gnostics were nothing other than psychologists."[26] The Gnostics enjoyed a special kind of *"psychological knowledge whose contents derive from the unconscious."*[27] More precisely, the Gnostics recognized the fusion in the Unconscious of good and evil. Their God was not only intuited directly within the self; such a God did not admit of moral or rational distinctions. "He" was the "dark" God who contained within himself the unity of all polarities: masculine and feminine, transcendence and immanence. The Gnostics did not circumscribe God by imputing to him a moral conscience or personal characteristics. The Gnostic Deity was impersonal and timeless. He remained "beyond good and evil." The Gnostic God, so far as Jung was concerned, is veritably an emblem of the "Self." The Self is the underlying order in the human personality, "the whole circumference which embraces both conscious and unconscious."[28] The Self mediates and combines the antitheses of conscious existence; it welds together *persona* and shadow. The whispered "immorality" of the Gnostics, Jung pointed out, was simply a caricature of their psychological acumen. Unbeholden to a rigid and rationalized moral system which brooks no place for evil propensities, they affirmed instead the bivalent features of the human mind. Jung detected the same openness to the combination of opposites in alchemy. Alchemy, through endeavoring to convert gross matter into a "spiritual" substance, set before itself the unstated aim of overcoming the cleft between the tangible and the intangible dimensions of nature. The myth of the *hierosgamos,* the sacred marriage or what the Rosicrucians called the "chemical wedding," was such a symbol of unification apparent in alchemical lore.

The task of modern man in Jung's estimate, therefore, is to conquer the alienation and division within himself by following a path which Gnostics and spiritual adepts have already prepared. The accent must fall not on a revision of doctrines or beliefs, but on revelatory *experience* of the abandoned self. Modern humanity, which has let slip away the once comforting myths and ideas about the world nurtured within Christendom, in fact hungers for new and intense experience. The benefit of such experience will be the facilitation of personal growth toward what Jung tabbed "individuation." Individuation is "becoming one's own self" by way of the reconciliation of opposites within the personality. The collective archetypes reel and clash with each other until the person, by dint of his own unique life experiences and increasing self-knowledge, has brought them into harmony with each other at a higher plane of consciousness. It was Jung's view that man has little choice when it comes to assimilating the contents of the Unconscious. The sole question is whether he will become aware of what is happening to him and on the same score *accepting* it. In this regard Jung was stirred by Nietzsche's conception of *amor fati,* buoyantly committing oneself to personal fate or destiny. "Fate," according to Jung, is scarcely anything more than the historical road mapped out by our Unconscious. To appropriate willfully one's fate is to harken to the inner "daimon," to countenance one's private calling or "vocation." "Only the man who is able *consciously* to affirm the power of the vocation confronting him from within becomes a personality; he who succumbs to it falls a prey to the blind flux of happening and is

destroyed."[29] Individuation, or integration of personality, ensues from
drawing up into consciousness and bearding squarely the dark, ancient
"spells" of the gods—the archetypes and their powers.

In Jung's discussion of individuation there persists a reminiscence of
the Romantic concept of "genius," the self-conscious and assiduously
self-critical individual who harnesses his passion with insight, who
brings the profound mysteries of life to scrutiny. Jung conceded his
admiration for the Romantic *Weltanschauung*. His premier hero was
Faust, the wizard of the spiritual. Like the Romantics, with their
Gnostic antecedents, Jung undertook to uncover the transcendental
sparks of the self smoldering within nature. Nature was the sperm fluid
that harbored the "higher" potencies of soul. It was the ground in
which were merged the unsurpassable unity of the two greatest
opposites—not just the conscious and the Unconscious, but man and
God.

Jung testified in his memoirs that he had sought all along to chart
"that great territory of the self which lies beyond the segment of
Christian morality, taken into the wholeness of nature and spirit in
which conflicts and contradictions are resolved."[30] By the same token,
his psychological investigations edged toward reducing the distance,
implicit in the Christian demand for "faith," between Creator and
creature, between the infinite and the finite, divinity and the self. The
God "symbol," Jung averred, is something more than a mental
representation or fiction; it draws into the collective unconscious, where
we find "the God within." Indeed, it is difficult to "tell whether God
and the unconscious are two different entities."[31] God, not as symbol
but as reality, corresponds to the Self. The Self, or "soul" of humanity,
"is assuredly not small, but the radiant Godhead itself."[32] One cannot
deny the "existence" of God without at once repudiating the demands
of the unconscious. "The God-image is not something *invented,* it is an
experience that comes upon man spontaneously—as anyone can see for
himself unless he is blinded to the truth by theories and prejudices."[33]
In Gnosticism, more incisively than in Christianity, such an experience
is given central significance. By pronouncing God and man incommen-
surable, Christianity had inadvertently erected a wall between the
conscious and unconscious sectors of the personality. Christianity has
spotted the footprints of God on the trail of consciousness, in the
temporal process and in history. And for that reason Christianity has

impaired man from innate self-understanding. Mysticism and Eastern wisdom, on the other hand, with their ahistorical and introspective approach, fall closer to the mark, in the same way as Gnosticism, which in its affinity with the Oriental method constituted a breakthrough for the Western mind, only to have been anathematized as "heresy." The Eastern tradition has been psychologically astute, insofar as it has concentrated on the "inner" rather than the "outer" mind. It has not committed the error of Christianity, which left man "alienated from his innermost being" and which consigned the "One Mind, Oneness, indefiniteness, and eternity" to "the prerogative of the One God."[34]

But man, regarded from the depths of his own consciousness, is the vessel himself of God. He is *eternity incarnate*. In contrast to experienced, historical time, the "unconscious certainly has its 'own time' inasmuch as past, present, and future are blended together in it."[35] The coexistence of all temporal moments in the unconscious was the cincture of Jung's doctrine of "synchronicity"—the theory that events in the ordinary universe that are not causally related or temporally prior to each other nevertheless can be linked together meaningfully. Dreams or premonitions of the future, occurrences which from one standpoint may seem to be the bare product of chance or coincidence—these are explicable from the vantage point of the collective unconscious. For all reality is ultimately an eternal interlocking skein of potentialities and purposes which unfold or manifest themselves sequentially in the realm of time. The unconscious is thus the clue not only to history, but everything which transpires in the orbit of matter. In order to "know" who he really is, the individual must avert his eyes away from external circumstances and inward toward the ground of all life and matter. Bergson has urged that one intuit the *élan vital* or underground flow of life. Jung gave both a psychological and metaphysical name to the process as the very cipher of all spiritual phenomena.

Regarding social thought, Jung spoke up for the favored Gnostic position of exclusivity and magical prowess. To become "awakened" is to enter into psychic accord with nature, and "nature," Jung professed, is inveterately "aristocratic." Similarly, Jung perceived a momentous peril in modern secularism's elevation of the "mass man." In 1932 he confided to Max Rychner, "Everything to do with the masses is hateful to me. Anything popularized becomes common."[36] Mass consciousness and morality serve to distract the individual from an authentic grasp of his vocation. The collective *conscience* of the social herd stifles and gradually silences the oracle of the interior man. The nation or State is raised up to a rational and abstract divinity whose adoration is incompatible with self-awareness and reflection. The ego-obsessed "leader" of the State becomes an idolatrous voice of authority where in reality there can be only one touchstone of truth—the promptings of the individual's own "soul." Jung did not consider the totalitarian movements of his age and their psychologies as merely aberrations of democracy. Such "inflations" were inherent in the modern drive to egalitarianism. Secularity, science, and "humanitarian" politics (all spin-offs of Christianity) were alike to blame. In *The Undiscovered Self* published during the 1950s Jung made his most tart attack on the social premises of modernity.

> Under the influence of scientific assumptions, not only the psyche but the individual man and, indeed, all individual events whatsoever suffer a levelling down and a process of blurring that distorts the picture of reality into a conceptual average. We ought not to underestimate the psychological effect of the statistical world picture: it displaces the individual in favor of anonymous units that pile up onto mass formations. Science supplies us with, instead of the concrete individual, the names of organizations and, at the highest point, the abstract idea of the State as the principle of political reality.[37]

The problem with democracy is not its *prima facie* view of man. Democracy at least gives lip service to the ideal of individual value and independence. But democracy fails because it gives precedence to political rather than spiritual causes. It extends to the individual a measure of social or material freedom, but it squelches in the name of "progress" or patriotic conformity the liberty of the unconscious. Whenever the person is not given latitude to grapple with his own interiority, the collective unconscious will do its necessary work through the group in the form of mass psychosis. The challenge of modernity is a psychic one, but the challenge can only be addressed in the arena of solitude. Only the self-conscious individual is capable of "applying the energy of the unconscious."[38]

Early in his career Jung flirted with the promise of Nazism. His Romantic leanings disposed him, like many Germanic intellectuals in the late 1920s and early 1930s, to construe the political mysticism of

Hitler, Rosenberg, and Goebbels as a natural development in Teutonic history which served to absolve the modern divorce between Christianity and naturalism, between the hyperrationality of the modern period and the archaic survivals of the spirit. The Germans under the Third Reich were giving vent to the long obscured collective unconscious. Jung, however, quickly forswore any political allegiances with Nazism, and remained content to exonerate his own stance as "unpolitical."[39] Over time he came to despise the holocaust which the Nazis had unleashed around the globe, and the ruination which he saw all around him only confirmed his latent historical pessimism. During and after the Second World War Jung could only continue to bewail the tumultuous collapse of modern culture. In 1933, with the inauguration of Hitler's tyranny, he had remarked of "the continuing divisions and upheavals" that would "gradually lead to a state of balance which will form the basis for a reconstruction." At the same time he reminded his reader that "this, of course, is not identical with what used to be called the march of civilization."[40] In 1949 he sounded more cautious and quite gloomy. Modern Europe, like "Old Rome," stands on the threshold of its own disintegration, even with the defeat of the Axis armies. The overshadowing menace is not a military one. It is the putrefaction of the *soul*.

> Technology and "social welfare" provide nothing to overcome our spiritual stagnation, and they give us no answer to our spiritual dissatisfaction and restlessness, on account of which we are threatened from within as from without. We have not understood yet that the discovery of the unconscious means an enormous spiritual task, which *must* be accomplished if we wish to preserve our civilization.[41]

All the glitter of progress is tawdry. All that history has taught us so far is that we must pass beyond history itself into the eternity of archetypes and symbols. The alternative is our spiritual demise and in the long run the return of chaos.

ABRAXAS REDIVIVUS

In the 1920s Jung published a strange, sententious, and lyrical little book entitled *The Seven Sermons of the Dead*. In the text Jung descanted on "the god whom ye knew not, for mankind forgot it," the god by the name of "ABRAXAS."[42] In Jung's own words, "Abraxas begetteth truth and lying, good and evil, light and darkness, in the same word and in the same act. Wherefore is Abraxas terrible."[43] Abraxas, of course, was an obscure, but magically powerful Gnostic divinity whose mode of veneration remains as enigmatic as his nature. For Jung, Abraxas represents the shadowy union in the unconscious of archetypal meanings. Abraxas is the "true" God, which Christianity unfortunately has closeted away in its archives of antique heterodoxies. References to Abraxas pop up now and then in occult traditions. But Jung saw Abraxas as something more than just another cultic divinity. Abraxas was the holy *name* for psychic power, for the new principle of human salvation.

The name Abraxas also figured in an important novel by Herman Hesse which came out and gained widespread interest in the immediate wake of the First World War. In *Demian* Hesse composed a story that was timely and prophetic, notwithstanding its autobiographical accent, and it pricked the emotions of a bewildered and distraught new generation. *Demian* is a tale of one Emil Sinclair's youth. Sinclair, the narrator, is an introverted, brooding, and toadying lad who finds himself cowed by the moral authority of his parents and sisters, and he winds up being blackmailed by a bully named Kromer for having stolen some apples. Too craven and self-pitying to stand up either to Kromer or his household, Sinclair finally comes across his "salvation" in the person of a boy called Demian. Demian turns out to be more than merely a friend who helps Sinclair get Kromer off his back. Through his words and deeds Demian is portrayed by Hesse as perhaps Sinclair's "shadow" personality: a derrick of courage and resolve which Sinclair himself can be if he only knows himself better. Demian introduces Sinclair to the untold secrets of the Biblical legend of Cain, who killed his brother and whom Demian praises as a "noble" figure. Demian explains to Sinclair that the reprobation of Cain in customary Christian morality is false. Cain's "mark" of evil is simply a capricious stigma which society has placed on stalwart and valiant men of will while denigrating their assertiveness as "sin."

> People with courage and character always seem sinister to the rest. It was a scandal that a breed of fearless and sinister people ran around freely, so they attached a nickname and a myth to these people to get even with them, to make up for the many times they had felt afraid. . . .[44]

Demian convinces Sinclair that Abel, the victim, who represents in

Christian eyes goodness and innocence, is really the "evil" one, whereas Cain is a hero. Sinclair relates that he began to see himself as "a kind of Abel," at least in terms of his deference to authority and weak conscience. He comes to realize that Cain, the wicked one, embodies the dark and unacknowledged side of his own character. Through Demian's guidance he discovers the play of moral opposites in his character.

In addition, Demian familiarizes him with the Gnostic spirit of Abraxas, whom Sinclair adopts as a symbol of his psychic transcendence of good and evil. At the end of the book Sinclair comes to unify the split image in himself, the gulf between his "female" dependency and his "male" power drive, the gap between his anxiety about sin and his instinctive egoism, through the archetypal symbol of Abraxas. He discovers the complementary facets of both Sinclair and Demian, and he acquires a whole new perspective on himself. The book closes with the now remade Sinclair going off to the Western front. The war experience serves to synthesize his conflicting psychic urges, and it exposes the decadence and hollowness of the old social morality to which he had earlier been captive.

> Many, very many, not only during the attack but at every moment of the day, wore in their eyes the remote, resolute, somewhat possessed look which knows nothing of aims and signified complete surrender to the incredible. Whatever they might think or believe, they were ready, they could be used, they were the clay of which the future could be shaped. The more single-mindedly the world concentrated on war and heroism, on honor and other old ideals, the more remote and improbable any whisper of genuine humanity sounded—that was all just surface, in the same way that the question of the war's external and political objectives remained superficial. Deep down, underneath, something was taking shape.[45]

What was taking shape was, of course, an inkling of a new spirituality and new values out of the corpse of the old. As a metaphor of destruction, Sinclair is wounded severely by shrapnel and taken to a military hospital where Demian, whom he has not seen since he went to war, returns for a brief visit, reassures him, and steals away as Sinclair falls unconscious. On coming to, Sinclair finds himself transfigured.

> Next morning someone woke me: I had to have my wounds dressed. When I was finally wide awake I turned quickly to the mattress next to mine. On it lay a stranger I'd never seen before.
> Dressing the wound hurt. Everything that has happened to me since

has hurt. But sometimes when I find the key and climb deep into myself where the images of fate lie aslumber in the dark mirror, I need only bend over that dark mirror to behold my own image, now completely resembling him, my brother, my master.[46]

Demian and Sinclair had fused into the mysterious being Abraxas.

Before writing *Demian,* Hesse had undergone analysis with Jung in Switzerland. Thereafter Hesse became, in a fashion, the literary ambassador for Jung's depth psychology. Hesse's novels of the 1920s and 30s tussle with the problem of the modern soul's division against itself, with the dilemma of moral rectitude versus the shadow. In *Steppenwolf* Hesse recounted the psychological junket of Harry Haller, the good bourgeois who has a dark, private alter ego which materializes in his fantasies. The flip side of Harry Haller is a cruel, friendless beast, the "wolf of the Steppes" (the *Steppenwolf*). Harry is slowly torn apart by the teeth of this contradiction within himself, and he is tempted to try suicide. While strolling through the streets, however, Harry comes upon a playbill for a "Magic Theater" into which admittance is "not for everyone." The magic theater, as he soon discovers, is a psychic cinema where all the archetypal forces in the soul, the cerebral and the sensual, the moral and the brutal, are juxtaposed on the screen together. Harry meets a strumpet named Hermine, who personifies the labile and protean life of pure experience which stands in opposition to Harry's regimented, bourgeois style. Hermine teaches Harry to dance and to abandon his inhibitions to the strains of jazz music. She helps to break down the brittleness of Harry's conscious self and leads him into the immediacy of the unconscious, the "magic theater" where the contrapuntal forms of the mind glide by in a series of "sideshows." Harry is immersed in a dream which is at the same time a foretaste of total reality. In the dream Harry has the sense that the Magic Theater is actually hell in disguise. He catches sight of grotesque war pictures of amassed bodies and the faces of the dead. He has finally had an undiluted taste of the "wolf world."

But just as he assents to the horror of it all, the mood dramatically changes. Now the dream carries him into a youthful springtime where he has fallen in love with a girl named Rosa. Chastened by the horrifying experience of his own depths, he passes from a haunted solitary courting psychosis into a new phase which points toward sanity and psychic integration. Love has started to heal his sutures. Through simple and natural love Harry casts off his case-hardened obsessions

and wades into the "stream" of existence. The fragmented and empty
time of his former life dissolves into an eternal flux. As in a "mirror"
he sees the characters of both Harry Haller and the *Steppenwolf* as
transient effects of the mind which have no more substance or
importance than a fleeting ripple. No longer need he take himself or life
so seriously, and for the first time he learns to *laugh*. Harry Haller, the
fretful and scrupulous comic figure of his now ridiculous past, receives
his "death" sentence from the "prosecutor" of the Magic Theater. He
is condemned to "eternal life" within the fullness of the unconscious.

In *Siddhartha* and *Klingsor's Last Summer* the same theme receives
extensive treatment. But now the resolution of the psychic conflict
which Hesse incessantly limned comes in the guise of Oriental wisdom.
The discovery of Abraxas is taken up, as suggested in Harry Haller's
encounter with the flux, into a vision of life as embracing all joys and
sorrows, all serious goals and velleities. The unity of conscious and
unconscious, good and evil, as adumbrated in the idea of the dark god,
is reaffirmed over and over in terms of the individual's capacity for
limitless experience. The cure for the psychic disease of civilization is
not a brash nihilism, but a serene mysticism.

Klingsor's Last Summer concerns the travails of an avant-garde
painter who has experimented with all new forms and colors, has
violated all traditional conceits, and is drinking himself toward death at
the age of forty-two. Klingsor, the artist, is steadily slipping into a self-
willed fantasy world, an enchanting delirium, in which he spews
feverishly onto canvas a stream of oneiric images churned up from his
possessed soul. His friends are mysterious and mythical figures as well,
and he gives the Chinese sobriquet of Tu Fu to one of them. In his madness,
however, Klingsor envisions prophetically the downfall of European
civilization, the unavoidable doom of a society in which he himself has
affected a necessary role. He rhapsodizes over wine to his friend Tu Fu:

> We are driving in a carriage on the edge of an abyss, and the horses
> have already shied. We are immersed in doom, all of us; we must die,
> we must be born again. The great turning point has come for us. It is
> the same everywhere: the great war, the great change in art, the great
> collapse in the governments of the West. For us in old Europe
> everything we had that was good and our own has already died. Our
> fine-feathered Reason has become madness, our money is paper, our
> machines do nothing but shoot and explode, our art is suicide. We are
> going under, friends; that is our destiny.[47]

But Tu Fu only mocks Klingsor's self-indulgent Cassandraism. He chides the vanity of his apocalyptic melancholy. The presentiment of upheaval and chaos which Hesse belabored in *Demian* gives way to a promise of a new consciousness in equipoise. Tu Fu explains that all presentiments, like current ideas, are "illusions." Even doom and death are illusions. Beyond illusions lies the stillness of *nirvana*, the void. Beyond the illusion of good and evil is perfect peace. "Everything is good. Nothing is good. The wisdom of the Magi abolishes illusions. It abolishes the worst of illusions which we call 'time.'"[48] Art seeks to immortalize the person, abolishing time and death, the destruction of worlds, as Klingsor in his mania has sought to do. But art cannot pierce the final barrier which is the ego. Klingsor does not seem to take this object lesson seriously. He sticks with art, with the discharge of his own unconscious drives which reaches a climax in his last esthetic fusillade, a stupendous self-portrait, in which he "insanely" draws his own death.

Whereas *Klingsor's Last Summer* remains a kind of tragic interlude, *Siddhartha* approaches an idyll. *Siddhartha* is Hesse's most eloquent statement of the meaning of wisdom. The tone of the novelette is reserved and dispassionate; it is carefully measured and stylized like an Oriental landscape. The young Siddhartha symbolizes Hesse's own Western rendition of the historical Gautama Buddha. Like Hesse himself, Siddhartha quests not so much after an answer to the riddle of suffering as the innermost meaning of life. Siddhartha hungers for a more searching spirituality than is offered to him by the ceremonial duties of his Brahmin caste. He leaves home, as did the real Buddha, and practices asceticism with a wandering troupe of Samanas. But the draconian denial of the senses and the moral rigors entailed in the life of a Samana leaves him still in want of a full understanding of his destiny. He becomes acquainted with the Noble Truths of Gautama, the Buddha, from which he obtains the supreme insight that life is an unremitting flow of all experiences and qualities, which in Hindu thought is called *samsara*. No longer an enemy of the senses, he leaps into life at flood tide. Siddhartha becomes the lover of Kamala, a beautiful courtesan, and gives himself over to a profligate career of business, drinking, and gambling. In these pursuits he incurs great wealth and material security, but he soon recognizes that pure sensuality and abandon are pointless goals for existence. In this respect he has overcome the kind of compulsive libertinism which proved to be the wrong path of salvation for Klingsor. Unlike Klingsor, he finally harkens to the Oriental message of perfect freedom in the abolition of the self and the stilling of unconscious desire. Just before he is about to take his own life by jumping into a river, he meets a mysterious ferryman who day in and day out plies the current. The ferryman instructs him that the purpose of existence is to become as one—genially, tranquilly, and guiltlessly— with nature. He teaches "the secret of the river," namely, that in the totality of the flow, the stream of life from beginning to end, "there is no such thing as time." Siddhartha must learn how to accept and appreciate every eventuality, every twitch of consciousness, every emotion and intention. He must discover how all forms of experience are bound together through "love," love of the river. He must even love death. Siddhartha goes to his former lover, Kamala, who is dying, and it is at her side as she expires that the "secret" becomes transparent to him. "In this hour he felt more acutely the indestructibleness of every life, the eternity of every moment."[49]

The later Hesse achieved through his stories the sort of cosmic composure which, he felt, Western man needs to reach in order to put behind him the anguish of watching civilization die. Novels such as *Journey to the East, Narcissus and Goldmund,* and his crowning masterpiece *Magister Ludi,* attest magnificently to this point of view. *Journey to the East* is a sustained dream in itself which leads past the dream state, and sweeps the reader beyond his own nagging sense of time, failure, and mortality into a luminous eternity. *Narcissus and Goldmund* conveys this timeless implosion of consciousness by being set in the idealized context of the faraway Middle Ages. It is the story of two friends—Goldmund, a young artist of deep, restless feeling and sensuality, and Narcissus, a monkish thinker and scholar. The two friends part ways in carrying through their respective destinies. Goldmund wanders off into the vast world and is corrupted by its very worldliness. He returns at the end of his life to be reunited with Narcissus who does not condone his sins, but yet accepts him without qualification as he is in a transforming attitude of love. Hesse perhaps endeavored to pose Narcissus and Goldmund as the eternal and necessary opposites that make up the "whole" personality. Goldmund, the man of instinct, is incomplete without Narcissus, the representative of sublimated drives, of prudence, and compassion. The same holds true in reverse. The two opposites are conjoined in a love which is both physical and spiritual. This harmony of conscious and unconscious power is the timeless objective which draws all lives irrespective of their historical setting.

In *Magister Ludi* (the German edition of the book is translated as *The Glass Bead Game*) Hesse projected the same tension between human aims into a utopian future. The protagonist of the novel is Knecht ("Servant"). Knecht has climbed to the topmost perch of success which the new civilization affords for any mortal. He has become master of the Glass Bead Game, an allegorical trope for the pure and disinterested intellectualism to which the academic mind aspires. But Knecht is uncomfortable in his lofty station. He senses that the intellectual elites have grown too far removed from the affairs of ordinary people. The ideal of "truth" enshrined in the Glass Bead Game jars drastically with the mundane passions and engagements of the common people. He becomes disenchanted with pure rationality and fears that the Glass Bead Game is fated to go the way of all rarefied and sublime accomplishments of high culture. The most likely prospect is a return to barbarism. Out of conscience he asks to be relieved of his titles and august responsibilities, but the "Castelian" order of intellectuals to which he belongs refuses, invoking the usual airy platitudes about "mind" having "its own independent history." Soon after this rebuke Knecht meets the kind of ironic fate that typifies Hesse's manner of resolving profound personal, cultural, and historical conflicts. Knecht drowns while swimming in a mountain lake and trying to keep pace with a vivacious and athletic boy named Tito. Thus Hesse capped his career as an author with sober tidings to humanity. History is a charnel house of futile designs and tenacious delusions. Time and history are a harlequinade of one-sided and overly specialized knaves who seek progress rather than "wisdom." Ultimately, the former is a chimera, the latter what endures.

Unlike Jung, who thoroughly retained the Gnostic animus toward modern culture, Hesse could resign himself to the perennial foibles of humanity. His ideal of psychic unity was predicated less on the refurbishing of individual souls, in contradistinction to the blind and vicious masses, than on a *rapprochement* between a person's private vocation and society, between self-knowledge and moral accountability. Hesse, for example, was never hypnotized even for an instant by the siren song of Nazism, and after the Second World War he made a concerted appeal for the intelligentsia to renounce its detachment from politics and social issues. Such was the not-so-hidden agenda, in fact, of *Magister Ludi*. Although the overhaul of the individual psyche is the chief precondition to arresting man's inhumanity, it is not the sole precondition. Man is a stitch in the endless web of institutions and history, and he therefore must become aware of his overall situation. The later Hesse tamed the Gnostic *hubris* by fidelity to a ripening, humanistic outlook. But he still was only a meager voice straining into a gale. The tide had always been flowing in the dangerous direction of which Jung had warned. The apocalypse intimated in *Demian* and *Klingsor's Last Summer,* rather than the spiritual quiescence of *Siddhartha,* remained from 1919 onward ominously near at hand.

THE SEASON OF THE DEVIL

Jung had admonished Westerners entranced with Hindu pantheism, Yoga, meditation, and the occult arts that the straightest way to the center of consciousness was strewn with many unexpected snares. Eastern man, Jung implied, already lives in a kind of naive relation to nature. His sensitivity and imagination have etched inside the unconscious an archetypal cosmos. Thus the endemic split within the Western soul between ego-awareness and the collective unconscious, between persona and shadow, has never arisen in the Oriental mind. In consequence, the Eastern mystic is able to dive right into the vortex of spirituality. He can make himself at home with the unconscious as effortlessly as a bird takes to the air. But Western man labors under a handicap of his own making. Before he glimpses the "inner light," he must first confront starkly his own repressed psychic contents.[50] Before he rises above good and evil, he must contend with the devil within him; and it may be that, if he does not proceed wisely, he will succumb to the nervous energies which are pent-up beneath the membrane of consciousness.

Though Jung continually argued that the collective unconscious must be given its due, he shuddered at what happens when it finds expression outside the individual personality in the historical sphere. The violent "inflation" of the unconscious is like a small tropical disturbance that bursts into a hurricane, and woe to the civilization which it lashes. By the same token, the Gnostic sense of "truth" raised to the level of the political can prove more insidious than moribund

Christian faith. A volcano of the archaic magma will spill out onto the plane of history and cause far-flung devastation. Privy as he was to the German experience, Jung thought that the tension within the Teutonic soul was extreme, and it would be in such a self-directed but fractured culture that a tremendous historical earthquake would occur.

The German poet Heinrich Heine, in an oft-quoted passage, had espoused the same forebodings a century earlier. Heine declared:

> It is the fairest merit of Christianity that it somewhat mitigated that brutal German *gaudium certaminis* or joy in battle, but it could not destroy it. And should that subduing talisman, the Cross, break, then will come crashing and roaring forth the wild madness of the old champions, the insane Berserker rage, of which Norther poets say and sing. . . . The old stone gods will rise from long-forgotten ruin, and rub the dust of a thousand years from their eyes, and Thor, leaping to life with his giant hammer, will crush the Gothic cathedrals![51]

No sensible historian would take Heine's words as a literal forecast of Hitler. But Heine, like Jung, was psychologically shrewd enough to foretell how the inflamed mythical imagination of Germany could ultimately kindle conflagration. In the German soul was the pressure of the irrational most intense and fraught with danger.

The Nazi firestorm was touched off by certain fortuitous circumstances of postwar Germany's history, such as the Great Depression, the ineffectuality of parliamentary politics in the Weimar Republic, the failure of democratic habits to take root in a society that had always been monarchical and authoritarian, the smoking resentment among the German people toward the victorious allies in the previous war and the conditions of the Versailles Treaty. But, as many studies over the last three decades have shown, the origins of the Nazi phenomenon are sunk in Germany's own legacy of popular symbols. We have already discussed (see Chapter 3) the threads joining the Nazi mind with Teutonic Romanticism. The mystical image of the *Volk* or "people" with an autonomous will and soul, crafted in the literature of the Romantics, mingled with crude theories of social evolution and racism justifying Western imperialism in the latter part of the nineteenth century to forge the Nazi idea of a nation of Aryan overlords. The Nazi ideology was a mish-mash of long-standing political aspirations on the part of particular fringe groups in Germany and arcane, quasi-religious fantasies. And it is the influence of the latter type of thinking that we shall be primarily concerned with here.

The background of the Nazi revolt as a *political* development can be traced, however, to the cultural turbidity of the prewar and postwar periods. Though Nazism was for the main part a middle-class movement, Hitler and the propagandists of the Third Reich tirelessly excoriated the bourgeoisie. Bourgeois man came to be identified as the bearer of all the modern and "decadent" innovations which had, in the Nazis' estimate, polluted the ancient spiritual marrow of the German race. Science, rationalistic philosophy, utilitarianism, democracy, and individualism were all hobgoblins which bourgeois society had allegedly brought along with it. These lamentable "facts" of modern life were compared with the old and "noble" spiritual virtues of German ancestral stock, who supposedly stressed feeling more than reason, mythical thought and martial virtues over morality, autocratic leadership of the *Führer* or "leader" who through his actions executed the tacit will of the *Volk*. The Jew, who historically was absent from the blood ancestry of the people and had now begun to assimilate modern ways, was the epitome of everything bourgeois and invidious. He was the germ behind the infection of modernity in the folkish body. He was nation-less, secularized, and wholly "unspiritual." He was the hated partisan of democracy, egalitarianism, Bolshevism—just about every-thing which competed with the ancient values of strength and aristocracy. The Jew was the carrier of modern culture, and therefore would perish along with it when the resurgent Teutonic spirit appeared. Nazi enmity toward the bourgeoisie became a wholesale opinion of the alienated shepherds of German culture in the first years of the twentieth century. Nazism was a proclivity long before it became a genuine undertaking.

The yearning for a bona fide new Germany of the spirit was couched in a revived nature mysticism during the 1890s that found an outlet in the *Wandervögel* (literally, "migratory birds") youth movement. The *Wandervögel*, as they were called, were passionate, idealistic young men who like Romantics of all eras reviled the superficial and materialistic character of society. Drifting through the woodlands with rucksacks on their backs, bellowing the praises of old German folk heroes beside campfires, and brandishing their manly talents, the members of the youth movement struck many as harbingers of a breathtaking new order. The *Wandervögel* in this respect were precursors of the mythical collectivism of the *Hitler-Jugend* ("Hitler youth"). They stressed the soaring notion of *Freundesliebe* ("love between friends") which had slightly scandalous overtones for polite society because of its suggestion of homosexuality. *Freundesliebe* later was translated into the ideal of "comradeship" among the German soldiery in the trenches. The avid sentiment of man's union with the natural world through fraternal loyalty thus became the basis of a new political cult of perseverance and valor, a streak of enthusiasm which the National Socialists smartly exploited.[52]

The Bible of the *Wandervögel* movement was a curious, polemical, and largely incoherent book by a free-wheeling intellectual and esthete called Julius Langbehn. The book bore the title of *Rembrandt as Educator*, even though it was hardly a biographical account of the great Dutch painter. Instead Rembrandt was drawn as a culture hero, a model of the "superman" which modern Germans in their inferior and errant ways were supposed to emulate. By and large *Rembrandt* consisted in a panegyric to the mystical, soulful, creative "type" of German man, a diatribe against the bourgeois philistine. The book was an indictment of everything mediocre, unheroic, and factitious, which in Langbehn's view infected nearly all of Wilhelmine society in the latter part of the nineteenth century. The only possible therapy for a sick Germany was a rebirth of the proto-German soul. The folkish soul was in itself an entity which transcended all modern ideologies and class distinctions. In the beginning, Langbehn asserted, the Germans were cemented together into a spiritual unity, but modern social democracy and various bourgeois, "Jewish" experimentations had been responsible for the shattering of the people's religious solidarity. Modern history has been a dire account of Germany's tragic and seemingly irreversible fall away from its marvelous origins. In opposition to the contentious and divisive individualism of bourgeois society, Langbehn proposed the reinstatement of corporate politics, the reconciliation of competing social groups such as industrialists and proletarians within a spiritual hierarchy. Equalitarianism would be replaced by the rule of superior, charismatic persons. Social democracy would bow out to what Langbehn termed "social aristocracy."[53] The new nobility would be both ruthless men of action and vigilantes of German sensibility. Their political legitimacy would be derived from both their skill at shepherding the masses and their attunement to the people's deepest emotions. And, of course, they would do their best to keep the Jew from soiling the purity of Nordic institutions and consciousness. Langbehn, like those of his age which included Stefan George and Moeller van den Bruck who coined the phrase "Third Reich," had primarily an esthetic and antiquarian temperament warped into the unsettling pipe dreams of a political high-flier. The combustible combination of Gnostic fantasies and political ambitions was the very torch which the Nazis used in their attempt to incinerate liberal civilization. The terror of time and history could be assuaged by enacting the new "German" idea of truth within the circus of history itself.

The rabid anti-Semitism of Nazi ideology, in equal measure, becomes intelligible in light of Gnostic estheticism and spiritualism. Mystical Teutonism, as it cropped up in Wagner, Langbehn, Moeller, and of course Hitler, always established itself over against the attitudes of modernity, against the rational and scientific orientation, against positive law and contractual relationships. On the social level it appealed to the disinherited *literati* and to their envy toward the professional classes, many of whom were Jewish. The German intellectual, in comparison with practical men of affairs, was usually steeped in some subtradition of Romanticism. And his declining social status in modern industrial Germany left him even more susceptible to cajolery from learned crackpots. As a result, he turned for relief to offbeat theories about human destiny and nature. He valued spontaneity and intuition over authority and law. Just as the ancient Gnostics reviled the "Jewish" elements in Christianity because of that religion's emphasis on moral scruples and obedience to a distant God, so the German intellectuals, in their protest against the formalism of bourgeois culture, were wont to project their hatred of authority onto the alien culture in their midst—the congregation of Israel.

Furthermore, the Jews, because of their ancient "historical" outlook, were anathema to a kind of thought that saw no meaning in history and endorsed absolute and transcendental goals. The Jew was a fateful reminder of the relativity of historical existence. A landless and transnational figure, he was uprooted from the mystical "soil" which Romanticism claimed lent a nation identity.[54] Jewish religion in Biblical times at least has warned against the exorbitance of the unconscious as the foundation of nature worship; it had condemned magic and the narcissistic grab for power by the individual self while pointing to the majesty and sovereignty of the Creator God. God was always "Other" than man, and therefore could *not* be readily reduced to man's private fantasies. Psychologically speaking, we can detect this extramental standard of truth in Hebraic religion as the basis for the modern alliance of Jewish culture and rationalism. The Gnostic, who located truth within the dark alcoves of his own imagination, and the Jew, who gave himself over to objective testing of his hunches, were a classic and recurrent match for each other. The strife between these two forms of mind lay behind the anti-Semitism of the inward and pietistic German.

The Gnostic mind, moreover, as we have seen, is stalked by the fear of contamination from without. The stain of evil, the corruption of matter, the menace of the rational organization of society—all these threatened to extinguish the limpid and pristine light of inner reality. The "soul" was forever in combat with the world. When Romanticism made the soul collective and associated it with the animating principle of a physical people (of the "race"), the inevitable outcome was a demented politics of racist fanaticism. The Gnostic's despisal of historical pluralism and his rage for psychic unity would drive him to purge all foreign matter from his environment. And the classifications of race were the most available target for this impetus. Finally, he would conduct the purge with the conviction of his own magical omnipotence.

Nazi politics were born, some have argued, out of occultism. While we cannot discuss all the ramifications of the occult origins of Nazism,[55] we can at least point up the uniform vision which aroused both the seers of the "ancient religion" and the men around Hitler. The Nazi emblem of the swastika (colored red and black to symbolize blood, the fluid of life, and death) was an ancient fertility symbol found in many primitive mythologies associated with worship of the sun. In the Nazi mind the swastika or "broken" cross may well have represented the crucifixion of the bourgeois, moral conscience derived from Christianity and the resurrection of man's primeval identification with the currents of nature. The racist myth, of course, was a desperate, unconscious affirmation of the "natural" man in the face of the historical particularities of modern culture. Though the modern world had erased all vestiges of man's spiritual identity with the cosmos, there still lingered the surviving "fact" of racial homogeneity, which in itself was threatened by the bitter acids of "Jewish" cosmopolitanism. Hence in the magical-political conception of the Nazis, the venerable anxiety of Gnosticism and occultism with regard to the dissolution of man's eternal soul in the tempest of "progress" and social change, was transposed into a brutal policy of exterminating all "unnatural" intrusions into life of the folk. *Gnosis* was modified by cheap, Darwinian speculation to support an assurance of the timeless validity of the Aryan people's right to rule over the globe.

The early Nazis of the 1920s, according to some historical evidence, took inspiration from the tenets of a secret society, founded in 1918, and dubbed the *Thule-Gesellschaft*. A "front" for a confederation of racist, anti-Semitic and occult groups, the *Thule-Gesellschaft* or "Thule Society" may very well have taken into its confidence the very personage of Adolf Hitler.[56] Maintaining contacts with the Golden Dawn in England, the Thule Society was a German registry for various Gnostic and theosophical doctrines which had been preserved for centuries. The Thule Society also had a political clout, as it helped engineer an abortive *putsch* or coup against the new German republic in April of 1919.[57] The Thule Society thus composed a significant link between esoteric idealism and the embryonic social designs of Hitler and his compatriots.

A *habitué* of the Thule Society, who perhaps more than any other individual served as the architect of Nazi racial *gnosis*, was the "mad" philosopher Alfred Rosenberg. Rosenberg's ideas were systematized finally in his *Myth of the Twentieth Century*, which came out in 1930, and won him such acclaim among Nazi theoreticians that Hitler awarded him an important administrative post in the Third Reich. According to Rosenberg, world history to the present has consisted in the steady degeneration of ancient wisdom which flowed from the genius of the Aryan people. In the West the "Jewish" conspiracy of Christianity was instrumental in blotting out this wisdom, inasmuch as it superimposed the Mosaic Law and the "dogma" of Christ's sacrifice on the primitive "blood thinking" of the barbarians. A remnant of the ancient wisdom, however, is to be detected in the magical and occult world view of Brahmanic Hinduism. India was one of the first locales in which the Aryan or "Nordic" spirit bloomed.

> A born master, the Indian felt his own soul expand to become the breath of life filling up the entire universe, and by the same token he experienced the breath of the world working in his own bosom as his very Self. Nature—strange, rich, pouring from herself virtually everything—could not sufficiently constrain him from this metaphysical profundity.[58]

In India the "noble" Aryan paraded his greatness by founding the caste

system, the bedrock of timeless spiritual understanding. But gradually
his power and sublimity became submerged in the dark wave of inferior
peoples. His knowledge was eclipsed by the popular religions of the
subject peoples. Indian philosophy in which "only soul is the essential
thing" originally affirmed the identity of God and man and reflected the
creative virtues of the Aryan rulers. Yet, as is the case with all exalted
and "spiritual" standpoints, the historical decline of culture hastened
by the diffusion of races meant the near extinction of the Aryan *gnosis*.
The modern era has witnessed the final attempt of the hybrid races to
expunge the glorious Nordic spirit from human consciousness, and it is
the task of the leaders of the new order to revive that spirit. A new
Germany would enable not only a reawakening of the spirit, it would
rebuild the vanished Aryan culture and re-educate the masses as to
racial consciousness and right thinking. In *Mein Kampf* Hitler scorned
the "Jewish nonsense" that modern, bourgeois man with his
technology has "conquered nature" and therefore brought about
progress in history.

> . . . so far man has never conquered Nature in any affair, but . . . at
> the most he gets hold of eternal riddles and secrets . . , in reality he
> does not "invent" anything but only discovers everything . . . he does
> not dominate Nature, but . . . based on the knowledge of a few laws
> and secrets of Nature, he has risen to the position of master of those
> other living beings *lacking this knowledge*.[59]

In Nazism, therefore, we have the politicization of the Gnostic claim of
"eternal secrets" which license some to be "masters" over those
without "knowledge." The idea of the Gnostic adept seeking to liberate
himself from gross matter becomes that of the "folkish soul"
(Volkseele) struggling to make itself "clean of Jews" *(Judenrein)*. Just
as the Gnostics divided the world into three types of humanity (the
"pneumatics" or spiritual ones, the "psychics" or conscious beings,
the "hylics" or persons of a purely material and bestial nature), so the
Hitlerians distinguished among the "supermen" or Nazi elite, the
Aryan collective, and the subhuman beings *(Untermenschen)*, mainly
Jews. Both the Gnostics and Nazis reviled the great majority of the
world's population as locked into inferior status and incapable of deeper
spiritual insights. They must remain "slaves" whose only function is to
gratify their born masters. Gnosticism's view that particular individuals
are precluded by the very order of the cosmos from participating in

divinity stands behind the Nazi tendency to treat its conquered adversaries as filth or vermin. The abasement of Jews and political prisoners in the concentration camps, the obscene torture of victims as part of "scientific" medical experiments, for example, were logical consequences of the dehumanizing separation in the Gnostic mind of a person's body and his soul.

Historically speaking, Nazism signalled a political uprising of natural, preconscious man against a modern and complex civilization which he could not fully accept or understand. Bourgeois secularism had the double effect of both destroying the traditional Christian universe and its symbolic mysteries and weakening man's ties with nature. The result was a nostalgia for a lost unity of life which could only be slaked by relapse into an arcane and irrational state of existence. The ersatz "myth" of the new century became a murky vitalism, the "philosophy of life," which lurked behind the delphic pronouncements of a Bergson and, in a more sophisticated and critical mode, analytical psychology.[60] National Socialism merely used political expediency to realize this myth in a grisly manner. The National Socialists saw their own "calling" as involving something much more than "mere politics." They regarded their role as that of manifesting on the historical stage the "will of God," who was not the providential and judgemental Deity of Judeo-Christian religion, but dark, volatile, unconscious Will, Nature herself, above good and evil, the cosmic alternative to "automatic progress."[61] In his writings and speeches Hitler frequently affected such a pseudo-religious air, referring to an indomitable "Fate" which galvanized his own ravings and crazed plans. The ambiguities of human history were now subject to the force of occult knowledge, to the magical will of the *Führer,* the highest of the high priests.

In the 1930s Carl Jung made an insightful observation. "I believe," he wrote, "that history is capable of anything. There exists no folly that men have not tried out."[62] In the white-hot glow of their own musings, a cenacle of twentieth-century Gnostics became storm troopers who accomplished perhaps history's superlative folly which was also its greatest depravity. At the close of *The Two Sources of Morality and Religion* Henri Bergson observed:

> Mankind lies groaning, half crushed beneath the weight of its own
> progress. Men do not sufficiently realize that their future is in their

own hands. Theirs is the task of determining first of all whether they want to go on living or not. Theirs the responsibility, then, for deciding if they want merely to live, or intend to make just the extra effort required for fulfilling, even on their refractory planet, the essential function of the universe, *which is a machine for the making of gods.*[63]

In the hands of the Nazis the machinery of god-making became at once a juggernaut of incalculable wrath and unbounded savagery. The fury of Wotan tethered for centuries became the devastation of the *Luftwaffe* and V-2 missiles. The American nation which finally quelled the frenzy was outraged and aghast at the violence it had overcome. Out of the rubble of history's most shocking war arose for the moment a flurry of democratic and modern social idealism which aimed to set humanity's record straight again. But the Gnostic seed had not completely withered. It had only found another top layer of humus in which to sink its taproots.

Chapter 7

The American Mind Cure From Massachusetts to California

Mind is the only reality . . .
—Ralph Waldo Emerson

Woodrow Wilson once proclaimed that "America is the only idealistic nation in the world." After the traumas of the Cold War, Vietnam, and Watergate, such words may sound tinny and inane, if not supercilious, to contemporary sophisticates. But they at least distill much of the once robust, sanguine spirit of national purpose and self-confidence which shaped the history of the people of this country. American "idealism," of course, has been the colophon of the republic throughout its history. The term recalls a tradition, both popular and academic, which came down on the perennially positive in human affairs. Such a tradition confirms the lofty aspiration of modifying significantly the human condition, and can be traced all the way from the Puritan ideal of establishing a "holy" commonwealth in the Massachusetts wilderness through the Declaration of Independence and the Revolution of 1776, the Abolitionist agitation and the Civil War, the crusade against tyranny which inspired the Spanish-American and First World War, the Civil Rights movement of the past decade. In the cultural sphere the idealistic impulse has been expressed in the thinking of the American Transcendentalists from Ralph Waldo Emerson to Walt Whitman, in the philosophy of Josiah Royce and George Santayana, and in such indigenous religious movements as spiritualism, Christian Science, and New Thought—the torch bearers of "positive thinking."

It is something of a paradox that a mass society favoring materialistic values has frequently represented itself ideologically in terms of psychical or "spiritual" goals. Critics of the American heritage will point out that the preoccupation with the "ideal" merely camouflages a refusal to come to grips with the fateful contradictions of history and society: a land of "opportunity" ruled by the rich, a democratic and egalitarian ethos besmirched by a record of slavery, discrimination, and the persecution of minorities. The theologian Reinhold Niebuhr, for one, has faulted American idealism as clutching a posture of national "innocence" while covering over at the same time the shortcomings and ambiguities of the country's experience. Yet, as Whitman himself observed, it was the very power of the "Idea" which has propelled the growth of both the American landscape and the American dream—the "fervid and tremendous IDEA, melting everything else with resistless heat, and solving all lesser and definite distinctions in vast, indefinite, spiritual, emotional power."[1]

The "idea" of America which has animated motley poets and barroom sages was never a clear and distinct one. It had vaguely to do with something called "freedom," as enthusiasts from Whitman to the antiwar protesters of Berkeley have described it. Emerson noted the primacy of the concept when he remarked "America is the idea of emancipation." It was not only the freedom to be one's own person, to homestead land or amass capital, to reap the material rewards of labor. It was also the freedom to think for oneself, to materialize in the mind's eye refulgent new possibilities of life, to dream impossible dreams, and so on. The American "experiment" was not solely a political and social project; it constituted a trial of the expansive imagination as well. The inflated claims which American pitchmen have made for generations concerning the errand and destiny of the republic has always been a puzzle and source of perplexity for Europeans. But it has likewise proven the backbone of democratic idealism and the mainstay of the personal dynamism and self-assurance which individual Americans habitually exude. The seemingly ingenuous, but buoyant line from the song *Invictus* intoned well into this century by school children ("I am the captain of my fate") enshrines this central strand of folk optimism. Individual freedom and a conviction in the unlimited powers of mind and will to take control of events were the key tenets which Whitman had in mind when he rhapsodized: "Great—unspeakably great—is the Will! the free Soul of man!"[2] America has always been regarded as more than a praiseworthy accomplishment; it has been marvelled at for the grandeur of its notion, for its daring design.

The historical reality juxtaposed with the American image of itself, however, has always been somewhat at variance. The magic of the Idea has led Americans either to rationalize or to carp excessively on their own historical failings. In the first case the result has been the smug and sometimes saccharine veneration of the "American" legacy—the jealous superpatriotism which makes porcelain gods of the nation's leaders, gilded causes of even the more sordid ventures such as the Mexican War or the extermination of the Indians, and has thrown up a false sanctity around the economic system. In the second instance the reverse process has taken place. Recognition of the contrast between actuality and ideal has spurred prophets or reformers to abominate American society for a multitude of wrongs and to seek to establish an order of moral perfection and righteousness. The radical passion exhibited in such diverse movements as pacifism, "moral rearmament," and the New-Left diatribes during the Johnson and Nixon eras illustrates such a tendency. It was the German sociologist Karl Mannheim who commented in his *Ideology and Utopia* that ideological conservatism and unyielding utopianism are really two sides of the same coin: the one envisages the status quo in terms of an ideal conception and the latter endeavors to overturn it in keeping with the same touchstone of truth. In both cases it is the ideal model of social arrangements which conditions a people's perception of present facts and its evaluation of history.

Indeed, it may be argued that the tenacity of American idealism has left this country blind to the subtleties of its own historical experience and has contributed to the cheapening of the view of history itself. Though it was a monumental historical event in 1776 which gave birth to the new nation and which is constantly celebrated as the warrant for the country's existence, a genuine appreciation for its chastening of history of human pride and pretension has been largely absent in the American outlook. Though it was an overwhelming feeling of historical vocation which guided national programs and policies for at least two centuries and which was emblazoned in such mottoes as "manifest destiny" or "redeemer nation," the American mind over the long haul has appeared unable to grapple with the uncertainties of its own successes and misadventures. Current stumbling over the meaning of the whole Vietnam episode serves as an object lesson in this connection. Perhaps the trouble lies with the fact, as the American historian Sidney Mead has suggested, that the United States is still too young to have a mature perspective on history and thus retreats from taking the historical drama seriously. The root metaphor for American history, Mead proposes, has not been time, but *space*. "He who would understand America must understand that, through all the formative years, space has overshadowed time—has taken precedence over time in the formation of all the ideals cherished by the American mind and spirit."[3] While Americans "have never had time to spare," they have always enjoyed space—immense space—in which to enlarge not just their physical presence, but their consciousness too. The "wide open spaces" of the Western frontier acted as a magnet to draw the restless, land-hungry immigrants ever onward and even today quickens the yearnings of the nomadic, "mobile American" who drifts from Vermont to California, from Ohio to Florida, in quest of the "good life." But in the same vein the concept of space was spiritualized as a token of the American craving for new visions and experience and for stoking up the mind with everything it saw and sensed. Again, the words of Whitman have captured this American enchantment with the magnificence of space and the negligibility of time in its plodding course. "I know I have the best of time and space, and was never measured and never will be measured."[4] Whitman's *Leaves of Grass* is a protracted paean to the vast beauty and complexity of American life from coast to coast to the sheer vigor and quantity of human action dispersing into seemingly boundless space. In beholding the giddy panorama of surging humanity, Whitman transforms the mere moment into a timeless horizon, an equally capacious eternity.

> The past and present wilt—I have fill'd them,
> emptied them . . .[5]

Time submerges in the ecstasy of the mind contemplating the tidal momentum of present existence.

The obsession with space, moreover, goes hand in hand with the glorification of freedom. For the American, freedom is primarily, according to Sidney Mead, the lack of limitation in movement, the unshackled urge to change, grow, and subdue the environment. A paramount American myth has been that of the "new Adam" arriving after all the hardships and tribulations of history in the new Eden that was the unspoiled wilderness sprawling from the Carolinas to the Rockies. And there in the garden the American Adam would be free to develop and express himself without restriction. He would become as a god again; he would be redeemed from his mortality by the union of the self with all of life and nature, and he would become *deathless,* impregnable to the catastrophes of time and becoming.

> Ages and ages returning at intervals,
> Undestroy'd, wandering immortal,
> Lusty, phallic, with the potent original
>   loins, perfectly sweet,
> I, chanter of Adamic songs,
> Through the new garden in the West, the great
>   cities calling,
> Deliriate, thus preclude what is generated,
>   offering these, offering myself . . .[6]

The liberty of unconfined space is transposed by Whitman's glance into the total freedom of the mind or "spirit" to embrace and conquer all, the puissant creativity signified by sexual prowess. The self or "I" of *Leaves of Grass* becomes a tireless, divine presence in all things, a ganglion of creative power which carves myriad experiences into a scintillating, personal vision. Thus Whitman calls himself a "cosmos" filled up with the very amplitude of American humanity. It is the swarm of humanity on the tireless trek, the great "En Masse." And the mind of the poet imbibes all this movement, all this energy, this "Life immense in passion, pulse, and power." The individual self hypertrophies to become what Emerson termed the "Over-Soul," the mystic force within all nature and human personality. The whole of history is compressed into the joy of subsisting in the "Now": the return to paradise is a *fait accompli.*

The hale, expansive character of American idealism with its naive disregard of the rude contingencies of human history constitutes, in one sense, a peculiarly New World form of Gnosticism. Man is spared the terror of time and history by becoming replete with the spirit of bigness and newness. The flushed consciousness of living in a new heaven on earth, a promised land with fertile possibilities never before imagined, annuls all the nagging anxieties about life which have stalked the human race since time began. The familiar American sense of exclusivity, of being set apart from the corrupt, Old World civilizations which had fallen away the Edenic ideal, has some parallels with the Gnostic's thought of himself as having found the secret gateway to eternity. The presumption of already existing in the true, spiritual kingdom rather than awaiting it with faith and humility has marked both the Gnostic and, in a certain measure, the American world picture.

On the other hand, if the American stance can be called "Gnostic," it has been a vibrant, outgoing version of Gnosticism. The classic Gnostic cowers before flood of historical life and rues the concept of progress. He pines for a primordial age of glory antecedent to history. He wants to halt time because he dreads the ruination of his soul. The American, in contrast, rides the crest of history; he looks upon his nation as the apogee of man's progress; he regards the creation of the republic as the restoration of the golden age which had lapsed at some unspecified time in human memory. The rankling mood of alienation which characterizes the classic Gnostic standpoint toward the world thus is missing from American idealism. To talk about the rise of American Gnosticism in the usual sense of the word requires that we move forward to a later age of disillusionment and the brutal awakening from the American dream. Gnosticism represents a kind of febrile search for past innocence, a quest for power in the face of historical failure. Such a search typifies the present and recent past, which we shall discuss in the final chapter. Yet the makings of the contemporary Gnostic pathos have been latent in American idealism itself, in the myth of national perfection and innocence. The fact that the American mind was never in key with the vagaries of history made it ripe for the Gnostic solution once the lustre of the dream wore off. The inattention of America to the realities of history left it susceptible to extreme remedies for its social ailments.

THE TRANSCENDENTAL MIND CURE

The Gnostic filament in American thought winds out of the collapse of Puritan culture at the end of the eighteenth century. The moral values and general historical vantage point of colonial America had been molded predominantly by Puritan theology, which conceived of society as under the ordination of God and human events as piloted by the all-encompassing hand of the Deity. Puritanism held that social morality and politics derive from a Covenant instituted between God and his people with church and state exercising virtually the same power of governance and discretion in watching over people's lives. With the growth of the English colonies and the spread of the secular philosophies of the Enlightenment during the 1800s, however, theology became less important, except in the churches and universities. Dislodged from the political arena, Puritanism was steadily supplanted by liberal, democratic ideas authored by men such as John Locke. The American Revolution for the most part spelled the end of Puritan dominance in American culture, and in its aftermath arose a thoroughly secular order presided over by wealthy merchants, financiers, and landowners whose religious ideology was that of English Deism. The God of the English Deists was an abstract and remote Being who did not intervene in the affairs of his creatures, but left them free will to decide for themselves and cultivate the "moral" life.

Such an ideology, of course, was distinctly suited to the interests and motives of the mercantile classes. God upheld the rule of *laissez-faire* in the universe with the same reserve as government was supposed to have in economic transactions. Significantly, however, there were those intellectuals—chiefly members or sons of the clergy—who resisted the encroachments of the new business world upon their traditional, genteel culture. Heirs to the Puritan avidity for religious experience, but barren of belief in an otherworldly, wrathful God, they reacted to the growth of commercialism and secularism by devising a religious intuitive, mystical sensibility. These "Transcendentalists," as they came to be called, substituted Nature instead of God as the wellspring of divine inspiration. In the footsteps of the Puritans, as Perry Miller writes, they "sought with renewed fervor for the accents of the Holy Ghost in their own hearts and in woods and mountains."[7] They responded to the modern scene by adopting a rarefied, esthetic, and cerebral approach to human problems. They called for salvation from the grimy toils of materialism through the wondrous expansion of the visionary capacities of the psyche.

It is not coincidental that Transcendentalism was the stepchild of Unitarian Christianity which, contravening orthodox Puritanism, laid aside the doctrine of Christ's divinity while at the same time to the tune of eighteenth-century rationalism exalted the potentialities of man. Both Transcendentalism and Unitarianism stressed the superior virtues of humanity; but Transcendentalism broke with the Unitarianism over the issue of "enthusiasm," insisting that the greatness of man is evidenced not so much by his use of reason as by his aptitudes for spiritual wisdom, for *gnosis*, as it were. One hears reverberations of the old Gnostic credo in the writings of William Ellery Channing, who stands as a strait between the Unitarian and Transcendentalist mentalities. Channing spoke of "the likeness to God" which "belongs to man's higher or spiritual nature."[8] Man's likeness to God is verified by "traces of infinity in the human mind."[9] The clue lies in what the Transcendentalists, as well as the German Romantics who influenced them and to whom they bear some resemblance, dubbed "genius," the genius of thought itself. "Great thoughts," gushed Bronson Alcott in his *Orphic Sayings,* "exalt and deify the thinker."[10] Through visionary thought which is "transcendental" the soul of "spirit of truth" struggles "to *transcend* itself, and soar ever higher and hear the great source of Truth, Himself. Thus declared Christopher Cranch in his essay on Transcendentalism.[11] Whereas Unitarianism had preached that man possessed a modicum of freedom to understand the divine nature and to act morally according to the dictates of conscience, Transcendentalism made the autonomy of mind and will an absolute premise. The Transcendentalists moved from a liberal theology adhering to the need for cooperation between divine and human to a mystical apotheosis of the individual self. Their cardinal assumption was what one commentator has denoted as the drive for "self-realization." At once they vaunted "the expansive or self-transcending impulse of the self, its desire to embrace the whole world in the experience of a single moment and to know and become one with that world," and secondly "the contracting or self-asserting impulse of the individual, his desire to withdraw, to remain unique and separate, and to be responsible only to himself."[12] Spiritual privatism and intellectual individualism decked out the Transcendentalist enterprise.

In many ways the Transcendentalists were not only the first homegrown idealists, but forerunners of a tradition in American culture that has been called "mind cure," manifesting itself later on in the school of "positive thinkers" associated with Norman Vincent Peale and, by extension, in the current vogues of popular psychology. The mind-cure attitude has always been tantalizingly simple: it vends the notion that right and unwavering thoughts will not only energize the will to act, but glorify the individual and help to surmount adversity. It also contends that reality is what one conceives it to be. In religious terms mind cure theology frequently links the finite, personal mind with the divine or transcendental Mind to which ordinary consciousness must be assimilated. Mind cure, therefore, consists in a special and quite practical brand of idealism suited to the composed and aspiring individual in a society prizing intensive self-reliance and fortitude. The Gnostic texture of mind cure is spun from the individualistic and success-oriented quality of American morals and social expectations. Balking at the subservient and less "spiritual" image of man which Transcendentalism and mind cure as a whole detected in conventional Christianity and Calvinism above all, the American Gnostics turned to Romantic and Oriental literature for their musings, and therein discovered a view of the universe which not only magnified the individual self, but also relieved them of the problem of learning how to live as a social animal. One could revel in the divine "All" without broaching the difficult, and everyday tasks of ministering to the mundane needs of others.

Ralph Waldo Emerson, the philosopher of Transcendentalism *par excellence,* articulated those idealistic precepts which were to be later seized by the popular mind-cure religious and metaphysical schools, including the irrepressible Christian Scientists. By Emerson's reckoning the whole visible cosmos is governed and brought into existence by Mind. "Nature [is] always the effect. Mind [is] the flowing cause," Emerson penned in his journals.[13] This Mind Emerson termed the "Universal Spirit" or "Oversoul," though he only employed the latter word rarely, contrary to conventional belief.[14] The cosmic Mind exhibits itself most directly in the contemplation of Nature and becomes active and vital in the spiritual genius, the philosopher or scholar who cultivates "a sensibility to the laws of the world."[15] In the spiritual genius the universal Mind demonstrates itself as Will, as the occult power of making over the world in one's own conscious imagery. "One after another [man's] victorious thought comes up with and reduces all things, until the world becomes at last only a realized will. . . ."[16] Thought as will "is divine in doing;"[17] it bends human fate to the deepest spiritual desire. It penetrates the subterranean secrets of life and transports the individual soul beyond body and matter into the transcendental realm of "pure Being." At the same time, mind and will overtake the vicissitudes of time and change and secure the delights of eternity.

> Thought; Will, is co-eternal with the world; and, as soon as intellect is awaked in any man, it shares so far of the eternity,—is of the maker, not of the made.[18]

The individual's will, galvanized by the Oversoul, shields him from the blows of a destiny not his own. For Emerson, we are only what we make of ourselves through the timeless force of mind.

The liberation of the mind, moreover, guarantees an eternal life in union with God. Emerson was influenced by Hindu religious literature and attracted to the idea that the soul, or finite mind, can divest itself of the weight of mortal existence by merging with the infinite Consciousness out of which it came and to which it must return. Through "higher thought," Emerson avowed, man "is rising to greater heights, but also rising to realities; the outer relations and circumstances dying out, he entering deeper into God, God into him, until the last garment of egotism falls, and he is with God,—shares the will and the immensity of the first Cause."[19] At the same time, Emerson betrayed the Gnostic conception of life in the world and of the labyrinthine route to salvation. "Life is the sleep of the soul,"[20] the incarceration of pure intelligence in matter and the senses. The soul seeks to leave the body and go winging on a journey through a vast universe which is "like an infinite series of planes" and which affords us no ground on which to plant our feet.[21] The wandering of the soul or mind on the way to its final rendezvous with the absolute Mind allows the opportunity for unlimited "experiences." Such experiences accumulate until the soul is satiated with particular and fleeting impressions—with pain and delight, sadness and joy—and then at last finds surcease from the world in the divine, in the Spirit which the Hindus named Brahma. Even dreams, in which the soul has "a sharp, synthetic power," according to Emerson, afford "real knowledge"[22] which leads to consummation in infinite awareness.

The magical flight of the mind leaves the mundane plane of reality far behind. And it dissolves the illusion of time. Time is nought but "the inverse measure" of the power of the soul, Emerson declared. The man who subsists in time and suffers its hardships and disappointments has not learned to use his mental competence and poke through the veil of Maya, the mother of illusion. The value of life, Emerson says, lies neither in longevity nor in the future aims individuals set for themselves and work strenuously toward. Rather,

> . . . an old French sentence says, "God works in moments,"—"*En peu d'heure Dieu labeure.*" We ask for long life, but 'tis deep life, or grand moments, that signify. Let the measure of time be spiritual, not

mechanical. Life is unnecessarily long. Moments of insight, of fine personal relation, a smile, a glance,—what ample borrowers of eternity they are!"[23]

By becoming reverentially absorbed in nature one is swallowed up in the "eternal now." Nature is vastly more significant than history. In his "Lecture on the Times" Emerson explained that the main value of looking at history, including the present era, is to glimpse the evidences of the eternal Spirit present in man's activity. The meaning of any historical epoch is to be found nowhere "but in Ourselves . . . in that Thought through which we communicate with absolute nature."[24] The mind overreaches history and annuls it. The individual experiences himself as belonging to another dimension of reality even amidst the clatter and distractions of workaday involvements.

The interruption of eternity in everyday affairs casts away the illusion not only of time and change, but also of evil. The mind-cure school uniformly insisted on the insubstantiality and inconsequence of moral evil when viewed by the mind under the aspect of eternity. The optimistic tenor of American idealism, of course, has never made room for the existence of an evil force in the universe, and Transcendentalism offered no exception to the rule. If Mind is all-powerful, then it can also rub out the stain of evil with its cauterizing slime following a metaphysical line drawn by Neo-Platonists and Saint Augustine, Emerson dismissed evil "as merely privative, not absolute," as "so much death or non-entity."[25] The effectiveness of evil is correlated with the power of mind to think it away. The greater one's knowledge of transcendental or spiritual things, the less a real threat does evil pose. In this respect Emerson anticipated the doctrine of Christian Science that regarded evil as an impurity in the material order, and that disparaged matter in turn as an illusion nursed by the absence of proper thoughts.

The problem of morality thus became for Emerson and many of the Transcendentalists a matter of right intuition. Emerson contrasted "mere morality"—conventional ethics or traditional values—with a higher sensibility which discerns laws of action through insight into the operation of the universal Mind. Morality is primarily an intellectual affair, a vision of how all happenings in nature are connected to each other. Emerson called this system of connections the rule of "compensation" whereby every time a person acts, or is acted upon, an equivalent effect is generated. Such an idea was comparable to the

Indian notion of *karma,* and Emerson advanced a teaching similar to its Oriental counterpart, to wit, that the universal skein of actions and occurrences balance out in the end and must not be valued as either good or evil in their own right. They simply *are*. Like the Hindu sage, Emerson's man of knowledge expands the mind so far as to encompass all of reality, to find the unity behind the multitude of phenomena. He learns how to detach himself from the petty worries of the world, from moral bagatelles; he becomes "a dweller in ages, mocker at time, able to spur all outward advantages, peer and master of the elements."[26] The ego collapses and is filled with the cosmic Spirit so that it is no longer tortured by decisions as to what is right and wrong. "I am representative of the whole," Emerson exclaims, "and the good of the whole, or what I call the right, makes me invulnerable."[27] In concert with their Gnostic forbears, many Transcendentalists resolved the ethical dilemma or correct action—whether in the personal, social, or political context—into a feat of mind. The appeal to "nature" was always a reference to the mysterious spirit which was supposed to supply the appropriate answers. Ascertainment of the good in life would be left in the hands of an aristocracy of seers. Transcendentalism was America's first wholesale defense of the right of spiritual geniuses to high social status.

Emerson himself had laudatory words for a "natural aristocracy." Such a sentiment seemed oddly out of place in a new nation built on democratic principles and bent on excising the remnants of European feudalism and hereditary privilege. Emerson, of course, was talking not about the old aristocracy of blood, but (like Nietzsche) of a *new* aristocracy of spirit. It was Emerson's belief that individuals are *by nature* unequal in spiritual talents, and that those endowed with superior gifts should be entitled to utilize them in the governance of society. "It is the interest of society," Emerson asserted, "that good men should govern, and there is always a tendency so to place them."[28] Nowadays the notion that the most fit should manage the affairs of the lesser able might be called a *meritocracy*. But Emerson's canon of merit was decisively intellectualistic. The "real" instead of the "titular" nobility which Emerson envisioned for America would have the charge to "guide and adorn life for the multitude by forethought, by elegant studies, by perseverance, self-devotion, and the remembrance of humble old friends, by making his life secretly beautiful."[29] He would be a poet, a contemplative, a corona of spiritual genius. "The idea after which each community is aiming to make and mend its law, is the will of the wise man."[30]

He is "Man Thinking" who stands forth as a bulwark against the materialism and the mean, utilitarian mind-sets of the horde.

> He is the world's eye. He is the world's heart. He is to resist the vulgar prosperity that retrogrades ever to barbarism, by preserving and communicating heroic sentiments, noble biographies, melodious verse, and the conclusions of history.[31]

As a lot, the Transcendentalists were disturbed by two major shifts underway in American society: the burgeoning population and its spread westward, the growth of an industrial and manufacturing economy. The administration of Andrew Jackson during the 1830s had ushered in an era of egalitarianism and had meant a concomitant loss of power and authority on the part of the traditional propertied classes, especially the Boston Brahmins. Throughout the 1830s and 40s this trend was evident in the Northeast as well. Western New England and upstate New York became a promised land for immigrants, who brought to the frontier a riot of new customs and religious enthusiams which ran the gamut from prophecies of the world's end to the beginnings of Mormonism and spiritualism. It was also a time for some radical social thought prompted by the widespread economic depression of the late 1830s and much actual utopian experimentation, such as John Humphrey Noyes's Oneida Community.[32] On the whole society seemed to many to be unravelling thread by thread. Religious and cultural traditions fell into disarray and a search was launched by a number of intellectuals for respite from what Emerson branded "the most vulgar times." Likening the present to the mythical bronze age which constituted a fall away from some primeval era of the spirit, Emerson however looked for ransom from the predacity of history by "a class of imaginative men" who would "give a new and noble turn to the public mind."[33] In *The Young American* he summoned his anonymous charges "to obey your heart and be the nobility of this land," to become "pure and purifying, the leaven of [the] nation."[34] The fractious rabble would be steered by right thinking and high-minded rudders of intellect. A world all askew would be set aright by Thought alone. Emerson's elitism, aestheticism, and dilettantish fancy for obscure sprigs of wisdom, though, was softened by his native admiration for the immensity and vitality of the new America. Even though he rued the developments of his century, he could still speak admiringly of America's "progress" in the material realm, a kind of progress he hoped would eventually veer toward spiritual goals. Instead of turning its back on the social world, therefore, American idealism aspired to the redemption of corporate life through the altering of the individual's mental disposition. This ideological strain persisted in various movements from evangelism up to the recent notion of "greening America" by revolutionizing "consciousness." By the end of the nineteenth century it had been transformed from the rarefied literary sensibility of the Massachusetts Transcendentalists into the more metaphysical variety of religious cultism evidenced in Christian Science and New Thought.

THE POSITIVE THINKERS

"New Thought," as it came to be called, was America's pragmatic and simplified version of Gnosticism. The name did not refer to any one particular sect or school of thinking, but was a label that could be slapped on a host of kindred popular philosophies bruiting the capacity of the individual mind to perform the difficult or even impossible. It had to do with what Norman Vincent Peale about two generations thereafter would dub "the power of positive thinking." And, although New Thought *per se* had major doctrinal differences with the teachings of Mary Baker Eddy and Christian Science, it is not unfair to say both exercised much the same appeal. New Thought and Christian Science together supplied a pat and enthralling solution, so far as the well-established were concerned, to the increasingly complicated problems of a pluralistic, individualistic, and success-oriented capitalist America. It was idealism in a convenient wrapper and with the "cash value" which the American pragmatists contended should be the criterion of true ideas. It pledged to use thinking not for the sake of thought alone, but as a refuge from uncertainty and failure in the grueling contest of getting and spending. It explained away the harsh symptoms of modern industrial life and served as an analgesic for the soul. It was the sort of religion which Donald Meyer describes as "purely the projection of wish, neither humbling the ego nor requiring action to reform the world."[35] As the average American became more prosperous and a pretender to Emerson's "aristocracy," so positive thinking passed into the main current of letters and culture.

America's second half of the nineteenth century has been called the Gilded Age, corresponding to the "Age of Materialism" in Europe. The principal icon of the age symbolizing middle-class ambitions was the Robber Baron—the Andrew Carnegie, the John D. Rockefeller, or the Jay Gould who piled up tawdry fortunes from their manufacturing or transportation empires and lived in ducal splendor like the titled gentlemen of the previous century. The only difference between these parvenus and the old nobility was that the former had "made" their fortunes and inspired many smaller entrepreneurs, or at least those who believed in social myths, to emulate them. In the intellectual arena the great mute hero was the scientist, but more specifically, "science" in the abstract. "Science" was the marvelous method of "trained and organized common sense," as Thomas Huxley phrased it, which made possible industrial progress and the diffusion of economic well-being.

The social climbers and the *arrivistes,* of course, were more concerned with making money according to the first model than in the dissemination of scientific knowledge. They became objects for pondering, if not envying, by the intelligentsia. The ambivalence of the Northeastern Yankee with his urbane culture and traditions toward America's new materialism surfaced in the attitudes of the positive thinkers. For example, Christian Science was supposed to be worldly, practical, and "scientific," as its name and official pronouncements implied. But it was also somewhat exotic and decidedly "spiritual" in its approach. Did not Mary Baker Eddy herself proclaim the shadowy and insubstantial nature of matter and the all-covering reality of divine Mind? Yet tapping the energy of Mind, or becoming "in tune with the Infinite" (a phrase in the title of a book by Ralph Waldo Trine, a New Thought apostle), could in the same breath produce material miracles, such as the healing of illness, and—more important—wealth and financial accomplishment.

Mary Baker Eddy (so-named by her third marriage), the architect of Christian Science, was the daughter of a Massachusetts sea captain and a monument of sorts in the city of Lynn, where she first gathered together her flock. Widowed and divorced before wedding one of her own converts, Asa Gilbert Eddy, she quickly gained fame as a faith healer and freethinker who scandalized many as a woman who dared not only to write theological tracts, but also to subvert Protestant orthodoxy. Her early work, launched during the 1870s, exhibited the influence of one Phineas Quimby, a Maine faith healer who inspired the

New Thought movement as well. But Mrs. Eddy quickly ensconced herself in the public mind as the original recipient of a new kind of "revelation" as to the character of God, the potentialities of man, and the way to salvation. By and large Mrs. Eddy's new tidings attracted a wide assortment of defectors from proper, middle-class society and by the same token from conventional religion. Christian Science rapidly installed itself as a new faith for those who might be called respectable, but somewhat nonconformist types. In addition, it made an unconscious pitch toward the partially "emancipated" middle-class woman of the period, who because of greater longevity and the new prosperity had forfeited many of her once time-consuming housekeeping functions and longed for a purpose and identity outside of family, particularly on the metaphysical plane. It was not coincidental that Mary Baker Eddy dethroned the masculine principle in Protestantism, not merely by assuming the role of a female hierophant, but also by describing God as impersonal and as traditional Mother-Father fused into one.[36] Christian Science not only undermined the traditional patriarchal subjection of woman to her husband (Mrs. Eddy divorced one spouse and virtually anointed the other herself); it called for a subtle insurrection against established mores and against time-honored religious presuppositions. It was an idealism that energized the individual will to conceive rather than believe, to assert the truth of one's consciousness against the many false and shallow mere "opinions" held by the masses of humanity.

Christian Science entered upon the ruins of Transcendentalism. The aging Bronson Alcott even came to bid Mrs. Eddy his respects. Transcendentalism had always been overly clubby, too magisterial for popular tastes. Christian Science, however, was evangelistic and stripped down to the sheerest essentials of Mrs. Eddy's own intuitions, to be marketed as authoritative witness. A bridge between Transcendentalism and Christian Science was the fad of spiritualism, which had its heyday in the 1850s and drew together the occult manifestations of the religious and intellectual ferment which had set in the decade before. Spiritualism, a religious cult preoccupied with intercourse between the living and the dead, was launched when two young girls in upstate New York, Katie and Margaretta Fox, alleged to have communicated with a disincarnate spirit which answered any question they posed with ghostly knocks. The phenomena at the Fox home were soon exposed as a hoax perpetrated by the two mischievous teen-agers; but true believers were hardly dissuaded, and in no time parapsychological oddities were a subject of special curiosity and investigation on the part of many thirsting for a new faith. The metaphysical basis of spiritualism was confirmed in the writings of the eighteenth-century occult philosopher Emmanuel Swedenborg, who had stirred significant interest among the Transcendentalists. Spiritualism sought to rediscover certain psychic forces just latent in the universe and to study them as clues not just to personal immortality but to the potentials of mind as a whole. Christian Science and New Thought considered spiritualism *per se* as arrogant, vulgar, and vain tinkering with the unseen, yet shared its ambition to unlock the miraculous powers of mind nevertheless. And both spiritualism and its Christian Science and New Thought counterparts sported a fundamental optimism about a harmonious universe which could be disclosed to those who honed their privileged sights on the universal, divine energy of Mind. Altogether, spiritualism presented itself as a straightforward and practical salvation cult that bested the merely contemplative and speculative features of Transcendentalism. Emerson's Oversoul took on a concrete and comprehensible aspect— the earthly intervention of the spirits of deceased friends and ancestors.

Andrew Jackson Davis (1826-1910) erected the theoretical framework of spiritualism in the United States. Having toyed with hypnotism and clairvoyant techniques, Davis claimed to have visions of persons and things existing in the spiritual world, including an encounter with the long dead Swedenborg, who agreed to act as his tutor in esoteric matters.[37] From his insights he was reputed to have gained extraordinary mental powers among which were telepathy and healing. The metaphysical system which emerged from his considerations was finally outlined in a lengthy and rather turgid set of volumes entitled *The Great Harmonia,* published during the mid-1850s. The universe, Jackson explained, is not untidy. For "all things were created in accordance with an eternal code of immutable laws; that operate under a Divine and universal system of End, Cause, and Effect. . . ."[38] The prime mover in all life is what Jackson referred to as the "Great Positive Mind." The Great Positive Mind suffuses all of nature, reaching its fullest expression in the human soul. But the human soul is wrapped in impurities. It has lost consciousness of its own divinity and of the cosmic order in which it plays a part; it fails to see how it participates in the "Great Harmonia." For the soul to reintegrate itself with this harmony is "health," according to Davis. Health is the steady realization of the Great Positive Mind in individual awareness, which leads to a strengthening of the "Will Power." Once the Will Power is heightened, the human mind can achieve the creative and masterful deeds appropriate to the Positive Mind. "The Will-Power with which the soul is endowed, and of which it accomplishes many great and mighty works . . . is capable of repelling, overcoming, and banishing every disruption of discord and unhappiness from the spirits' illimitable domain."[39] Mind, or Will-Power, becomes the "source of [man's] seeming impotence."[40] By the "magic of MIND" whose "source is knowledge" all things seem possible.

It should be noted that Davis, like Mary Baker Eddy, viewed both the theory and practice of his system as exemplifications of a new "science." Moreover, he saw that spiritualism held great promise for promoting "the rich blessings and advantages of improved machinery, and other applications of physical knowledge."[41] Davis felt that spiritual discipline would keep individuals happy and "adjusted" to society, would mean a less troubled polity in America. But primarily the goal of spiritualism was to offer the individual an opportunity for his own private self-actualization in spite of the pressing problems which society faced and history forced upon him. In this sense, spiritualism by Davis's reckoning, Christian Science, and New Thought stood on virtually the same ground. The secret springs of mind can be plumbed and harnessed for health, wealth, and contentment. "Mind" could be a social anesthesia that lets the tumors of industrialism grow while lessening their pain and giving the patient the impression that the body has not been damaged at all. Davis' very metaphysics reflected this attitude of psychic withdrawal. Nature itself is a grand, clanking machine into which the "heavenly germ" of human mind is placed. The mind must attune itself to the machinery, just as it must learn to adapt itself to prevailing social conditions, without sacrificing its own composure. Yet, once the attunement is accomplished, it can enable countless personal benefits. The spirit, cloistered in the matter, becomes all-pervasive and dominant. The hubbub of time and history is muffled in the eternal peace of a positive mentality.

Davis's ideas were more seminal than consequential. Spiritualism gradually slipped into obscurity because it probably struck the public as much too infatuated with the feats of mediums and occult dodges, many of which were proved fraudulent; and Davis's more difficult notions were shelved by the movement. Christian Science, on the other hand, combined metaphysical subtleties with practical prescriptions for the improvement of life. In her *Science and Health with Key to the Scriptures* Mary Baker Eddy expounded the rudiments of her teaching. The four cardinal precepts of the book were as follows:

1. God is All-in-All.
2. God is good. Good is Mind.
3. God, Spirit, being, all, nothing is matter.
4. Life, God, omnipotent good, deny death, evil, sin, disease—
Disease, sin, evil, death, deny good, omnipotent God, Life.[42]

By "Mind" Mrs. Eddy always meant the divine Mind. Indeed, there is in reality no other kind of mind.

Immortal man was and is God's image or idea, even the infinite expression of infinite Mind, and immortal man is coexistent and coeternal with that mind.[43]

What man takes to be his own private and confused consciousness is merely a mirage. "Mortal mind," or thought conditioned by the body, is the chief illusion from which man suffers. Mortal mind perpetuates a profound ignorance of a person's identity with the Divine Mind. Man is inherently spiritual and perfect. The material order by the same token is an illusion. Disease, death, and suffering—all notes of discord in the material realm can be silenced simply by convincing oneself of their lack of reality. For "health is not a condition of matter, but of Mind."[44] By "the might of Mind," that is, by thinking it away through meditation on the Infinite Power in all things, unhealthy disorders can be vanquished. Christian Science eschewed doctors and medicine, because these were only material and thereby wrong solutions to what were categorically spiritual problems. Hence, Mrs. Eddy wrote, "we must abandon pharmaceutics, and take up ontology,—'the science of real being.'"[45]

Christian Science was bare-bones idealism—American style— embroidered with religious psychology. Divine Mind not only is a formidable agency for getting results: it is all that exists whatsoever. Christian Science culled Gnosticism from American popular sentimentality. Radically individualistic, and perfectionist, Christian Science represented, according to Mrs. Eddy, a "Declaration of Independence" from matter and everything that entangles individuals in mortal life. Belief in the human being in all its dimensions as identical with the Divine Mind "sets man free to master the infinite idea." Such mastery, Mrs. Eddy compared to a soul flight which the ancient shamans and Gnostics regarded as release from the ambiguities of quotidian existence.

> In dreams we fly to Europe and meet a far-off friend. The looker-on sees the body in bed, but the supposed inhabitant of that body carries it through the air and over the ocean. This shows the possibilities of thought.[46]

There were negative possibilities of thought too, Mrs. Eddy averred, spawned by the "lower" mental powers. Mrs. Eddy anathematized "animal magnetism," witchcraft, necromancy, and just about all occult pastimes—not because they were frivolous superstitions, but because they constituted demonic opposition to positive thinking and mental healing. Indeed, Mrs. Eddy fumed that her husband Asa, who expired in 1882 (according to the coroner) of a heart attack, had been murdered by the evil thoughts of an adversary, by "mesmeric poison."[47] One who had shucked the mortal mind could not possibly succumb to physical infirmities. A Manichean[48] vision of struggle between the pure, knowledge-filled soul and dark, material forces thus stalked into Mrs. Eddy's theology, even though to her critics it flatly contradicted her monistic belief in the singular actuality of Mind. If positive Mind alone had existence, it was silly to rail against the machinations of adversary spirits. But Mrs. Eddy was mortal enough herself to let go with some howlers at times. She was not a trained philosopher, and the veracity of Christian Science to its devotees did not rest on the consistency of its theories so much as on the effects it wrought. "Human language had lost its power of expression, for no words came to me; and in all this six years of bliss I still have found no words to tell my new-found life in God," a jubilant reader of *Science and Health* who had been healed by Mrs. Eddy's counsels exclaimed.[49]

But Christian Science was too narrow in its scope for a good number who craved the nutriments of a new wisdom. There were two main drawbacks to Christian Science, so far as the secular-minded were concerned. First, Christian Science suffered from being excessively "Christian." Mrs. Eddy considered her ideas to have a firm ground in Biblical theology, and she made as much ado about the importance of

Jesus as any liberal Protestant author. The would-be transcendentalist aristocrat, however, wanted a more eclectic and metaphysical creed which did not identify so intimately with the Biblical religiosity that was the stuff of ordinary, American Protestant culture. He liked his God cerebral and impersonal, his faith more sublime and ahistorical, even though at face value Mrs. Eddy's teachings seemed only to use Biblical exegesis as window dressing. Second, Christian Science tended to preoccupy itself with healing and the damnation of doctors. Mrs. Eddy's animus against medicine may have appeared a bit irrelevant to the "higher" challenge of the soul—the pure pursuit of individual happiness through the pacification of the psyche. Indeed, the loose web of other cults and movements which took their origin from the gospel of Phineas Quimby, fiercely competing with Christian Science for a time, and which finally acquired the name of New Thought, addressed themselves to just that higher challenge. New Thought had no recognized founder and therefore was not embarrassed with the quirks of Mrs. Eddy. It could be more free-ranging in its appropriation of alien ideas and more attuned to the basic desire of Americans to have their cake and eat it too, that is, to have a novel but responsible kind of religion which promised nothing less significant than complete personal well-being.

New Thought, which in the long run embraced a plethora of different religious denominations with such titles as Divine Science Church, Church of Religious Science, Unity, and INTA, sought to rifle nearly every metaphysical religious tradition and philosophy. It mined sources as diverse as Hindu Vedanta and Emerson. At the same time New Thought, like the historic hybrids of Gnosticism, claimed both to be both "new" and "old." It was "new" inasmuch as it mixed different strains of speculative idealism into one palatable concoction for the modern American. It was "old" to the extent that it purported merely to rehabilitate and synthesize the "eternal" truths of nature and the universe which had always been reflected in the religious philosophies of the world. Finally, it picked up on a theme running through Andrew Jackson Davis's effusions on the great harmonia which also squared with the world view of the late nineteenth and early twentieth centuries. It lent eminence to the notion of evolution which Darwin had introduced into popular thinking and was now elicited to explain and justify everything about why the universe was the way it was, especially in the doctrine of social Darwinism which maintained that affluent Anglo-Saxons clung to their positions in society because the process of natural selection had made them most fit to rule and be successful. Every being, New Thought argued, "is an invisible spiritual dweller within a human body, continuing and unfolding as a spiritual being beyond the change called physical death."[50] Of course, the major strides in spiritual evolution took place on this side of the grave. The common Protestant idea of the period that the duty of man is to constantly improve his moral character before the sight of God was stripped of its theistic and ethical trimmings, and in its stead was raised the notion that perfection depends on developing the positive mind. What was the rationale for this total mental overhaul? The mind must be refurbished in order to secure such virtues as "Power, Peace, and Plenty," to be the pilot of one's own destiny, which meant to learn how to be a rugged individual and get ahead of society, to become well fixed and well liked, in short, to "make it."

The compendium of New Thought books is massive and for the most part redundant. Yet the tenor of New Thought theology can be guessed from inspecting the titles of its publications: Charles Fillmore's *Prosperity*, Elizabeth Towne's *Practical Methods of Self-Development*, Emmet Fox's *Power Through Constructive Thinking*, John Garns's *There's a Thrill in Business*, Ervin Seale's *Success is You*, Robert Bitzer's *All Power to You*. The nub of New Thought's pragmatic metaphysics is summed up in a passage from Christian D. Larson's *Mastery of Fate* which appeared in 1908: "To master the creative power of thought is to master the personal self; and to master the personal self is to master fate."[51] "Fate" naturally was a theological code word for all eventualities which inhibit the individual from realizing his true desires, such as the most sacred wish to succeed in business. You can succeed in business, Larson wrote, when "you think that you can succeed in business," because "by thinking that you can succeed in business you draw all the creative energies of the system into these business faculties."[52] The unsuccessful however, have only themselves to blame. "The average person who thinks he is underpaid, will find himself to be the real cause."[53] The key to rectifying any injustice "remains wholly with the individual." Social Darwinism took on a Gnostic hue. The afflicted must come to know why in the cosmic scheme of things he is afflicted, and how he can overcome that affliction through absorbing himself in the eternal Mind. If a person suffers poverty or discrimination, it is assuredly because he is ignorant. Right knowledge will lead to forceful action and ultimately the attainment of one's goals.

The genius of New Thought, from the psychological vantage point, was that it gave the individual an immediate sense of cosmic importance while laying open the possibility of achieving all sorts of worldly ends. The anxiety of everyday coping and managing the tremendous pressures of work, status-seeking, and the scramble for recognition in a competitive industrial society could be allayed by the conviction that one was secure in the transcendental bosom of his own thoughts. New Thought's message offered some analogy with the Protestant tenet of "justification by faith" with the patent difference that one was justified or accepted not so much before the judgement seat of God, but in the assurance that the Infinite dwelt in one's paltry little self. From this assurance flowed the will to do good works, or more pointedly, works that paid off in success. New Thought bestowed a preponderant meaning on trivial tasks. For instance, it showed forth, as Nellie Friend wrote later in 1945, "the importance of you and me in a mass production era." One could belong to the "mass", ply a humdrum job in business, live just like the Joneses, and yet *be conscious* of one's more exalted situation in life. "The individual does count today as he never has counted before," Friend bubbled, because he is aware of his relation to "that Highest Good, that Super-Intelligence, that Human Inspirer and Unalterable Principle, which sustains and stimulates all living things."[54]

New Thought marked the maturation of a *middle-class Gnosticism* in the United States. It acted perhaps as a psychic prophylactic to the fear of many comfortable and established middle-class Americans concerning the menace to their self-esteem and sense of identity caused by rapid social change, by the requirements of industrial capitalism that they either perform well in their regimented roles or be left to flounder. The fear of social change and the loss of security, of course, was manifest on the metaphysical level as an uneasiness with existence in time, as the terror of history. Whereas mere middle-class success-striving without the religious factor postpones satisfactions indefinitely in the future and creates a longing for a meaning to life hidden by the daily passage of time, New Thought spoke of the presence of eternity here in the moment. "The spiritual life, it was pointed out, is continuous—we already live in eternity."[55] One makes his eternity with every correct thought and performance. Nellie Friend wrote:

> As each twist of the thread counts in the woven tapestry, so every thought, word, and deed counts in weaving the eternal life-pattern. The deed acts as does the shuttle of the loom, in locking the threads together and making the fabric itself secure. The shuttle is the clinching gadget; the individual's commitments, the clinching device in character building.[56]

New Thought styled itself "the science of that which eternally *is*, as distinguished from that which merely *appears* in outer, temporary manifestation." It emphasized, according to Egbert Chesley, "the kingdom of God to be established in this earth of ours, here and now."[57] The upsurge in New Thought thus remained in keeping with America's yeasty impulse to realize its high-flown expectations not in the far-off future, but in the immediate present. America's characteristic lack of appreciation for history and tradition has conditioned its people to believe that the final goal of life has already been consummated, that aspirations have been met. The "fullness" of time is already at hand. But New Thought, despite its innovations, was not truly esoteric. The Gnostic demand for an exclusive and thoroughly unmediated intuition of a world beyond history could only be satisfied outside the context of Western religion. The more uncompromising aspirants of the American mind quest thus turned their backs on homegrown success cults and bowed to the mystic East.

THEOSOPHY AND THE TURN EASTWARD

New Thought had puttered with Oriental metaphysics, chiefly with its monistic assumptions about an impersonal, divine energy in all life and thought. It had digested completely the Oriental-Gnostic understanding of salvation as the cultivation of the powers of the mind and the attainment of a privileged, supersensible insight. It twisted America's indigenous ethic of individualism and self-reliance in the social and economic sphere into a quietistic concern for untroubling the soul and the separation of one's own personal destiny from others. Oriental Gnosticism, like commonplace American morality, has borne along a stricture that each individual must pull himself up spiritually as well as socially by his own "bootstraps." But New Thought did not make an unqualified break with Western faith. On the main it kept much of the language of Christianity and refused to make much out of such notions as reincarnation and ascetic self-denial. New Thought had a breezy, businesslike, and wholly pragmatic outlook on spiritual problems, which distinguished it from the complicated and abstruse formulations of orthodox Indian gurus. One might draw a comparison with the contemporary fad of Transcendental Meditation which has shriven itself of most standard Hindu associations in an attempt to supply a mass-market panacea for America's nervous maladies. New Thought also shied away from the extravagances of occultism, unless such occult beliefs proved congenial to its success orientation.

Nevertheless, there was in the America of the last quarter of the nineteenth century a small, but receptive congregation for a profoundly foreign teaching; one might even say for an imported Messiah. In the summer of 1873 there landed in New York a mysterious, middle-aged Russian woman by the name of Helena Blavatsky. Though she was without much of any funds and traveled across the Atlantic in steerage, she was soon revealed to be the free-wheeling daughter of petty Ukranian nobility, who already had left a trail of gossip about her rakish activities over the years in various European capitals. Madame Blavatsky had journeyed to America in hopes of making a reputation as a spiritual wonder-worker. Her adepts claimed that she had possessed magical talents since birth, and she deliberately put on at once the air of mystical Russia, remaining delphic and aloof in a manner which confounded, but utterly enchanted her American audience. Her debut in the United States came a year or so after her arrival when she encountered Col. Henry Steel Olcott at a spiritualist seance on a Vermont farm. Olcott was a shrewd and intelligent Yankee, who practiced law, farming, and spiritualism. He teamed up with Madame Blavatsky to fabricate a new cult which appealed to Bohemian tastes and which combined the eccentric personal inspirations of its female founder with a farrago of Oriental and occult notions gleaned from the religious literature of the world. Such a cult was finally christened *Theosophy*, which meant the "wisdom of God" but which was more volatile and encompassing than most private revelations of the same ilk that had been peddled before.

Theosophy distinguished itself by breaking with moderate, religious idealism and plunging into the unknown and offbeat side of the spiritualist legacy. It was so *outré* that it could not even be casually assimilated, like New Thought, to familiar religious beliefs, and thus made a noticeable impact among the alienated urban intellectuals in such cities as New York (where it established its first headquarters), not to mention a sizeable number of less educated opportunists and outright crackpots. The outlandish and largely unsystematic quality of theosophical doctrine mirrored the undisciplined, brooding mind of Madame Blavatsky herself. In 1877 Madame Blavatsky published her *chef d'oeuvre* entitled *Isis Unveiled*, a hodgepodge of Asian wisdom snippets and bits of arcana. One of Madame Blavatsky's less flattering biographers has written that basically *Isis Unveiled* "was the expression of a brilliant and frustrated woman rebelling against the humdrum routine of life, escaping like Alice through a looking-glass into a world where everything was fascination because it was different, off the normal."[58] The same sort of rebellion could be ascribed to many of her admirers. Madame Blavatsky displayed, particularly during her youth, all the traits of a spoiled Russian countess who could inject purpose in her life only by flouting the conventions of society, by gambling and dallying with a succession of male suitors across Europe, living the life of a wayward expatriate. When such behavior was blended with her charm in parlor rooms and a gift for beguiling talk about supernatural affairs, Madame Blavatsky easily drew into her ambience the sort of people who were disaffected with their part in modern society, who yearned to have their confusion cleared up and be given some unprecedented answers to their questions.

Isis Unveiled, not to mention later theosophical affirmations, purported to divulge to nescient mankind a "secret doctrine" eclipsed throughout the ages. Esotericism was the escutcheon of Theosophy, and Madame Blavatsky shored up her own authority with uncounted, baroque references to little known creeds and pseudoscholarly minutiae. Subsequent critics accused the Russian sibyl of shameless plagiarism. The "secret doctrine," they protested, was nothing more than a ragbag of manuscript excerpts fobbed off as an original theory. But it was precisely the elaborate and befuddling mishmash of often disjointed ideas which probably impressed her disciples. She quoted virtually everybody and everything to drive home her point of view. The Hermeticists and the ancient Gnostics came in for special commendation as well as Zoroastrianism and the Vedas. Magic, miracle, and veiled mystery larded almost each page. A classical reference to Ovid, a citation of the Old Testament, a passage from Daniel Defoe—these and other wafted along on her windy exposition until the reader lost the train of argument and became hypnotized by her erudition, if that was what it could be called. The book aimed to introduce the reader to the principles of "pure seership," to intimate knowledge of the ethereal planes which could be wrought by "conscious withdrawal of the inner man," to execution of the "movements of the wandering astral form" to which "neither time nor space offer obstacles."[59] The mind was not merely a passive vessel; it was compressed into the faculty which Madame Blavatsky denoted as "pure will-power," the ability to transcend all illusion of time and common sense premises about the universe, the capacity of the soul to become God through increasingly refined *gnosis* until engulfed in the great cosmic vision of reality. "Our fervent wish," Madame Blavatsky declared in conclusion of the book, "has been to show true souls how they may lift aside the curtain, and, in the brightness of that Night made Day, look with undazzled gaze upon the UNVEILED TRUTH."[60]

Who were the "true souls"? Madame Blavatsky, of course, was one. Theosophy, in spite of its effluent rhetoric about the brotherhood of man on earth bound together by spiritual knowledge, was coolly elitist.[61] It followed the Gnostic habit of selling salvation like membership in a supper club; it made the apprehension of inward truth as arduous as possible. Theosophy also had its cosmic leadership clique—the Mahatmas or Great White Brotherhood which Madame Blavatsky said resided in the far-off Himalayas and materialized before her in their astral bodies now and then to instruct her on policy. No one but Madame Blavatsky, though, ever saw the Mahatmas. On the more mundane level Theosophy's courting of the pure and chosen ones had certain racial overtones, which dovetailed nicely with the Anglo-Saxon chauvinism and racism which had made deep inroads among the Western ruling classes in the late nineteenth century and found its legitimacy in social Darwinism. The emphasis on race crops up in *Isis Unveiled*. "Races of men differ in spiritual gifts as in color, stature, or any other external quality," Madame Blavatsky contended, and "among some peoples seership naturally prevails."[62]

Seership also had a eugenic explanation. Theosophy took the line that the race of "spiritual sensitives" would gradually emerge from the mingling of the various racial stocks, engendering a small class of higher types. Thus, Madame Blavatsky insisted, America was the optimal breeding ground for seership, since in its melting pot were brought together more divergent strains of humanity than anywhere else on the globe.[63] Years later, after Madame Blavatsky's death, a group of Theosophists sought to hasten the advent of such a racial elite by founding the Point Loma community overlooking the Pacific Ocean near San Diego, California.[64] Though overt racial propaganda was never a staple in Theosophical pamphlets, the insinuation that the most spiritual race was the white European one was ever alive. Or at least the best possibilities for spiritual ascent lay in the "Aryan" race which had first imparted eternal wisdom long ago to India and would continue to evolve upwards along the ladder of perfection here in America, bringing forth a new, "sixth race" which would outshine the dark, uncivilized, and savage beings who had occupied the planet in the preceding stages.

Outward features of the person, however, could only be temporary accidents concealing the inward character of a soul. Man, Theosophy stressed, was principally a soul who *happened* to possess a body. The soul was a "divine spark" which had fallen into the body "from on high."[65] Having become encased in a body, it accumulated various "experiences" which determined what its further destiny would be. Theosophy invoked the doctrine of reincarnation not only to account for an individual's current life circumstances, but also to underwrite the notion that the soul is ever "progressing" in the scheme of evolution toward a final state of perfection. Evolution can be hastened or hindered by having a proper or wrong "thought." For "all we can do" in aiding our advancement, one Theosophist asserted, "is to have thoughts of good quality."[66] Thoughts of good quality, of course, involved the special application of psychic forces; and those who reeled from adverse conditions of life undoubtedly did not know yet, having not gone far enough on the evolutionary path, how to avail themselves of their psychic and spiritual endowments. Annie Besant, Madame Blavatsky's appointed heir, put the matter less delicately. Whatever one is results from his own act of "self-creation." In an urban slum, according to Mrs. Besant, one finds criminals and harlots, so accursed because of their own cosmic ignorance. Their wretched birth testifies to their lack of spiritual vigilance. Yet in another home is born a child "with every advantage, amid pure surroundings and welcomed by tender, parental love; his head is marked for the indwelling of genius, with well modelled skull, with delicately chiselled features, that tell of sensitive emotions and high ideals."[67] The difference between the two set of circumstances is nought but "justice"—impersonal, cosmic justice, according to the law of moral compensation for one's deeds in successive lives. The end of the individual life, however, is to escape the wheel of action and compensation. Theosophy posited a fantastic cycle of ages (in concert with traditional Hindu notions) spanning millions of years in which races appear and decline, nations rise and fall, and nomadic souls labor onward from one evolutionary plateau to the next. The meaning of existence is for the most part irrelevant to the social and historical contingencies of one's time. One must crane beyond the present into the eternity of spiritual life shut out by the senses. That is the key to becoming "noble."

Theosophy was a heady wine for all but the most stalwart initiates. But it wanted within its ranks only the strongest and most self-possessed free spirits. Unlike New Thought, Theosophy prescribed much more than success. It vouchsafed the reward of supreme spiritual status in a universe overcrowded with inferior, unenlightened beings. It excoriated the false values of "commercial" civilization and built a munificent palace of symbols and dreams for those who could not find contentment in modern America. Theosophy promised to convert society's failures and estranged ones into new aristocrats of the mind. It would make shamans of all upon whom the American tribe had turned its back. Moreover, it offered the glib assurance that "invisible helpers"—mahatmas and celestial guardians with assorted names and functions—were leading their privileged protégés by the hand on the pilgrimage to perfection. Main-line Theosophy was cosmopolitan, entreating the blue-bloods of society to divest themselves of any parochial interests and embark on a mission into eternity.

It was tempting fruit for those who found themselves buffetted by social change, who had become uprooted from firm cultural soil, and who no longer were bound in any real nexus of social relations. America during the post-Civil War period and into the twentieth century was constantly undergoing the shocks and transformations which left individuals socially and spiritually homeless. Rapid industrialization, the ongoing march westward, the billowing waves of immigrants who splashed onto Ellis Island contributed to the acceleration of motion in

American society. Theosophy flourished particularly throughout the so-called Progressive Era—that decade or two before the First World War when reformers undertook to ameliorate poverty and populist politicians made fiery speeches about breaking the backs of the trusts and corporate finance. Yet Theosophy was not progressive in any social or political sense. It took note of America's festering social ills in a way that betrayed the nervous social awareness of the privileged strata. Theosophy on the one hand sought to make legitimate poverty and unhappiness among the masses as the unfolding of karma and on the other hand proffered the idealistic sop of piecemeal social improvement through the rehabilitation of man's inner spiritual nature. It was better to *understand* the justice of one's condition than to change it. As Annie Besant said, ". . . let me bear my pain. Rather let the evil that I have done work itself out to the uttermost expiation."[68] For "social evils have their roots in mental faults."[69] "The slum-dweller and the prince, the middle-class man and the nobleman, they have all cooperated in the Past to make the slum. It is the outcome of their own ignorance, their own folly, and their own crime."[70] A later spin-off of Theosophy, the I AM Movement founded by Guy and Edna Ballard in the 1930s, was to mix the sorts of esoteric bluster and revelations bequeathed from Madame Blavatsky's school of thought with superpatriotism and with hints of fascism. Ballard saw the I AM Movement as engaging in the "Protection of America," which is the "Land of the Light of God That Never Fails." The movement even contrived political auxiliaries entitled the Minute Men of St. Germain and the Daughter of Light, who sported uniforms and marched in parades.

Theosophy more than occasionally drew the hostility of academics, news writers, and various spokesmen for the general public, who accused it of melodramatics, hucksterism, and plain flimflam. The I AM Movement received a blot on its name in the early 1940s when a federal grand jury indicted the Ballards for mail fraud. Theosophy and its satellite organizations clearly betokened the baleful side of Gnostic religion in America. Theosophy claimed to have decanted for the layman the nectar of Asian spirituality, but in the final tally it was through and through an American consumer product. The "light from the east" may have seemed harsh and perturbing to the uninitiated who read mostly of the Theosophists' own strange antics and squabbles and who wondered at the unsavory reputations acquired by some of its representatives. Paradoxically, it was not Theosophy which made the interest in Oriental wisdom respectable, but the gentler and less obtrusive votaries of mystical knowledge who remained apart from the movement.

Lux ex Oriente

"Asia today is not further away than the East River or Gettysburg," Francis Hackett noted in *The New Republic* in early 1957.[71] Indeed, such a remark must have sounded queer to the ears of an America still wallowing in the barkbound and bellicose provinciality of the Cold War, and Eisenhower years, an America riding the crest of the Main Street sort of Christian "revival" that made church going as *de rigeur* as watching television and taking an automobile vacation each summer, and having not yet beheld Hare Krishna followers chanting and soliciting on the street, or heard of Maharishi Mahesh Yogi, the Guru Maharaji, tarot cards, or *karma*. Perhaps they had picked up news scraps of a strange, imported Japanese craze called "Zen" among the beatniks in San Francisco. But *that* was California, in itself a Shangri-la of oddballs as far removed from the normal American scene as the Asian mainland.

Yet the light from the Orient was slowly filtering into middle-class consciousness, and it had been doing so ever since the Second World War when United States servicemen in the Pacific facilitated the first omnibus contact between WASPish American culture and the eccentricities of the Eastern style. That was not to say that Eastern religion and philosophy had not already fascinated the peripheral intellectuals and cultists for some decades. The graph of Theosophy's rise and fall was ample affidavit to the power of alternative belief systems among the restive, rich, and disengaged. But now the Eastern point of view was no longer monopolized in the primarily Western-flavored borrowings and ad libs of self-made messiahs who were generally concerned with the *outré* and the occult. It had ceased to be mere grooming for the indigenous metaphysical movements, and had established its own pedigree.

During the 1920s and 30s, a number of Hindu teachers, who were unqualified Indian masters and not Theosophical dabblers, presented their credentials to American audiences. Small in membership, but curious enough to attract sporadic attention, the circles of followers around these teachers grew fast enough to give them some institutional credibility. The Parliament of Religions in 1893 had been the site of a modest, initial breakthrough. One of the highlights of the Parliament was the debut of a young Bengal, Swami Vivekenanda, who stirred considerable excitement among the audience and went on to introduce centers for the study of Hindu Vedanta in California and New York. Essentially traditionalist and conservative, Vivekenanda expounded the unalloyed gospel of Vedanta from the *Upanishads* through Shankara down to the preachments of his own guru and mentor, the Hindu saint Ramakrishna. Vivekenanda was a Hindu "fundamentalist" in the sense that he defended the ancient Brahmanic faith as veracious "in every respect." In his usual glib fashion he praised Hindu orthodoxy as a counterpoint to the "scientific" and "materialistic" preoccupations which he sniffed everywhere in America.

By and large, however, Vivekenanda had a singular message which made relatively the same points as the Theosophists, but with greater verve, more erudition, and less obfuscation. And here was the one, true timeless philosophy of light spouted by a bona fide, swarthy Indian divine. One no longer needed the stave of Madame Blavatsky's mysterious Mahatmas. The phenomenal universe, Vivekenanda said, is a trap and illusion. To extricate ourselves from this universe we must have self-knowledge, which comes from taking to heart the Hindu Scriptures. Such knowledge is not chiefly theoretical, but *practical*. Through self-knowledge the individual can shimmy up heights of success and ascend toward personal perfection. Vivekenanda tickled the fancies of those weary of their own Christian superegos by demonstrating the detached, alpine, perspective of Indian wisdom.

> The Vedanta recognizes no sin, it only recognizes error; and the greatest error, says the Vedanta, is to say that you are weak, that you are a sinner, a miserable creature, and that you have no power and you cannot do this or that.[72]

Not to have power, that is, *will-power,* was the most monstrous defect an American mind-quester could conceive. The deeper, cosmic mind was the unexploited source of power for Americans of practical bent. The truth of Vedanta was implicit in American thinking itself. Vivekenanda's successor in the Ramakrishna order, Swami Abhedananda, in fact busied himself with finding glimmerings of Vedantist idealism in the Transcendentalists and in Christian Science, whose "science" was closer to the metaphysical systems of yoga than to the gray, empirical golem found in Western laboratories.

Vivekenanda goes on. "Who makes us ignorant?" he asks. "We ourselves." What is the motive force behind evolution? The *will*. "Continue to exercise your will, and it will take you higher still. The will is almighty. If it is almighty, you may say, why cannot I do everything?"[73] In the train of Vivekenanda came other preceptors of the Hindu way. There was the voluble Yogananda, who by the 1920s had put together the Self-Realization Fellowship. At least in form Yogananda anticipated many of the Indian gurus of the 1960s and 70s who emigrated to the United States and set about stripping down the complicated symbol and thought configurations of normative Hinduism in order to promote an irresistible mind-cure. Hitching his doctrine to the New Thought vernacular, Yogananda spiked with occasional subtleties in Sanskrit such notions as the "fusion" of science and religion through meditation and "philosophic insight." In contrast to Vivekenanda who had condemned "science," he talked of "scientific healing affirmations," "material success affirmations," "healing methods" and so on. He admired American free enterprise and the self-reliant spirit behind it, while he esteemed Henry Ford as an American "missionary" from whom India could learn.[74] Besides Yogananda, there was a passel of quaint and long-forgotten names (if they were ever *known* except to monitors of obscure trends) like Baba Bharati Krishna, Yogi Hari Ram, Deva Ram, Yogi Ramacharaka, Swami Omkar. The Vedanta Society in California was most active, and attracted among others two articulate English gentlemen, Christopher Isherwood and Aldous Huxley, who in numerous articles and essays hymned the bliss of the supreme consciousness.

But Hinduism as a whole was too thick and rich a sauce for average American tastes. For it to remain real Hinduism, rather than become an embellishment to the American mind cure, would have required a cross-fertilization of cultures as difficult as the mating of a mayfly with a hippopotamus. The Hindu gurus became captives of American society, relinquished their own rigorous traditions, and succumbed to the techniques of salesmanship and gimmick packaging. Unfortunately, even these labors were hardly successful. The majority of Americans were just not quite alienated enough to commit apostasy *en bloc* from historical Christianity. The mind-cure stripe in American culture was still connected to the American dream. It would take a noisy demolition of that dream before a full-blown metamorphosis into Gnostic escapism on the mass level became apparent.

Chapter 8

Where the Wasteland Goes On

It's just people's confusion that there is a society. What is society, tell me? Society is always wrong.

—*Guru Maharaj Ji*

HEALTHY-MINDEDNESS AND HAPPINESS

In the fourth chapter of his oft quoted classic *The Varieties of Religious Experience* the American philosopher William James dissected the type of personality associated with "the religion of healthy-mindedness." While James did not straightforwardly attribute "healthy-mindedness" to the religious mind-set of Americans, he could easily have done so. For James's whole philosophical approach which he called "pragmatism" was an outgrowth of the American experience. The term "pragmatism" itself has become a signet for describing the underlying American orientation toward reality. Similarly, in *The Varieties of Religious Experience* James makes numerous approving references to the attitude of healthy-mindedness which comports with his own ideas about God, the individual self, and the way of overcoming evil. James places the religion of healthy-mindedness in a uniquely American setting by citing the literature of Christian Science, New Thought, and spiritualism which had won considerable advocates around the turn of the century when he was writing. The expansion of healthy-mindedness, James suggested, was a new and surging wave in the transformation of Christianity. "The advance of liberalism," James noted, "during the past fifty years, may fairly be called a victory of healthy-mindedness within the church over the morbidness with which the old hell-fire theology was more harmoniously related."[1]

But the religion of healthy-mindedness had a deeper meaning than its role in combatting "hell-fire theology." Mind cure, or healthy-mindedness, as we have seen, was a this-worldly version of the Gnostic faith which articulated the characteristically American quest for individual autonomy, prosperity, and power through a mental inflation of the positive data of experience. James made a pertinent observation about Walt Whitman in this connection: "the only sentiments he allowed himself to express were of the expansive order."[2] Healthy-mindedness, according to James,

> . . . is an abstract way of conceiving things as good. Every abstract way of conceiving things selects some one aspect of them as their essence for the time being, and disregards the other aspects. Systematic healthy-mindedness, conceiving good as the essential and universal aspect of being, deliberately excludes evil from its field of vision; and, although, when thus nakedly stated, this might seem a difficult feat to perform for one who is intellectually sincere with himself and honest about facts, a little reflection shows that the situation is too complex to lie open to so simple a criticism.[3]

For the American, the toughest belief to criticize is the proposition that all are entitled to the "pursuit of happiness." And, if the Declaration of Independence guarantees that objective, then *so must the universe*, which mind cure made over in the image of the appetitive self's aspirations. The objective, James insisted, is warranted by the ceaseless striving of all human beings in that direction. "If we were to ask the question 'What is human life's chief concern?' one of the answers we should receive would be: 'It is happiness.' How to gain, how to keep, how to recover happiness, is in fact for most men at all times the secret motive of all they do, and of all they are willing to endure."[4]

The healthy-minded pursuit of happiness, therefore, had inevitably become a trademark of American popular piety. The rude contingencies and tragedies of life, which stall the drive for self-perfection and personal enjoyment, would appear in the American scheme of interpretation not merely as an anomaly; they would seem quite *unreal*. Were James surveying the state of American culture in the aftershock of two world wars and Vietnam, he might have poignantly reported, along with other commentators, the proverbial loss of America's "innocence," the deflowering of its mythical purity. James himself was not so "tender-minded" (as he called it) as to banish from sight the rueful counterevidence to the native anticipation of health, wealth, harmony, and success. Yet James, even though he sipped and imbibed its waters, was not a creature who swam comfortably in the main spate of ethnocentric idealism. James may have been willing to concede a stage at which the therapy of mind cure is perverted into quackery. James did not survive long enough to witness the religion of healthy-mindedness turn into an obsession, where the tamer confidence in the powers of mind become a widespread means of escape from the desolate confusion of an ailing society. Healthy-mindedness gradually changed into the syndrome of the "sick soul," which like a damaged gland converted its stabilizing hormones into a poison. The mind cure way of thinking which in its own tacit style quietly celebrated the earlier American mood of vitality and expansion now became a palliative for old age. The irrelevance of historical existence, such as the Transcendentalists had hinted, passed into a horror of where history was going. The desire for happiness, innate in all men, was transmuted into the neurotic's preoccupation with emotional and spiritual perfection. The code words for such a preoccupation in the 1960s were "bliss" and "ecstasy," terms which the level-headed philosophers of Boston in the 1840s, or even the New Thought enthusiasts, would have found queer and misplaced. But the founding generation of mind cure had not had to come to terms with the apocalyptic monsters of the mid-twentieth century.

The Beat Generation and the Bomb

It has been pointed out recurrently that the children who grew up after World War II could set little store in the future. Indeed, it was questionable during the 1950s, especially, whether mankind itself would persist into the next decade. The exterminating angel of nuclear holocaust hovered in the imaginations of young people who read in daily newspapers about the Cold War and "brinkmanship," who watched their parents dig bomb shelters, who ran through weekly "survival" drills in school and saw motion pictures (to impress callow minds with the value of such exercises) that showed melted girders, blasted buildings, and disfigured dummies following the detonation of *the bomb*. When combined with a realization of the colossal slaughter and devastation wrought by the global war, the mood of those sensitive souls who also had to contemplate the hideous majesty of the mushroom cloud could only turn to a kind of psychic catalepsy. The radical insecurity of all human endeavors would prompt a total revaluation of past and future. The immediate moment would seem infinitely more precious. The method of justification for one's own personal life would entail a search for durable meaning in the available present, rather than in the "sweet bye-and-bye." Louis Pauwels and Jacques Bergier in *The Morning of Magicians* have eloquently limned the despairing twentieth-century spirit:

> Cut off from the past, suspicious of the future, man looked upon the present as an absolute value, seeing in this frail frontier a promise of eternity. Like despairing travelers, they embarked in solitude on a raft on the seas of eternity, the Noahs of some future Flood, living on plankton and flying fish.[5]

Many hunted for the holy grail of wisdom, as Pauwels and Bergier recount, in the dark and perennial mysteries of occultism, in a vanished Atlantis or Lemurian civilization, in the world of extrasensory and paranormal phenomena. Others ripped their ties with modern society, including both its comforts and illusions, and became wanderers, subsisting on cheap wine and bread, if not plankton and flying fish.

In the mid-1950s there sprung up in California a subculture of defecting youth and Bohemian intellectuals known popularly as the "beats" or "beatniks." The "beat generation" marked perhaps the first wholesale apostasy on the part of children of the American middle classes from the standard culture of respectability, upward mobility, and economic success. Forerunners of the "flower children" of the next decade, they scandalized the guardians of bourgeois style with their unashamed bad manners, indolence, and a primitive sort of hedonism. The ethic of the beats was an informal sort of *carpe diem*, sacrificing future gratifications for the immediate pleasures of jazz music, alcohol, drugs, and of course, free love. The conspicuous materialism of their parents and peers they denounced as decadence. The social rituals of suburban society they shunned as "square" and opted instead for nonconformity in dress and spontaneity of feeling as expressed in underground poetry and art. For the beat generation, the world had become too much with them; the future was no longer radiant and was fraught with impending catastrophe. They could no longer view themselves as participants in the drama of American "progress," as organized society seemed now to be rattling on toward self-destruction.

In short, the beat generation was to gain attention by daring to adopt a whole manner of life founded on the joys of immediacy. Their clamor for personal identity was voiced in terms of the dilation of the senses and the cultivation of inner experiences. In the realm of religion the beats tossed aside Christianity, which they saw as fatally wrapped up with Western cultural values, and embraced the gospel of Zen Buddhism, recently imported from Japan. The appeal of Zen to the San Francisco hipsters was something of a novelty. The mind cure schools had coquetted with assorted Eastern philosophical systems, especially those of Indian origin, but they had not given any real attention to the playful, irreverent, and *unmetaphysical* technique of enlightenment from the land of chrysanthemums and cherry blossoms. The reason Zen had not caught on earlier had to do with two obvious factors. First, Japan before the Second World War did not afford Westerners contact with its indigenous traditions, unlike India which had been opened up by British colonialism. Second, Zen was not a comprehensive set of doctrines inscribed in ancient and readable texts as was, for example, Vedanta. But, more important, Zen had an entirely different flavor from Hindu monism, and could not be integrated easily into the Western body of symbols in the same fashion that New Thought had crossbred theosophical notions with Christianity. Zen was not for old-line "positive thinkers" who merely wanted a reputable, personal ideology propping up the *status quo*. It was a flashy, new evangel of healthy-mindedness that emphasized not adjustment, but *detachment*. The Zen disciple was to relinquish his worship of middle-class idols; indeed, he had to renounce all worldly aspirations. He had to become serenely conscious of the relativity, the "emptiness," of all conventional concepts and moral principles, which D. T. Suzuki says "conditions all our knowledge, all our deeds, and is our life itself."[6] The Zen practitioner, in short, had to learn to immerse himself in *samsara,* in the "flow" of life. He had to discover how to let things be as they are, to consecrate the temporary and contingent aspects of life as a way of uncovering the "Buddha-nature" in oneself as well as in all persons and objects. He would float with the tide, take the fillips and velleities of life as they come and release them as they go. That would be his *dharma,* his "rule" for living which was not actually a rule at all.

Of course, the traditional Buddhist *dharma* of the Japanese monks was a far cry from the breezy abandon which the beats themselves tried out. Their *dharma* was thoroughly Americanized and made over into an

undisciplined style of hedonism. Consciousness of one's Buddha-nature
was easily confused with sensuality and self-indulgence. The relativity
of ideals and morals could be uncritically taken as an invitation to
nihilism. Not surprisingly, one of the heroes of the beats and eminent
"master" of the new free-wheeling California Zen was novelist Jack
Kerouac. Kerouac first captured the secret yearnings of the post-war
generation with his *On the Road,* which was published in 1955 and was
about wild rides across the highways of the United States from San
Francisco to Washington and about fast women and hard liquor, not to
mention tireless tousles with local gendarmes who symbolized the
slapstick of provincial law and mores. The uninitiated still read *On the
Road* as a kind of adolescent diary of obstreperous pranks, a witty bit of
juvenalia. But for Kerouac's admirers the book had a mystical
undertone. The jacket of a recent paperback edition of the book
expresses the sort of cultish blandishment which Kerouac's fans were
wont to engage in. *On the Road,* the jacket blurb says, "is an explosion
of consciousness—a mind-expanding trip into emotion and sensation,
drugs and liquor and sex, the philosophy of experience and the poetry
of being." All of these epithets with the possible exception of the last
one do not sound anything at all like Buddhism. But the Beat
Generation *called* it Buddhism; and in *Dharma Bums,* which came out
three years later, Kerouac had preempted enough of the terminology of
legitimate Zen to devise a rhetoric that would lend credence to the
laisser-passer life-style by representing it as somehow profound and
spiritual. Mind cure had been revamped into a total titillation of the
nerve endings, which was what it meant to be "aware."

The Dharma Bums tells also of omnibus sensuality and foraging for
"experience," of adventurous rides on freight trains, of pot-sotted
carouses in Berkeley apartments, of bracing hikes in the Sierras—all of
which are supposed to add up to a kind of mind explosion. Yet in the
narrative Kerouac was self-consciously attempting to depict the whirl of
sensation as the key to cosmic understanding, as a vehicle of liberation;
though he left little disinction between the liberation of the mind and the
libertinism of the youthful rake and rebel. A passage from *Dharma
Bums* illustrates this loss of discrimination. Kerouac's friend Japhy is
rhapsodizing about the *dharma:*

> . . . that's the attitude for the Bard, the Zen Lunacy bard of old desert
> paths, see the whole thing is a world full of rucksack wanderers,

Dharma Bums refusing to subscribe to the general demand that they consume production and therefore have to work for the privilege of consuming, all that crap they didn't really want anyway such as refrigerators, TV sets, cars, at least new fancy cars, certain hair oils and deodorants and general junk you finally always see a week later in the garbage anyway, all of them imprisoned in a system of work, produce, consume, work, produce, consume, I see a vision of a great rucksack revolution thousands or even millions of young Americans wandering around with rucksacks, going up to mountains to pray, making children laugh and old men glad, making young girls happy and old girls happier, all of 'em Zen Lunatics who go about writing poems that happen to appear in their heads for no reason and also by being kind and also by strange unexpected acts keep giving visions of eternal freedom to everybody and to all living creatures. . . .[7]

The "rucksack revolution," with its affidavit of "eternal freedom" could only vaguely be compared with authentic Zen *satori,* but the beats were not at all concerned with upholding norms, even Buddhist ones. Since Zen in historical practice had been sufficiently free-form to allow certain contradictory adaptations and improvisations, the beats seized on its language and symbols to sanctify their glib rebellion against the "plastic" society. Like the former enthusiasts of mind cure, the beats craved a world that seemed blissful and scrubbed clean of pain and evil. Zen offered a perspective on life that miraculously resolved the tension between the traditional moral values of work and discipline, which now seemed bankrupt in light of runaway consumerism, and the instinctive thirst for happiness. The former could be smoothly abandoned for the sake of the latter, and happiness could be achieved in accordance with new definitions of what it meant to be spiritually "whole." The characteristically American conviction of the goodness of man and the virtues of natural innocence were rendered in Kerouac's idyll of the open road and of youth celebrating its own vitality. The harmony of life could not be gained by participation in the social order; it could only come within the sphere of mind through a revolution of "consciousness." The closure of the future, the loss of confidence in the familiar quest for earthly riches accentuated by the dread of the bomb, helped to translate America's impulse toward the conquest of physical space over time into an exploration of *inner space* apart from history. But the same basic values were present; they had merely been sublimated. The beats, like their "square" counterparts, were committed to full gratification of the senses. They were the sons and daughters of the middle classes who had never been weaned from the American dream. The difference was that they did not purport to regiment their lives in terms of education and career, always in pursuit of postponed pleasures. They wanted satisfaction *now*, because there might not be any tomorrow. Beat *dharma*, therefore, implied a form of instant transcendence, a route to complete enjoyment of the senses without having to work for it. The "poverty" of the beats was not austerity; it was simply a new economy of pleasure based on the orchestration of everyday "highs" and thrills. It was a colorful hedonism rather than a grey one, and it was present-oriented. It was a semi-sophisticated American instance of Epicureanism: "eat, drink, and be merry for tomorrow we die." It was the makings of a *Weltanschauung* that would reach full flower a decade later with the coming of the counterculture.

A FRANCHISE FOR GURUS

Kerouac was a writer with great verve and stylistic exuberance who galvanized the passions of the young. While his *dharma* was taken all too seriously, it lacked the central element of *mystique*. Even the beats' dalliance with Zen meditation and *koans* lacked a certain legitimacy. Zen ultimately needed a theoretical apologist who was a Westerner, but who at the same time could enunciate its mysteries without watering them down or cheapening them. In other words, the transmission of *dharma* depended on a learned person, a guru. Gurus, of course, usually belong within the Hindu camp and are traditionally wedded to some mode of Indian orthodoxy; but in the case of the beats the guru had to be unselective. His position required facility not just with Vedanta, but with all rudimentary motifs of Oriental wisdom. For the beat culture was itself eclectic. It picked and chose what it demanded from the East in order to build an alternative to Americanism-cum-Christianity. The vast cultural and religious distance between the integral traditions of India and Japan had to be blurred. *Samadhi* was interchangeable with *satori; koans* served the same purposes as *mantras*. And one could glide back and forth between the uttering of the sacred Hindu syllable, *OM,* and the recitation of the teasing Zen riddle "What is the sound of one hand clapping?" Such a new kind of adept in his own idiosyncratic fashion moved even further afield than the modern, liberal Protestant who holds no brief for the distinctions between Methodism, Episcopalianism, humanism, and sundry secular creeds. Whatever *worked* to arrest his soul was appropriate. And the guru he followed would have to be able to improvise the different mystical sublimities, the contrasting shades and tones of meaning, into an ebullient scherzo of mind-music.

One candidate for supreme guru was the unique poet Allen Ginsberg, who appeared as the character Alvah Goldberg in *Dharma Bums*. But Ginsberg was mercurial, and his poetry, a spuming, unedited, and uninterrupted effusion from his typewriter onto a roll of newsprint, could hardly count as holy instruction. Ginsberg wrote like Kerouac (though he turned out poetry instead of narrative) in both style and substance. He was oracular; he did not bother with form. He belched out feelings and inspirations in a verbal cloud of exhaust, which sometimes included precise images or clarified the meaning of certain mystical symbols, but which most of the time was sheer impressionism. Ginsberg endorsed Zen *à la* Kerouac, then moved onto the *Upanishads* and Hindu devotionalism when *that* style a few years thereafter seemed more congenial to his experimentation.

The other candidate, however, was one Alan Watts, also caricatured in Kerouac's book as Arthur Whane. Watts was later to become the preeminent American figure within the religious counterculture of the late 1960s and early 1970s, and he first received his renown as an exponent of Zen who was also a competitor to Kerouac. With respect to externals Watts was a good foil to the novelist. He was not a "bum." He was a paragon of probity for the most part with his clean-shaven face and crew cut and with his official position as dean of the American Academy of Asian Studies. He was an Englishman which in itself supplied a slight semblance of rectitude. He had already published a number of well-sold books interpreting the religious ideas of the East, particularly Buddhist ones; and he had served as an Episcopal chaplain at Northwestern University. Whereas Kerouac was merely voluble, Watts was composed and articulate. Kerouac's novels may have appeared as garish feats of self-exhibition, but Watts's works were didactic and at least made a pretense to scholarship, even though Watts usually oversimplified or fudged a technical point for popular taste.

Watts, in other words, came across to the public as a *philosopher*— not necessarily the academic kind, but one who could be authoritative as well as entertaining. And he demonstrated how his philosophy could be tied to a practical life-style. Watts had made his start all the way back in the 1930s in Britain (long before esotericism had become faddish) as a student of Buddhism and protégé of the noted Orientalist Christmas Humphreys. In 1940 he published *The Meaning of Happiness,* a spry and somewhat homiletical account of the Eastern religious "way" as a resource for solving the ageless human riddle of how to make life rich and rewarding. There Watts addressed himself to the same, fundamental concerns as tackled by legions of popular mind-cure writers; but, in contrast to them, Watts had an honorable command of the crucial concepts and phrases from the sacred texts of the Orient. His recipe for happiness was spelled out in essentially the manner he would continue to pronounce for three decades with minor variations and permutations. Happiness lies in what he termed the "way of acceptance." The affliction of unhappiness is due absolutely to a wrong-headedness which makes us desire things we really do not want and causes frustration and distress when we fall short of our aims. The problem resides in the mind, and the mind alone. Instead of investing our energy in the attainment of specific goals, we should develop a new attitude which helps us intuit the necessity and interconnection of events in our experience. The weal is bound up with the woe, the pleasurable good with the painful. We must perceive the hidden pattern which discloses a oneness in the multiplicity of phenomena.

> Thus if man is to realize again his fundamental unity and harmony with life he must proceed by the roundabout way of trying to get that which he already has until he convinces himself of his own folly. For it is only by *trying* to accept life as a whole that we can make ourselves aware that there was never any real need to try, and that spirituality is in fact a matter of "becoming what we are."[8]

Watts picked up on the insights of psychoanalysis. Our ideas of good and evil, the divine and the demonic, are all projections of our unconscious mind and do not have any *real* status. When we learn to view them as figments, rather than as objective beings or powers, then we are on the path to self-discovery. So far as we learn to recognize them as currents in the fluency of consciousness, we can accept them, neither fearing nor delighting in them. "Acceptance," Watts averred, is the resolution of the feelings of being chained to life, and acceptance is altogether and qualitatively distinct from submission to "fate." "Total acceptance" is veritably the "key to freedom," since "when you accept what you are now you become free to be what you are now, and this is why the fool becomes a sage when he lets himself be free to be a fool."[9]

Watts amplified the same theme in *The Wisdom of Insecurity* which came out in 1951. We must practice the art of "foolishness" which is largely taking life as it is, including ourselves as we are. We must become aware of ourselves, not as isolated egos, but as a fleck in the "great stream" of existence. When we discover how to drift with the stream, we give up resisting. And when we stop resisting, we realize that our selves are forever at a thin interface with the immensity of the cosmos. Acceptance of the world *as is* constitutes a kind of foolishness, inasmuch as it subtracts from our feeling of responsibility. But what is the sense of responsibility, Watts asked, but a craving for security, an obsession with our own paltry needs and a false dichotomizing of experience into what is "proper" and "improper?"

> We look for this security by fortifying and enclosing ourselves in innumerable ways. We want the protection of being "exclusive" and "special," seeking to belong to the safest church, the best nation, the highest class, the right set, and the "nice" people. These defenses lead to divisions between us, and so to more insecurity demanding more defenses. Of course it is all done in the sincere belief that we are trying to do the right things and live in the best way. . . .[10]

Affirmation of the "insecurity" of our persons with reference to temporal acquisitions and limited successes can usher us into a different sort of "security": the ecstasy that comes with drinking the plenitude of life. Lived this way, life is open and needs no "justification."

Here Watts introduced two notions which would be consequential for the elaboration of his own doctrines and for the ideology of the later counterculture—"creative morality" and "the marvelous moment." The word "creative morality" may have been cribbed from Bergson and was tied to the whole vitalist conception of ethics as a dynamic outworking of the mystical consciousness. In posing the principles of "creative morality" Bergson had in mind the spiritual heroism of history's saints. Watts, though, was advancing a formula that could be applied plainly by ordinary individuals. Creative morality is simply spontaneity, festivity, sportiveness, *joie de vivre*—all without the burden of guilt and the niggling thought that one should be doing something for a definite purpose or within socially prescribed bounds. Conventional morality straps the mind to both narrow standards of respectability and to future objectives. And in the pursuit of those objectives one naturally tends to sacrifice appreciation of the worth and significance of what he is doing for its own sake. Life becomes a means to an end and ceases being an end in itself. The alternative of creative morality, however, hands the individual a freedom to cherish the "now," to forget his motives and experience the *moment*. "The marvelous moment," therefore, stands as the point of intersection between time and eternity. The mind must overcome its habit of referring and directing present experience to future accomplishments. Dissatisfaction and its extreme form—despair—only arise when the mind registers a cleft between what it *expects* to have and what it does not *now* have. But, if all that counts in the official summation is the value and joy of the moment, then the future has no attraction, and the agony of *not* having something melts away. The experience of time with its forward movement propelled by deferred satisfactions and moral striving must be overcome, and in its place one must learn to accept the enchantment of the present, "eternity in an hour," as Blake said.

This sort of popular interpretation of Eastern religions sat well with those who were fed up with the money-grubbing, prestige-seeking rat race that had become a national pastime in the 1950s. It was also a honey-tongued counsel to self-enjoyment without social or institutional constraints, which chorded with the proclivities of the Zen set. Reading Watts's careful, but cookbook exposition of self-liberation, one might obtain the impression that he was more serious than he was. In fact, however, as Watts's frank biographer David Stuart lets it be known, Watts was actually an achiever in his own right; he was one who courted celebrity status, and did so by packaging a good deal of the playboy philosophy as the perennial one. Watts could not have countenanced for himself any of the austerities or restraints which the old, Buddhist Middle Way prescribed. He was a sensualist with a weakness for comely women, which drew him into untold affairs and broke up two marriages. He drank regularly (which Buddhist monks or gurus do not do), was a gourmand when it came to food, and his home displayed a fondness for sumptuous furnishings and beautiful surroundings. "He had," Stuart comments, "carefully nurtured the concept of a complete libertarian, concerned with his own pleasures, and of a showman-shaman."[11]

Watts did fall into some disputes about what was the authentic Zen approach with Kerouac and his groupies. Specifically, Watts was irritated by the portrayal of himself in *The Dharma Bums,* which implied that Watts's stance toward Zen could not be separated from Kerouac's.[12] Watts had harsh words for the kind of beat exploitation of Zen for which Kerouac was accountable. Whereas Zen offers an independence from moral authority, together with freedom from guilt, it should not, Watts declaimed, be promoted as an invitation to license, as a rationale for "anything goes." His article of 1958 entitled "Beat Zen, Square Zen and Zen" purported to correct the beat interpretation for what he considered a gullible literary audience. But Watts was in no position to come down very hard on this cut-rate version of Zen. Watts's own breezy and popularized presentation of the subject made it easy to construe Zen as primarily a means of flouting bourgeois decorum. Watts was himself a friend of Kerouac and a habitué of the beat social scene in the 1950s. His own life-style, his desire to be *un esprit fort,* disqualified him from censuring the beat practice of libertinage on any other grounds than it was sloppy when it came to concepts. In his later autobiography Watts admitted that his "easy and free-floating attitude to Zen was largely responsible for the notorious 'Zen boom' which flourished among artists and 'pseudointellectuals' in the late 1950s";[13] he also confessed that his attack on the beats in "Beat Zen, Square Zen and Zen" had been "somewhat severe."

Perhaps his change of heart had to do with the fact that Watts by 1960, when the pioneer beat culture was on its way to oblivion, had superseded Kerouac, Ginsberg, and company as the recognized mouthpiece for the *dharma.* Watts's own pennant was now flying, which he interpreted as a sign of a *true* reformation of culture for which (he now conceded graciously) the beats had been precursors. In 1960, Watts reminisces, one could discern "signs of an astonishing change of attitude among young people which, despite its excesses and self-caricatures, had spread far over the world by the end of the decade."[14]

Watts sailed into the 1960s as the guru/father figure of the nascent hippiedom. Though his dicta on Zen brought him his American renown, he was quick to put his flirtation with that method in its proper light. Watts wanted to be something greater than a Buddhist or a Zenist, or even a scholar. His message began to sound slightly more proselytizing. As it turned out, he was bent on working out a personal philosophy of life that would have repercussions throughout American

society; and if his ideas were to have impact, they would have to shed
the aura of an academic mediation of a live tradition. They would have
to crystallize into an American evangel with only an Asian overlayer.
Watts encouraged his audience to be unrigorous and eclectic in
appropriating what the East had to offer, for he himself had the same
strategy. Watts wrote:

> . . . I think it will now be clear that my own approach to Asian
> philosophy was part of an individual philosophical quest. I am not
> interested in Buddhism or Taoism as particular entities or subjects to
> be studied and defined in such a way that one must avoid "mixing up"
> one's thinking about Buddhism with interests in quantum theory,
> psychoanalysis, Gestalt psychology, semantics, and esthetics, or in
> Eckhart, Goethe, Whitehead, Jung, or Krishnamurti. I feel about
> academic "subjects" just as the Balinese feel about "Art" when they
> say, "We have no Art; we just do everything as well as possible."[15]

Watts was slapping the mortar on the groundwork of the countercultural precept "do your own thing." He was talking long before
Charles Reich about the "greening of America." He was looking
toward a "spiritual" renovation of American culture, in the tradition of
the mind-cure specialists, which would give everyone an Elysian taste of
their own consciousness. The nub of Watts's advice to those hungry for
a new spirituality was to dive into the gush of "experience." In *Nature,
Man, and Woman* (1958) Watts described more or less what the life of
"experience" could be. One must be mystically in tune with the
resonances of mind and body together. Historical Christianity has little
with which to equip the deeper human spirit. While it degrades the
body, it also blocks the flow of experience. It requires "belief," the
mindless assent to certain creedal propositions about God and Christ,
without allowing internal awareness as a guide to the world. What the
builders have rejected, however, the new illumined ones will take up.
They will recover "*gnosis,* or direct experience of God" as an antidote
to ritualism, rationalism, moralism, and dogmatism.[16]

A Gnosticism of untrammeled feeling and sensation, therefore, was
Watts's balsam for the injuries done to the modern soul. Watts outlined
the steps to attainment of the *unio mystica*. But the union was not
intended to be disembodied and ethereal; it was *carnal*. In *Nature, Man
and Woman* Watts touted Tantrism or "sexual yoga," which was his
next important gambit beyond Zen. He extolled sexual love as a
"revelation," orgasm as the physical or phenomenal-gateway to

transcendence. Tantric sexuality or *maithuna,* on the other hand, must not be done with ego-satisfactions in mind, or out of boiling lust. It must be done in full consciousness of its cosmic meaning, the conjunction of opposites, the confluence of the primal energies of creation. When the English translators of the Bible rendered sexual intercourse as "knowledge" (e.g., "Adam knew Eve"), they were not just coining a euphemism. The "consummation" of sexual activity constitutes *gnosis.* In the same breath Watts characterized sexual activity as the truest expression of "spontaneous feeling" which has a "timeless quality." It is that which brings time to a standstill and manifests the inner content of nature, if not the whole cosmos. The morality of sexual relationships is not worth considering. Promiscuity is as good as marital fidelity, because the physical and "spiritual" circumstances are the same. Such confining institutions as marriage are irrelevant to the magic moment. In this connection Watts followed his own impetus by divorcing his second wife and pursuing a third.

The sexual revolution was now in the early sixties *in statu nascendi.* Surburban hedonism was pushing away the old screen of prohibitions and taboos. The old values were washing out to sea and the old God would soon be pronounced dead. Young people as well as some middle-aged imitators were deserting the Protestant ethic first at a trickle, then in a torrent. They were turning inward from the other-directedness of the previous decade and finding an Eden instantaneity to such a degree they would come to be anointed the "now generation." Watts had the ready-mixed materials for immediacy with his glad tidings of "awareness." But most Americans could not sensitize their minds without some technological helpmate. Watts went along with them and tried out LSD. Thus *satori* and *samadhi* were transposed into psychedelics.

CHEMICAL INFINITIES

The embryonic "counterculture" was introduced to the marvels of psychedelia by one Aldous Huxley. That is not to say Huxley, who had already garnered fame in the previous generation among the *literati* and *cognoscenti* for his novels and essays treating such diverse topics as science and society (e.g., *Brave New World*), pacifism, and Vedanta, was the first to make the mind-exploding drugs physically available. Instead Huxley had written the definitive *apologia* for the use of hallucinogens. His *Doors of Perception,* composed in 1954, sought to give account of what happens to consciousness under the influence of mescaline, with which Huxley was experimenting at the time. Steeped as he was in Asian mysticism and other variants of the perennial philosophy, Huxley argued the analogies between the drug experience and the prototypical visions of the revered religious sages. Mescaline could "cleanse the doors of perception" in Blake's now well-warmed phrase. It did not distort reality in psychopathological proportions, but actually broke down the defenses of the conventional, conscious mind to lay bare the world in its shining essence. Huxley pointed out that the ordinary and familiar view of things is a result of selective cognition, whereby the mind only culls from a limited mass of data for the sake of satisfying animal needs, for its getting-and-spending, its "survival." The pleasures of "heightened" awareness, by the same token, supply a clue to a monumental fact. Reality is beyond anxiety! Goal-seeking and money-grubbing are only sums of a false felicific calculus. "Turning on" is an act of *consecration;* through increased awareness the mind allows the universe to exist as it *is* in its fullness and subtle intricacy. One's ego shrinks to a vanishing point where the survival requirements of the organism no longer exert force on the individual's habits of perception.

Watts could not let slip the opportunity to match his own dilettantish form of yoga with the interest in drug experiences. Watts met up with two offbeat psychologists at Harvard who were doing intensive research in hallucinogenic chemicals, one of whom was Richard Alpert, the other Timothy Leary. Both would eventually be fired from their jobs and go on to become doyens of the counterculture in their own right. Leary would emerge as "the high-priest of LSD," the author of the well-circulated aphorism "turn on, tune in, drop out" which soon became the shibboleth of the acid-heads in their assault on the Vietnam "death culture." Alpert would travel to India, meet his Maharaji, and reappear in the early 1970s as the esteemed spokesman for the way of drugless self-illumination. But at the beginning of the sixties it was not the internal powers of mind, but the easy nirvana of psychedelics, that served as the object of curiosity. Watts "tripped" on LSD, encountered new vistas, and reported them with his beguiling prose in *The Joyous Cosmology* which hit the book market in 1962. Watts now had co-opted Huxley as a prelate of the chemical infinities. And Alpert and

Leary even penned a forward to *The Joyous Cosmology*, flattering the book's readers with the opinion that they had purchased "a great human document" signalling "an important turning point in man's power to control and expand his awareness."

The Joyous Cosmology took off on the same theme that Watts in *Nature, Man and Woman* had embroidered, flaying the "greatest of all superstitions" that there is a "separation of the mind from the body."[17] But while *Nature, Man and Woman* had advocated the reunion of mind and body through self-reflective enjoyment of sex, *The Joyous Cosmology* suggested that the same effect can be brought on by ravaging the mind with drugs. With a little help from one's "friends" (as the Beatles would cryptically denote LSD), the mind can be pried free of its fixations so that "brain and world . . . seem to interpenetrate inseparably."[18] The chemical marriage of brain and world, however, has another advantage over the mere concentration of bodily energy in the sex act. The ecstasy of coitus evaporates as soon as the orgasm is spent, and the lovers draw back sadly into the flurry of time and renewed desire. But in the translated consciousness of the acid "high" there arises what seems like an ultimate abolition of both time and suffering. The "trip" takes the mind behind the proscenium of time and space and puts it in contact with an unchanging dimension of life. It throws open the gates of Eden, which has always been sequestered out of sight in the copse and brambles of everyday concerns. The eternal nature of the world now has an access.

> Everyone and everything around me takes on the feeling of having been there always, and then forgotten, and then remembered again. We are sitting in a garden surrounded in every direction by uncultivated hills, a garden of fuchsias and hummingbirds in a valley that leads down to the westernmost ocean, and where the gulls take refuge in storms. At some time in the middle of the twentieth century, upon an afternoon in the summer, we are sitting around a table on the terrace, eating dark homemade bread and drinking white wine. And yet we seem to have been there forever, for the people with me are no longer the humdrum and harassed little personalities with names, addresses, and social security numbers, the specifically dated mortals we are all pretending to be. They appear rather as immortal archetypes of themselves without, however, losing their humanity.[19]

Watts was waxing lyrical about what Theodore Roszak would some years thereafter dub "rhapsodic intellect," the envisioning of the universe in terms of its constant interrelations and the beauty of permanent form. There is a dreamlike quality to the scene he depicts, reminiscent of many of the descriptions in Jorge Luis Borges's writings, but dreaminess is exactly what he aims to communicate. The drug experience fractures the mental dikes which hold back the sea of unconscious meanings otherwise revealed only in dreams, and lets them wash and splash all over the visible landscape. The perception of the world in the camouflage of time, with its pimping problems and "harassed little personalities," breaks apart and resolves into an apprehension of all entities like still, colorful figures in the wax museum of eternity. Human life is no longer singular and transitory: it becomes timeless and "archetypal." History vaporizes and disappears, like a fleecy cloud beneath the hot summer sun. And everything "forgotten" is "remembered again," because it always was and shall be. In his autobiography Watts ruminated about such profound disclosures. LSD, while susceptible to misuse, is extremely valuable, because it can point people quickly toward an inner "knowledge" that is rigidly "repressed" in modern, Western culture, a knowledge with the "implication" that "there is nothing in life to be gained or attained that is not already here and now."[20]

But Watts's expectations concerning the promise of psychedelics was a bit too sanguine. Within three years after the publication of *The Joyous Cosmology* the hippies had made LSD the shewbread of Haight-Ashbury, and were causing a sensation with their indulgence of it. Many artless teenagers were "freaking out" on the stuff, victimized by "bad trips" which made them functional schizophrenics who thrashed around like madmen in dirty, backstreet rooms, or who fancied they could fly like birds and went crashing to their deaths from second-story windows. LSD was becoming a *cause célèbre* at counterculture parties. It was dropped in drinks and on sugar cubes, synthesized surreptitiously after hours in college chemistry laboratories, and released into the growing stream of underground drug traffic, which was rapidly cornered by the pushers, hard criminals, and other standard purveyors of vice. It was often adulterated with dangerous narcotics that had lethal symptoms, and by the decade's end it had well-nigh vanished from the pharmacology of the young. In a prologue to a subsequent edition of *The Joyous Cosmology* Watts was persuaded to retract a certain amount of the optimism he had betrayed before in regard to LSD as the philter of self-deification. LSD was not an automatic trigger to the vision of God, Watts reminded his audience. It required an "intelligent approach" which in its mass application was bound to be ignored by some. On the other hand, the trouble with LSD, Watts pontificated was in its *use*, not its character. Now Watts found it convenient to invoke the *Christian* theological idea of the *adiaphora* or "indifferent" things: nothing is evil in substance, only in the way it is employed. Besides, the real source of drug abuse lay in government prohibition, which gave LSD the appetizing allure of forbidden fruit. Were LSD made legal, Watts insisted, the "spiritual" possibilities ingredient within it might once more be realized. Watts could not have admitted that his original enthusiasm might have been misbegotten, that his own tendency to mistake fadmongering for insight was causing him grief.

But American youth culture outpaced Watts in one important respect. It was coming to recognize the perils of unlicensed experimentation with hallucinogens. LSD did reveal the "universe in a grain of sand" for some more blithe souls, but for others it afforded only a roller-coaster ride down into the bowels of hell. It permitted many a breath of genuine religious experience in the suffocating atmosphere of corporate capitalism now tooled up to fight a savage and senseless war in Southeast Asia; it could be interpreted as an opportunity for latter-day shamanism, as the popularity of Carlos Castaneda's books about a Yaqui Indian sorcerer, who showed to his anthropologist apprentice a "separate reality" through peyote and mescalito, would later indicate. Yet it also was capable of flushing out the latent psychoses of certain individuals, sending them reeling into the depths of their own bewilderment and depravity, as the murders at the Altamount rock concert and the Manson murders would in time also bring to light.

Drugs "expanded" awareness by fostering what Watts referred to as "polar vision," the apperception of the demonic along with the holy, and many unsuspecting initiates were caught up in the former. The attainment of a view of the universe beyond good and evil could easily precipitate the recurrent passion of the Gnostic to destroy the world around him which seemed hopelessly sunk in corruption. R. E. L. Masters and Jean Houston in their classic study of the effect of LSD on human personality observed in 1966 that psychedelics do not transform the mind so much as sweep away the bulkhead of normal consciousness while letting in all the repressed materials of unconscious life. In the drug experience there is a loss of distinction between outward perception and inward fantasy, between object and symbol; and the mind does not pierce the veil of sensory illusion (as is claimed by the typical mystic) so much as it wallows in a bubbling brew of distorted and magnified psychic images. The experience parallels the wrestling with one's own mental demons which the *Tibetan Book of the Dead* describes as the purgatory of the soul after death before it glimpses the Clear Light of the Void, which is true liberation.

In addition the drug experience has a dangerously seductive charm about it, because it invites a narcissistic state in which one no longer wishes to return to "reality." Thus the acid-head continues to rely on chemical inducements in order to take flight from the world. He can no longer arbitrate between the two, competing dimensions of experience—the workaday and "altered" conditions of consciousness—so that he compulsively (albeit without physical addiction) retreats into the latter, unlike the shaman and the yogi who have the facility for operating on both planes, for going back into the everyday "world" *in order to redeem it*. The difference between the legitimate mystic and the Gnostic, therefore, is one of versatility. The mystic seeks an eternity in which temporal salvation is realized; the Gnostic seeks the obliteration of time altogether. Masters and Houston cite the testimony of one of their patients who experienced the feeling of being "out of time" during a peyote session. Marvelling at the feeling of having been left afloat in "timeless space," which he envisaged as a bubble that seemed likely to "burst," he poignantly realized that his ecstasy was fragile. He became aware of his own "dull sort of sadness." He did not want to leave the womb of the eternal. "I wanted to remain forever out of time," he lamented.[21]

ON THE TRAIL OF THE TRANSCENDENT

But the bubble did burst. The "joyous cosmology" proved in the final analysis to be what Theodore Roszak in the *Making of a Counterculture* disparaged as a "counterfeit infinity." The infinity was counterfeit because, in the name of saving the world from the dread beast Roszak called *technocracy* (the domination and management of human thought and behavior according to the imperatives of technological development and scientific, social planning), the drug cultists had merely inaugurated another form of social control which helped to adjust the myriad of lost souls to their distraught condition. The chemical nirvana in which Leary and his retinue exulted, Roszak demurred, is "the most lugubrious of illusions." Drug-dependence, regardless of its enchantment for the user, is to the hippies what firewater was to the Indians. It keeps them happy and docile while the "great white father" steals their land and herds them onto reservations. In this case the Indians were the restless college students aghast at the predations of their government in rounding up its young men and shipping them off to the jungles around Saigon. The ecstasy of psychedelics is merely a fatal diversion from having to come to terms with the horrors of contemporary society, a diversion which plays into the hands of the taskmasters of the establishment. "The historical record certainly suggests that it is precisely the role of narcotic agents to tame and stabilize,"[22] Roszak remarked. Psychedelics *à la* Leary might be heralded as a new religion, but it was the religion against which Marx railed as the "opium of the people."

Moreover, Roszak pointed out, drug-highs can hardly be fobbed off as "revolutionary," as Leary claimed, since they are wholly compatible with truckling to the system. "Purged of its social non-conformity, [narcotic use] is becoming an integral part of the swinging society— like wife swapping in suburbia or the topless cocktail waitress."[23] Psychedelics are only an "emotional release," a "safety valve" which acts to purge the individual's consciousness temporarily, but not curatively, of its deeply infected disgust with the dehumanization of his social environment. Drugs can rub *out of mind* the brutality and vanity of the world as confronted from day to day, but they cannot eliminate objective misery. Had not Huxley primarily plunged into the delights of mescaline in order to numb the agonizing pain of terminal cancer? One of Huxley's last books, *Island*, in fact was another "utopian" novel which can be taken as an unintended allegory about the pipe dreams of the hippies seeking to bring in the kingdom of heaven with dope. *Island* is about a tropical paradise in the South Pacific where the natives traditionally have kept blissful with a magical drug known as the "moksha medicine." The island, rich in precious petroleum deposits, is coveted by a two-bit dictator from a nearby kingdom who is bent upon conquering it and bringing "progress" to the benighted natives. The book ends as the dictator invades the island with tanks and armor, while the central characters in the story remain oblivious to the unlovely truth of what is happening around them, since they are experiencing the piquant transports of the "moksha medicine."

In *The Making of a Counterculture* Roszak has a gruff reproach for the druids of drug-celebration, but his rancor is targeted more toward the means than the end. The harm inflicted by psychedelics traces to the fact that they are *artificial* inducements to higher consciousness. In the last chapter of the book, "Eyes of Flesh, Eyes of Fire," Roszak started to plot the kind of strategy for transcendence which would bank upon the natural and spontaneous powers in human beings. The secret was held by the shamans, but not those who relied on psychotropic plants. Roszak gave warm mention to the shamanism "by which men have lived since the paleolithic beginnings of human culture."[24] It was a shamanism which practiced the "old magic" which "opens the mysteries to all." In his second, and perhaps most important work, *Where the Wasteland Ends,* Roszak dilated extensively on the shamanic vision quest as a prototype of salvation in the twentieth century. The wonders of the shaman's imagination will serve to overreach the "artificial environment" which modern science and gray, technological expertise, abiding by the false reality-principle of "single vision," have fabricated. Technocratic culture has bewitched the multitudes of materially comfortable humanity into surveying the world with "a dead man's eyes." It has stifled and regulated the mind-body process in the narrow pursuit of tangible rewards with the whip of logic, calculation and empirical analysis, to such an extreme that most people have been denied the "inarticulate wisdom of the instincts." Not drugs, but the unleashing of the dormant energies of the psyche through self-scrutiny and of meditation, is the organ of wisdom. Roszak's shaman, however, is displaced from his quaint, prehistoric setting and transferred to the visionary present. We cannot go back to paleolithic times, but we can resurrect the figure of the shaman and update him in keeping with man's evolutionary strides as a special role-model for the current rebels against technocracy. In *Where the Wasteland Ends* Roszak undertakes to assimilate the shaman to the romantic hero, who shudders with "sudden ecstasy, an awareness of the heavens and earth swept by awesome presences, the mind on fire with rhapsodic declaration."[25] He issues a call for "romantic perversity" which, in its indulgence of "the full variety of consciousness," nevertheless splits open the crusty integuments of rational, surface knowledge. The shaman/romantic breaks through the vault of infinity; he steps over the skeletal remains of "objective consciousness" in order to raid the treasure of secret knowledge. The "old magic" now becomes, for Roszak, the "old Gnosis," which strips away the mind's limitations.

> The insights of eastern religion, the nonreductive study of primitive myth and ritual, the sympathetic investigation of occult traditions like those of the Sufis, alchemists, and Gnostics. All these begin to emerge from the dungeons where single vision had locked them away as superstition and heresy.[26]

The Old Gnosis has lay buried, but it still seethes volcanically in the subterranean crannies and lesions of the mind. The Gnostic is the civilized bedfellow of the shaman. As Stephen Larsen has put it, "there is an urge to immediate, ecstatic, shamanistic awareness in the psyches of many, many modern people right now."[27]

The controlling symbol of *gnosis,* Roszak rightly specifies, is the "vision flight," the ascent of the shaman's spirit from his body into the atmosphere where he beholds the timeless warp and woof of creation. The Gnostic, and Romantic, too, resist the "laws of gravity" in not so much a physical, but a *symbolic* or psychical sense. Their passion is *levity,* which according to Roszak represents the actualization of the total possibilities of mind, a mind no more weighted down with rational abstractions and a distrust of "subjective" intimations. The "visionary company" of rhapsodists and seers rises above the boundaries of time and space, projecting themselves into another reality where the "out there" and "in here" no longer conflict with each other. The arrow of transcendence points upward through an indeterminate, inner space, rather than forward in time and history—the blind alley of so-called "humanists," technocrats, and social "reformers." For Roszak, the ancient Gnostic myth of the soul descending from the primeval light and becoming lost in the dark density of the material order epitomizes the travail of the contemporary citizen of industrial society.

> We too have lost our way in the abyss, searching for divine goods dimly reflected there. For us, the entrammeling descent has been the pursuit of total human fulfillment *through the mastery of history and matter.*[28]

Rather than assuming greater "social responsibility," which is nothing other than complicity in the mad, machinations of the technocratic state, we must withdraw into the temple of the mind. We must break from the ranks of social and historical marchers snapping to the commands of "progress" and tarry in the "here and now." Thereupon we will realize that "there is nothing to do, nowhere to get. We need only 'stand still in the light' [of *gnosis*]."[29] The problem is modernism and technocracy run amuck; but in response to the problem we must not pose the familiar, but fatuous question "how do I save the technology?" Rather we must ask the "more pertinent question, how do I save my soul?"[30]

That form of dialectic, of course, pleased Watts as well as just about all the nonpolitical units of the counterculture. In *Beyond Theology* Watts discharged his fiercest volley against what he saw as the formidable, but unexposed alliance of Christianity and modern technocracy. The malaise of modern culture has ancient origins, which need to be rediscovered. The "fall" took place "thousands of years ago" when man surrendered to "the demonstrable efficiency of rational thought and the rule of law in social conduct" which at once "cast doubt upon the impulses and intuitions of man's organic and nonreflective being."[31] In yielding to such a point of view, man forsook the promise of enlightenment; he gave up trying to harmonize with his cosmic self. But a reconciliation can now take place by revisioning the sacred in terms of a playfulness and lack of seriousness toward secular concerns. The instincts and the unconscious must come to redefine nature. The metaphysic of rational ordering and the morality of "responsible" striving for time-bound objectives must give clearance to the unqualified joyous revelation of immediate existence as worthwhile, the unqualified precept that "it doesn't matter." To be a *tathagata* (the word is Buddhist meaning the awakened "guide" who lights the "way"), Watts proclaimed, "is to dance the day instead of working it."[32]

"Dancing the day" was, in a manner of speaking, exactly what the counterculture was bent on doing. By the late 1960s the drug mania had begun to wane and was steadily giving place to a variety of incipient religious groups with an Oriental decor which would soon be tagged "the new religions." The new religions were pulled out of the broad wreckage of middle-class values wrought by disgust with the Vietnam war. But they were also a product of the paralysis of antiwar politics which, despite constant mass demonstrations and marches on Washington, failed to shake significantly the policies of government. The violent repression of the "movement," evident in the squelching of the protests over the Cambodian invasion of May 1970, together with the Kent State shootings, marked the start of a major shift from political action among the young to inward voyaging. Robert Grant in his study of Hellenistic Gnosticism has proposed the thesis that the origins of the ancient cults of self-salvation can be explained in terms of the failure of apocalypticism, the loss of faith in an imminent and cataclysmic end to a wicked world, after whose destruction the "righteous" ones would inherit a new and utopian order.[33] Throughout the sixties the counterculture had been awaiting doomsday for "the American Babylon"; but Babylon did not fall and, in response, the counterculture, like the Gnostics of old, fled into the realms of immediate awareness. By the same token, the discredited pledge of "cosmic consciousness" through drugs left many in quest of a mind cure that did not have invidious, physical side effects and did not conjure up "demons." There was a rabid need to relieve the tremendous pressure of anxiety resulting from the thwarted pursuit of happiness and the recognition of the futility of social and politic alternatives. There was need for an all-absorbing and definitive "experience" of life as joyful, even though the bombs kept dropping on Laos and Hanoi and Nixon remained entrenched in the White House. Instead of trembling with fear and loathing at the terrible turn events had taken, one would now undergo a "conversion" of consciousness and accept things as they were. Watts had always alluded to this experience in his own writings, an experience that contains "the conviction that this entire unspeakable world is 'right,' so right that our normal anxieties become ludicrous that if only men could see it they would go wild with joy."[34] Some did see it and did go wild with joy. The Hare Krishna people sprung up on the streets of New York, Boston, and San Francisco, clanking their tambourines and tirelessly *dancing* and chanting the *mahamantra:* "Hare Krishna, Hare Krishna, Krishna Krishna, Hare Hare." The new religious "consciousness" was taking wing.

A Taste of Nectar

Enter Richard Alpert again, this time in his incarnation as Guru Baba Ram Dass. Alpert, alias Ram Dass, had returned from India and was, according to his own biographical notes, "floating about on an ocean of love."[35] Ram Dass preached a new, hybrid message of spiritual ecstasy

and "nowness," which he committed to print as a crazy pastiche of
bold-face words strewn all over the pages in scissors-and-paste fashion,
wild cartoons, and delphic sayings, all stuck together with a purple
cover, under the title of *Be Here Now*. *Be Here Now* was written with
the kind of abandon that one might expect of someone transcribing a
drug experience, but the book makes no mention of LSD or of any other
kind of psychedelic stimulus. The book is putatively about the
attainment of *samaj samadhi*, the paramount state of consciousness.
But, as the title implies, it is more a tribute to the "marvelous
moment."

> HERE WE ARE
> HERE & NOW
> THAT'S ALL THERE IS
> AND IF IT ISN'T BEAUTIFUL, MAN
> THERE'S NOTHING.[36]

"Nowness" supersedes striving toward a coherent and secure future.

> SO YOU SAY:
> WELL, I CAN'T HAVE IT BEAUTIFUL NOW. BUT, LATER! WHEN
> WE GET THE FOOD HOME IT WILL BE BEAUTIFUL
>
> LATER NEVER EXISTS
> WHAT'S HAPPENED TO LIFE INSURANCE, TO TENURE, TO
> PLANNING, SAVING, RESPONSIBILITIES?[37]

The "now" is "Shiva's dance of life." Through looking at life as play,
as necessity, as a *dance*—all of which vibrates together in a stunning
roulade of existence—the eternal composition of the universe, suffused
with the energy of consciousness, an amalgam of all things together,
becomes evident.

> NOBODY IS GOING ANYWHERE
> NOBODY IS COMING FROM ANYWHERE
> WE'RE ALL HERE
> WE'RE ALL HERE
> IN ETERNAL TIME & SPACE
> WE'RE ALWAYS GOING TO BE HERE
> WE'RE JUST DOING LILA RASA
> THE DIVINE DANCE WE'RE DANCING
> & DANCING & DANCING
> DANCE AFTER
> DANCE
> IN ONE BODY

IN ANOTHER BODY
& WE'RE ALL HERE
WE'RE ALL STAYING RIGHT HERE.[38]

The point is not to try to struggle with the complexities of one's external surroundings over which one has no power.

YOU WANT TO CHANGE YOUR ENVIRONMENT?
CHANGE YOUR HEAD! IT'S ALL THE
ECSTATIC MOMENT.[39]

In *The New Religions* Jacob Needleman discusses the appeal of the new religions in terms of their "instrumentality" or power to transform life, which he contrasts with the staid and familiar Western kinds which, denuded by secularism of their amazement and mystery, persist only as social conventions with little charm.[40] The instrumentalism of the new religions is comparable to the pragmatism of the older modes of healthy-mindedness. The new religions make one "feel good" while at the same time offering the heal-all of *happiness*. Indeed, that is why the new religions have succeeded in going further than the drug culture. For they retailed a "quick fix" which had a certain permanent quality about it, an ecstasy that depended on a particular kind of rigor and technique that was more than random agitation of the brain chemistry. They could also pass themselves off as more serious in purpose than dalliance with acid, since they claimed to belong within a venerable "tradition" of saints and spiritual seekers trailing back into the remote past of the Asian continent.

But the new religions were, first and foremost, an *American* phenomenon. They were utilizing the symbols and rules of discipline developed by the Oriental parent religions only so far as such were suitable for American habits. The Mahayana Buddhist doctrine of realizing nirvana by "convenient means" *(upaya)* thus became a warrant for streamlining and slickening the complicated philosophy and rituals to which monks and yogis had been beholden for centuries; and the doctrine was exploited to electrify (sometimes by outright sales gimmicks) the minds of the American middle classes. And the most important accommodation the new religions made in this connection was their concession to the American demand for *fast results*. No longer was the road to wisdom lengthy, arduous, rutted, and littered with many impediments to spiritual consummation. No longer was *the way* the way of the patient pilgrim. But the aim was to "get it" (as votaries of *est,* a popular and burgeoning cult that mingles shreds of psychotherapy with Zen, designate it) and get "it" quickly. The same pandering to the desire for effortless gratification appears in one of the slogans of the Divine Light people, who in the early 1970s were playing on the rhetoric of "peace" that rang subliminal bells with the counterculture. The gift of a great guru, the slogan proclaimed, was not just peace in the world, not just peace among nations, but that most coveted trophy *inner peace,* which comes when one gets "zapped" with the "knowledge."

"Getting it" swiftly and getting it *now* was the special pitch of Divine Light, whose meteoric growth in the early 1970s is an interesting case study in the character of the new "consciousness." Divine Light came about something like what in the sixties was known as a "happening." A "happening" was an untoward, unplanned, and wholly spontaneous event that stirred mass followings and grabbed media attention overnight, then receded back into the blur of frenetic social changes. In 1971 a chubby little bronze-skinned teenager from northern India, whom his *premies* (i.e., "lovers") called Guru Maharaj Ji, made his first tour of the United States, and within two years had attracted thousands of mooning, flower-throwing young supporters who staggered from the decimated platoons of former countercultural dropouts and antiwar veterans, the most renowned of which was Rennie Davis of Chicago Seven fame. In the eyes of the unregenerate, there was nothing particularly charismatic about the boy, who spoke halting English larded with clichés from the argot of hippiedom, wore natty and expensive clothes including gray, Western business suits, rode Rolls Royces and motorcycles, and gorged himself on Baskin-Robbins ice cream. But his supplicants hailed him as *sat-guru,* the "Lord of the Universe," the greatest of divine *avatars* or "incarnations," and they employed language alluding to him even as the Second Coming of Christ. The reason for such adulation, his followers protested, was not what he was *in appearance,* but what he *gave* to them—the divine "knowledge" comparable to the "energy" of a million supernovae. Anyone with a pure heart could obtain this knowledge, which was dispensed in mass conversion sessions by the guru's lieutenants or *mahatmas* (literally, "great souls"), not unlike the infusion of grace at Christian revival meetings.

The "knowledge" which the guru served up was not the sort of intellectual grasp of things which usually counts for the word. It was *gnosis* of the most dazzling and mind-bending type. Those who had "received" the knowledge described it as an unmitigated "high," exploding the casings of ordinary consciousness with "incredible energy." The knowledge was not so much a composed, mystical cognition as it was a highly charged and ecstatic modulation of the five senses. It was

> (a) *visual*—the flooding of the mind with pure "light" causing an ineffable feeling of joy.
> (b) *aural*—the hearing of the "divine music" supposedly analogous to the "most beautiful" sounds of an electric rock band.
> (c) *olfactory*—the aroma of the "holy fragrance" pervades the universe.
> (d) *gustatory*—the tasting of the "divine nectar" which was the sweetest sensation of all.
> (e) *tactile*—the experiencing of all the harmonious "vibrations" of all life in its "perfect" state.

The knowledge bore parallels with the drug experience. As one *premie* related, the first time he "had" knowledge he just "flipped out."

> I saw incredible colors and when I came out of it the walls were melting; it was like being on an acid trip. I couldn't believe it. I was way off the ground, very high.[41]

The difference was that one did not need drugs, only self-surrender before the person of the guru, and the sense of elevation was *constant*. There was no danger of "freaking out" as many had done on LSD. Rather, the mood was that of having been "blissed out." The mind cure was complete—no negative emotions, no anxieties, only the serene rapture of participating in an indescribable universe of *bliss*.

But the divine light was not the only form of knowledge from which seeped the pure and delectable nectar of ecstasy. In November 1973 the Divine Light movement held a convocation of the faithful at the Houston (Texas) Astrodome which they billed with much fanfare as "Millennium '73." The "Millennium" actually consisted in a three-day extravaganza of singing, devotional exercises, and impromptu homilies by the guru, his family, and various ministers. Millennium '73 was aimed at saving a benighted world and promised to inaugurate "a thousand years of peace for people who want peace," as one of the flyers said. Outside the Astrodome, however, there was picketing by members of the International Society for Krishna Consciousness (ISKCON) who attacked Maharaji as a false messiah. The Hare Krishna people insisted that the revered seraph was *not* the way and the light. The truth did not lie within the adolescent guru's style of knowledge, but in the "eternal reservoir of pleasure" that resides with Lord Krishna.

The Hare Krishna sect never approached the elephantine size of the Divine Light movement, mainly because of its strict, nonconforming standards of dress and general life style—the shaving of the head for men, the wearing of saffron robes, the severing of regular family ties, and so on. Yet its promise of undiminished bliss through the realignment of the mind was just as impelling. Surrender of one's personality and the dedication of one's life to God in the confirmation of the votary's "Krishna consciousness" would bring about the sort of unbounded "happiness" that those with profane thoughts could hardly dream of. The chanting of the familiar mantra "Hare Krishna, Hare Krishna" was the occasion; it would set the mind afire with the flame of *bhakti-yoga*.

The trouble with most Americans, according to A. C. Bhaktivedanta Swami Prabhupada, the former Indian businessman and wrinkled patriarch of the Krishna disciples, was that they craved mental peace and happiness, but in their materialistic diversions did not know how to possess it. It was not that cars and snowmobiles and beach homes were *evil;* they were defective because they failed to satisfy. Their marginal utility was quite limited, and thus they were bogus aids to pleasure. For those sated with a wide inventory of worldly amenities, but still aspiring toward some sort of consummation, the "transcendental" bliss of Krishna's paradise was the answer. Such bliss would no longer be ephemeral, but steady and everlasting. It would be the "eternal pleasure" of spiritual satisfaction. Prabhupada writes:

> Happiness derived from pure devotional service is the highest because it is eternal. But the happiness derived from material perfection is inferior because it is temporary.[42]

Similarly,

> We seek happiness by some extraneous, artificial means, but how does it last? It will not endure. We again come back to sorrow. Suppose, by intoxication, we feel happy. That is not our actual happiness . . . [which is, however,] union with the true identity, Kṛṣna, the reservoir of pleasure and eternal bliss.[43]

This writer once interviewed a male member of the Krishna temple in

Denver. The young man told me that, prior to his dedication to the service of Krishna, he had belonged to a rock band and was sunk in the desultory hedonism of the pop-music subculture. He had all the high living, so went his story, that one could withstand: free drugs, easy sex, and enough cash to buy the world. But none of these gratuities were adequate. For every revel there was always the morning after. From every pinnacle of pleasure there was the inescapable slide downward. Happiness in its crystalline and undivided essence eluded his reach. So he "discovered" Krishna consciousness, he informed me, and all at once he knew he would never experience unhappiness again. The Hare Krishna chant itself is magical; it works its divine effects, as Roman Catholics would say of the mass, *ex opere operati.*

> The words Hare, Kṛṣna and Rāma have a special quality because they are seeds of pure spiritual consciousness . . . They are names of God, as ceaselessly energetic as God Himself. When you pronounce these sounds, you are propelled into your eternal position as participant of spiritual energy, a person living in a transcendental nature. Hare Kṛṣna reveals to you the person you really are.[44]

The Krishna and Divine Light people, as part of the vintage of the late counterculture, represent some of the most forceful expressions of a widespread drift inward. They were the heirs presumptive to the legacy of American optimism which was battered brutally in the upheaval of the sixties, and they never claimed their birthright. Instead they closed off the future as well as denying truths of life in the current era. They harped on cosmic rather than social or political themes. They wove around themselves an enchanted web they dubbed the "eternal present," within which they feasted on the sweetmeats of happiness. Their special brand of *gnosis* was, therefore, a substitute gratification for the deep-felt loss of social significance. Their vision of eternity was an unconscious reparation for the experience of broken time that ensued from the prostration of the old social expectations and ideals. They were the first witnesses to the *Götterdammerung* of the nation's middle classes, to the wholesale exhaustion of the American faith in history.

WHERE THE WASTELAND GOES ON

The new religions, or what might be termed the "new Gnosticism," were in one vital respect a response to the clawing sense of powerlessness on the part of average American citizenry. It is, of course, the powerlessness which arises from the disintegration of

binding social institutions and the disappearance of all conscious
participation in them. As one Divine Light *premie* reports, his romance
with Guru Maharaj Ji was spurred by his desire to have mastery over his
situation.

> I never let myself become truly involved in anything. I always wanted
> to be in control and be responsible. Finally I was so desperate that I
> went up to a mahatma and asked him how I could become more
> involved in the Knowledge . . . He told me, "Oh, you must
> surrender."[45]

One must surrender to the guru, who gives knowledge and thereby a
feeling of control over circumstances. "The knowledge is powerful."
Through the knowledge one is able to engage in magical flight above
the misery of the world. In the words of the guru himself:

> Anywhere we go, people are suffering, right? Suffering is no good.
> We must get out of it. The only way to get out of suffering is by this
> Knowledge . . . if we want to leave suffering behind, we need to fly
> with this Knowledge, because it takes us high . . . into our
> consciousness.[46]

The new religions constitute a Gnostic escape route for the masses of
individuals in our society who, thrown out as the detritus of crumbling
communal groups and institutions, including the family, are desperately
looking for some kind of salvation by their own resources. In this
respect they are following in the footsteps of the ancient Gnostics and
mystery cultists who sought self-salvation in the confusion of the
decadent Roman empire. The dissolution of *real* and concrete ties
between people leaves a situation in which every individual becomes an
isolated atom of consciousness who has no relation to, or responsibility
for, the social environment. The only social imperative remaining is to
delve further into "inner space," to cultivate the subtle forms of
awareness to their maximal degree. According to Ram Dass,

> . . . *the only thing you have to offer another human being, ever, is your
> own state of being . . . you're only manifesting how evolved a
> consciousness you are.* That's what you're doing with another human
> being. That's the only dance there is![47]

In the intensification of awareness one gains the innocence of paradise
again. It is an innocence disembarrassed by the potentiality for
destructiveness which commissions the individual, as Charles Reich

describes it in *The Greening of America,* to "dance, seek out nature, laugh, be happy, be beautiful."[48] It is an innocence which "sees no evil" and thereby walls off the threat of meaninglessness from the outside.

The sociologist Robert Bellah, in his recent overview of the new religious phenomena, has set them against the backdrop of the transition from the last decade to the current one. Bellah has noted that "out of the shattered hopes of the sixties there has emerged a cynical privatism, a narrowing of sympathy and concern to the smallest possible circle that is truly frightening."[49] This cynical privatism has manifested itself, in part, in terms of a scrabble for purely psychic rewards and the attainment of personal power to compete against others in the pursuit of individual goals of success. A better word than "privatism," however, Christopher Lasch suggests, is "narcissism," which represents for many today, albeit as a pathology, the easiest way of coming to terms with a "dangerous world." Narcissism is the disease of "a society that fears it has no future" and is infected with "the ever present sense of historical discontinuity."[50] The narcissist subordinates all future concerns, even for his own children, to immediate satisfaction. The narcissism of the new religious consciousness has shown up in the way in which the supposed psychic good of "awareness" becomes a cloak for the will to power. One can point to numerous religious and parareligious cults which promote themselves as aids to personal wealth and happiness. Nichiren Shoshu, a militant Buddhist group with its counterpart called Soka Gokkai in Japan, for example, promises that everything from higher salaries to color television sets can be obtained by reciting a particular chant *nam myoho renge kyo.* Transcendental Meditation offers to its users the "fulfillment of true desires," comprising among other things better composure at work and success in business, and has been adopted as a technique by many top business executives. And there is the so-called Human Potential Movement, blending Eastern religious ideas and meditation methods with Western psychotherapy, which stresses the unlimited possibilities for "growth" (which can mean anything from having an affair to getting rich to becoming one's own guru) within the individual if he only becomes in touch with the "transpersonal" powers locked in his own consciousness.

Not too long ago the Arica Institute, one of the many proliferating "growth" centers which offers to its clients access to increasingly higher levels of "consciousness," according to a graduated fee schedule, advertised its programs with a slogan: "You are responsible for your own evolution." The language is reminiscent of Theosophy with the exception that in place of the old occult abracadabra, the Arica Institute peddles an impressive panoply of "scientific" tools for generating hidden knowledge. As with all Gnosticism, the picture is that of man having been consigned to complete autonomy without dependence on others or with a trust in any will or power other than his own. The ancient Gnostic image has been touched up slightly. Replacing the earlier Gnostics who conceived of man as a spark of divine fire trapped in matter, the new Gnostics patter about the transcendental "consciousness" that is blocked by man's robot-like actions. Werner Erhart, founder of *est,* declares that by nature we all are "machines," creatures of our own ignorance and insanity catapulting us toward destruction. Yet we can be "saved" from the cataclysm (we can "survive") if we untether the powers of mind within us. We no longer have to be "programmed" (here I am employing the parlance of John Lilly) to the bare requirements of eating, working, and raising a family, but we can inject into our biocomputers the "metaprogram" of infinite awareness.

The problem, however, is that an individual absorbed totally in the expansion of mind finds himself in a social desert. The anarchy and anomie which he perceives dimly around him gets reflected in the narcissism of mind cure. "You are responsible for your own evolution" becomes the radically individualistic ethical inference to be drawn from the solipsistic world view as stated in the maxim of *est:* "You are the creator of your own universe." Such a standpoint invites its adherent to affect a *mindless* indifference to other people's misfortunes. Peter Marin, for example, in his article on "The New Narcissism" tells about a woman who had finished *est* training and who was convinced that the individual will is omnipotent and that she should feel "neither guilt nor shame about anyone's fate and that those who are poor and hungry must have wished it on themselves."[51] The total loss of social conscience of the latest breed of Gnostics is a sign of the end of middle-class culture laid waste by the forces of modernity. The new Gnosticism does not signal, as Roszak suggests, an "end" to the wasteland, but is an extension of it. Gnosticism flourishes wherever there is a death of common purpose, a dread of the future, and a mad rush for personal legitimacy in a psychic war of all against all. The Gnostic does not reach out, but tucks himself away like a mollusk against the battering tides of history. He finds happiness as he luxuriates in the glow of his own consciousness, which may however turn out to be reflected light from the fire that is burning his own house down.

Postscript

The evolution of modern Gnosticism has in one measure been exponential, like that of population growth and man's technical mastery of the material world. "Progress" itself—a word which has fallen into both disuse and disrepute nowadays—has brought forth its own antithesis, the cult of antiprogress. Whereas the modern era with its record of ever accelerating social transformation has made man keenly aware of his character as a historical creature forever cruising the sea of change, it has also made him giddy with vertigo. Alvin Toffler has diagnosed the malaise of "future shock"—the paralysis of thought and will which eventuates from an inability to cope with the high-velocity shifts going on in our society. The "future-shocked" personality can no longer comprehend the future. Not only out of his bewilderment does he fear it, he spins in his head a silky web of wish-fulfillments and fantasies which insulate him from the temporal process around him. In his loneliness and isolation he imagines himself an all-powerful and magically competent "man of knowledge," who is (to use a cliché) "above it all." But, in actuality, he only cuts the pitiable figure of a latter-day King Canute, commanding the waves of the ocean to roll back. In this case the waves are the momentum of change and history.

It has been said that a cynic is an innocent who has been traumatized because of his own inadvertence. Likewise, many Gnostics of this century, particularly in America, have been "innocents" of the real, underlying forces of history until their own position was virtually swept away. The upsurge of Gnosticism in today's culture may very well have something to do with the fact that Americans have never truly possessed a tough, historical sense. They have always assumed that things will go their way, that the American experience is a special boon of Providence. The memory of the past has been idealized according to outsize expectations; and when present experience tends to disrupt those expectations, the inclination is to deny the significance of historical change. Certainly the story of the counterculture in the sixties and early seventies confirms this description. The "now" generation had grown up in the affluent fifties accustomed to the immediate gratification of needs, which when combined with the foreclosure of the social future because of the menace of atomic holocaust, gave rise to a sense of the all-important value of immediacy. The anticipation of a great and imminent social revolution in the sixties, partly as reaction to the horrors of the Vietnam episode, was bolstered by this orientation to the present. When the "revolution" failed, the response was not to extend one's hopes into an uncertain future, but to find a mystical fruition for them in the realm of "consciousness." As the mind cure advocates would say, "with right thoughts all things are possible."

The Gnostic flight by mind-magic into eternity is spurred by an unsettling realization of the loss of worldly *place,* the undermining of previous advantages and satisfactions by the movement of historical events. Those who give credence to history are the ones who can faithfully envision new possibilities for man and who are patient enough to wait for their realization, or sufficiently bold to bring about themselves the desired effect. Whoever denies history and seeks salvation in the timeless world has given up on the universal human prospect. *Historically* speaking, the Gnostic retreat from hope has been the sour grapes of the privileged classes, who have had their relatively secure worlds disrupted, their scheme of predictable satisfactions interrupted. Although many Gnostics may appear on the surface to be "revolutionaries," mouthing Jacobin or antiestablishment causes, their protest or antinomianism is against the perceived peril to their own self-advantage and not in the service of their fellows. "Radicalism" is an often misleading term which belies the special interests of the one characterized by unconventional views and behavior. The Gnostic radical is often, therefore, of the desperate and self-indulgent variety.

His *gnosis* bespeaks his fanatical certitude that he is in the right relationship to the cosmos, and that he has nothing more to learn from the experience of years or of generations.

The danger these days is that we are all becoming Gnostics of a sort. Yet the enthusiasts of the "new consciousness" will not see it as a danger. They will see the decline of historicist humanism as a salutary sign and the new Gnosticism as evidence of the widespread recognition of the "tremendous potential of individual consciousness." They will see no virtue in the continued struggle with the ambiguities, contingencies, and incalculable factors of historical existence. The irony is that while confidence in some definite but perhaps not completely translucent meaning in history is at its nadir in the Western world, the challenges and complexities of historical life have become so great that they cannot be ignored. Long ago the saying of Jesus that "the kingdom of God is in your midst" was mistranslated as the kingdom that is "in you," which served the Gnostic's skewed purpose. The contemporary imperative is not just to look inward, but to look outside the self as well, until the kingdom begins to grow, as in the parable of the mustard seed, from its first minute sprouts into the tree of life which overspreads the earth.

Notes

Chapter 1

1. "First Poems," *Translations from the Poetry of Rainer Maria Rilke*, by M. D. Herter Norton (New York: Norton & Co., 1938), p. 19.

2. Shakespeare, *King Henry IV, Part I*, V., iv, 81.

3. Thomas Browne, *Religio Medici* (1643), part i, #11.

4. Erich Przywara, ed., *An Augustine Synthesis* (New York: Harper & Row, 1958), p. 448.

5. Søren Kierkegaard, *Either/Or*, trans. David and Lillian Swenson (Princeton: Princeton University Press, 1959), vol. i, p. 439.

6. Friedrich Nietzsche, "Thus Spoke Zarathustra," in *The Portable Nietzsche*, trans. Walter Kaufmann (New York: Viking Press, 1954), p. 340.

7. Søren Kierkegaard, *The Gospel of Suffering*, trans. David and Lillian Swenson (Minneapolis: Augsburg, 1948), p. 44ff. "The longest schooling trains for the highest; the school which lasts as long as time, can only train for eternity. The schooling for life shows its results in time, but the life-school of suffering trains for eternity." Ibid., p. 61.

8. G. W. F. Hegel, *The Phenomenology of Mind*, trans. John Baille (New York: Harper & Row, 1967), p. 231.

9. Kenneth Boulding, *The Image* (Ann Arbor, Mich.: University of Michigan Press, 1956), pp. 25–26.

10. For an interesting discussion of how time awareness may be related to the development of thought and tool-making, see Robert Maxwell, "Anthropological Perspectives" in Henri Yaker, Humphrey Osmond, and Frances Cheek, *The Future of Time* (Garden City, N.Y.: Doubleday & Co., 1971), p. 36ff. The relationship between time and intelligence is also explored by J. F. Orme, *Time, Experience, and Behavior* (New York: American Elsevier, 1969), p. 161. The necessity of an intelligible time sense for the use of fire is argued by A. F. C. Wallace in *Culture and Personality* (New York: Random House, 1961), p. 77ff.

11. Jean Piaget, *The Child's Conception of Time*, trans. A. J. Pomerans (London: Routledge and Kegan Paul, 1969), p. 6.

12. Numerous studies have shown a close link between "changes in body

temperature and changes in time estimation." Orme, p. 145. This is probably because "a rise or fall in the inner temperature of an organism can produce an acceleration or a deceleration of its physiological processes, making its metabolic clock beat faster and slower . . . [for example] if flies are kept at an abnormally high temperature they age more rapidly and die sooner." G. J. Whitrow, *The Nature of Time* (New York: Holt, Rinehart, and Winston, 1972), p. 63.

13. See also Kurt Salzinger, "The Immediacy Hypothesis," in Yaker, et al., pp. 272–97; Henri Yaker, "The Schizophrenic Perception of Time—a Syntactical Analysis of Language," ibid., pp. 293–309; Bernard Aaronsen, "Behavior and the Place Names of Time," *American Journal of Hypnosis* IX (July 1966): 1–17.

14. The literature on the effects of drugs on time consciousness is fairly extensive. See *inter alia* Frances E. Cheek, et al., "The Time World of Drug Using Groups—Alcoholics, Heroin Addicts, and Psychedelics," in Yaker, et al., pp. 330–50; Stephens Newell, "Chemical Modifiers of Time Perception," ibid., pp. 351–88; Alan Hoffer, "Problems Connected with Evaluation of the Effects of Psychedelic Drugs on Time Perception," ibid., pp. 389–404; Claudio Naranjo, *The Healing Journey* (New York: Random House, 1973), p. 78ff.; R. E. L. Masters and Jean Houston, *The Varieties of Psychedelic Experience* (New York: Dell Publishing Co., 1966), *passim*.

15. Alan Watts, *The Joyous Cosmology* (New York: Random House, 1962), p. 33.

16. W. T. Stace, *Time and Eternity* (Princeton, N.J.: Princeton University Press, 1952), p. 75.

17. T. S. Eliot, "Burnt Norton," *The Complete Poems and Plays* (New York: Harcourt, Brace, and World, 1952), p. 119.

18. Harriet Mann, Miriam Siegler, and Humphrey Osmond, "The Psycho-typology of Time," in Yaker, et al., p. 162.

19. Alan Watts, *The Wisdom of Insecurity* (New York: Random House, 1951), p. 38.

20. Ibid.

21. Horace, *Odes,* I, xi, 7.

22. See also L. Melikan, "Preference for Delayed Reinforcement: An Experimental Study among Palestinian Arab Children," *Journal of Social Psychology* 50 (1959):81–86; Stephen Klineberg, "Future Time Perspective and the Preference for Delayed Reward," *Journal of Personality and Social Psychology* 8 (1968):253–57. Similarly, Leonard W. Doob writes: "The duration of an interval is likely to have significance whenever gratification is deferred . . . A considerable body of research exists which suggests that persons following non-Western traditions have a strong tendency to prefer immediate rather than delayed rewards." *The Patterning of Time* (New Haven: Yale University Press, 1971), p. 93. The same observation is made, as Doob notes, by Edward Hall in *The Silent Language* (Garden City, N.Y.: Doubleday & Co., 1959), p. 33. The consciousness of the future is based on "belief that gratification is attainable not at present, but in the future." Doob, p. 47.

23. See also Edward Banfield, *The Unheavenly City* (Boston: Little, Brown & Co., 1968).

24. The tendency of lower-class people to reject goal-directed behavior and to seek immediate gratification is reflected in their peculiar forms of religiosity, as Max Weber has shown. Whereas privileged classes tend to view salvation in terms of reward for cumulative personal achievement, nonprivileged groups are apt to stress the intervention of a savior who gives immediate relief to distress and suffering. The emphasis on magic as a means to manipulate the forces of the universe for a quick "payoff" is found especially among the faiths of the disenfranchised. See Max Weber, "Religion of Non-Privileged Classes," *The Sociology of Religion,* trans. Ephraim Fischoff (Boston: Beacon Press, 1963), pp. 95–117. However, there is also a common historical case, as the remainder of this book will show, when the privileged classes themselves become "disinherited" and thus lose faith in the future, preferring instead immediate gratification in the moment.

25. See Gary Schwartz, *Sect Ideologies and Social Status* (Chicago: University of Chicago Press, 1970).

26. See L. Bernot and R. Blancard, *Nouville: Un Village Français* (Paris: Institut d'Ethnologie, 1953).

27. See John Mander, *The Unrevolutionary Society* (New York: Harper & Row, 1969), p. 142ff.

28. Thomas J. Cottle and Stephen Klineberg, *The Present of Things Future* (New York: Free Press, 1974), p. 161.

29. Ibid., p. 34.

30. See Mircea Eliade, *The Sacred and the Profane* (New York: Harper & Row, 1963), p. 35.

31. Mircea Eliade, *Myth and Reality* (New York: Harper & Row, 1963), p. 35.

32. Stephen Toulmin and June Goodfield, *The Discovery of Time* (New York: Harper & Row, 1965), p. 23.

33. For a description of the *shalako* ceremony, see Frank Waters, *Masked Gods* (New York: Ballantine Books, 1950), p. 282.

34. For a summation of the Mayan concept of time, see Eric Thompson, *The Rise and Fall of Maya Civilization* (Norman, Okla.: University of Oklahoma Press, 1959).

35. Revelation 21:1ff.

36. The promised-land motif is first stated in Genesis 12:1ff. It is amplified and reinterpreted through the Old Testament and reaches truly eschatological dimensions in the Second Isaiah (Isaiah 40:1ff.).

37. Quoted in Aldous Huxley, *The Perennial Philosophy* (New York: Harper & Row, 1970), p. 189.

38. Paul Tillich, *The Eternal Now* (New York: Charles Scribner's Sons, 1963), p. 132.

39. *Bhagavad-Gita,* trans. Juan Mascaro (Baltimore: Penguin Books, 1962), p. 92.

40. Søren Kierkegaard, *Philosophical Fragments,* trans. by David Swenson

(Princeton, N.J.: Princeton University Press, 1936), p. 53.

41. Henri-Charles Puech, "Gnosis and Time," in *Man and Time* (papers from the Eranos Yearbook), Bolingen Series XXX.3 (New York: Pantheon Books, 1957), p. 65.

42. Aldous Huxley, *Time Must Have a Stop* (New York: Harper & Row, 1965), p. 265.

43. Ibid., p. 266.

Chapter 2

1. J. B. Bury, *The Idea of Progress* (New York: Macmillan & Co., 1932), p. 1.

2. Mircea Eliade, *The Myth of the Eternal Return* (Princeton, N.J.: Princeton University Press, 1954), p. 141f.

3. Ibid., p. 147.

4. Compare the definition of Gnosticism given by Arthur D. Nock: ". . . a pre-occupation with the problem of evil, a sense of alienation and recoil from man's environment, and a desire for special and ultimate knowledge of the secrets of the universe." "Gnosticism," *Harvard Theological Review* 57 (Oct. 1964):256.

5. Robert Haardt, *Gnosis: Character and Testimony*, trans. J. F. Hendry (Leiden: E. J. Brill, 1971), p. 161.

6. Mircea Eliade, *Images and Symbols* (New York: Sheed and Ward, 1961), p. 127.

7. *The Hypostasis of the Archons*, trans. Roger Bullard (Berlin: Walter de Gruyter, 1970), p. 27.

8. Ibid., p. 29.

9. Ibid., p. 39.

10. The origins of Gnosticism in the mystery cults is suggested by L. Gordon Rylands, *The Beginnings of Gnostic Christianity* (London: Watts & Co., 1940), p. 5ff. and by Paul Schmitt, "The Ancient Mysteries in the Society of Their Time, Their Transformation and Most Recent Echoes" in *The Mysteries* (papers from the Eranos Yearbooks, 1955), p. 93ff. Other scholars do not necessarily subscribe to the theory of the birth of Gnosticism in the mystery practices.

11. C. K. Barrett, *The New Testament Background* (New York: Harper & Row, 1961), p. 91.

12. See, for example, a discussion of the agrarian origins of the mysteries in Martin P. Nilsson, *Greek Folk Religion* (New York: Columbia University Press, 1940), p. 42ff.

13. See John Ferguson, *The Religions of the Roman Empire* (Ithaca, N.Y.: Cornell University Press, 1970), p. 129.

14. Harold Willougby, *Pagan Regeneration* (Chicago: University of Chicago Press, 1929), p. 20.

15. Quoted in Willougby, p. 208.

16. Barrett, p. 87.

17. *Thrice Greatest Hermes* ["Hermes Trismegistus"], trans. G. R. S. Mead, vol. 3 (London: 1960), p. 39.

18. Ibid., p. 9.

19. Ibid., p. 2.

20. Frederick C. Grant, *Hellenistic Religions* (Indianapolis, Ind.: Bobbs-Merrill, 1953), p. 33.

21. See Rylands, p. 73. The idea of the Word as having magical potency belongs to a primitive conception of the universe which has been eclipsed by the world view of advanced civilization. As Ernst Cassirer notes, "word magic" is a common feature of one primitive mentality, wherein "thought and its verbal utterance are usually taken directly as one . . . ." *Language and Myth*, trans. by Susanne Langer (New York: Dover, 1953), p. 46.

22. See Mircea Eliade, *Shamanism* (Princeton, N.J.: Princeton University Press, 1964).

23. Michael Rostoutzeff, *Mystic Italy* (New York: Henry Holt & Co., 1927), p. 138ff.

24. The bird symbol in shamanistic lore is discussed extensively by Joseph Campbell in *The Flight of the Wild Gander* (Chicago: Henry Regnery & Co., 1960), p. 167ff. See also Eliade, *Shamanism*, p. 69.

25. Haardt, p. 386.

26. Eliade, *Shamanism*.

27. Haardt, p. 39.

28. Eliade has characterized shamanism as "the earliest speculation concerning . . . the omnipotence of intelligence," the power of the mind to influence the material universe. *Shamanism*, p. 480.

29. Carlos Castaneda, *Tales of Power* (New York: Simon & Schuster, 1974), p. 59.

30. Hans Jonas, *The Gnostic Religion* (Boston: Beacon Press, 1963), p. 264.

31. Ferguson, p. 129.

32. Friedrich Nietzsche, *Joyful Wisdom*, trans. Thomas Common (New York: Frederick Ungar, 1960), pp. 248–49.

33. Some scholars trace the myth of the Redeemed Redeemer to an Iranian source, which may have influenced the tradition of *jñana-yoga* ("the yoga of wisdom") in the Vedic literature of India. The first to propound this thesis was R. Reitzenstein in *Der Iranische Erlösungsmysterium* (Bonn: 1921); the suggestion has since been amplified by Geo Widengren, *The Gnostic Attitude*, trans. Birger A. Pearson (Santa Barbara: Institute for Religious Studies, 1973).

34. Walter Schmithals, *Gnosticism in Corinth*, trans. by John Steely (Nashville, Tenn.: Abington Press, 1971), p. 38.

35. H. C. Puech, "Gnosis and Time," in *Man and Time*, papers from the Eranos Yearbook (New York: Pantheon Books, 1957), p. 63.

36. Robert M. Grant, *Gnosticism and Early Christianity* (New York: Harper & Row, 1966), p. 33.

37. *Thrice Great Hermes* (n. 17), vol. 1, p. 116.

38. See Andrew K. Helmbold, *The Nag Hammadi Gnostic Texts and the Bible* (Grand Rapids, Mich.: Baker Books, 1967), p. 28.

39. W. E. G. Floyd, *Clement of Alexandria's Treatment of the Problem of Evil* (Oxford University Press, 1971), p. 65.

40. Jonas, *The Gnostic Religion,* p. 329.

41. Such is the description of the Manicheans given by Saint Augustine. See Haardt, p. 342.

42. See Victor White's statement: "Gnosticism is essentially esoteric and sectarian and (in the Greek sense) aristocratic." *God and the Unconscious* (London: Fontana Library, 1960), p. 210.

43. Max Weber, *The Sociology of Religion,* trans. Ephraim Fischoff (Boston: Beacon Press, 1963), p. 123. More updated reviews of Gnosticism along these lines are H. G. Kippenberg, "Versuch einer soziologischen Verortung des antiken Gnostizismus," *Numen* 17 (1970):211–31; and John G. Gager, *Kingdom and Community* (Englewood Cliffs, N.J.: Prentice-Hall, 1975), p. 107f.

44. Ibid.

45. Ibid., p. 124.

46. H. Idris Bell, *Egypt from Alexander the Great to the Arab Conquest* (Oxford University Press, 1948), p. 41.

47. See W. W. Tarn, *Hellenistic Civilization* (New York: World Publishing Co., 1965), p. 207.

48. Norman Cohn, *The Pursuit of the Millennium* (Oxford: Oxford University Press, 1961), p. 160.

49. Ibid., p. 172ff.

50. See Francis Yates, *The Rosicrucian Enlightenment* (London: Routledge & Kegan Paul, 1972), p. 17f.

51. See Francis Yates, *Giordano Bruno and the Hermetic Tradition* (New York: Random House, 1969), p. 238ff.

52. The historical link between empirical science and the rising bourgeoisie is documented handily by Christopher Hill with respect to the thought of Thomas Hobbes. See his *Puritanism and Resolution* (New York: Schocken Books, 1964), p. 288ff.

Chapter 3

1. Carl Becker, *The Heavenly City of the Eighteenth-Century Philosophers* (New Haven and London: Yale University Press, 1932), p. 129.

2. Roy Pascal, *The German Sturm und Drang* (New York: Philosophical Library, 1953), p. xv.

3. J. W. von Goethe, *Egmont,* trans. Willard R. Trask (Great Neck, N.Y.: Barron's Educational Series, 1960), p. 120.

4. For the classic discussion of the Romantic origins of the Nazi mind, see Peter Vierick, *Metapolitics: From the Romantics to Hitler* (New York: Alfred A. Knopf, 1941).

5. J. W. von Goethe, *Faust,* parts i and ii, trans. Charles E. Passage (Indianapolis, Ind.: Bobbs-Merrill, 1965), p. 63.

6. Ibid.

7. Quoted in Pascal, p. 138.

8. See A. Lesle Willson, *A Mythical Image: The Ideal of India in German Romanticism* (Durham, N.C.: Duke University Press, 1964), p. 59ff.

9. Herder, *Sämtliche Werke,* edited by Berhard Suphan (Leipzig: 1877-1913), vol. xxvi, p. 412. Cited in the original German by Willson, *A Mythical Image,* p. 68. Translation author's.

10. *The Poems of Schiller,* trans. Edgar A. Bowring (New York: Hurst and Company, 1851), p. 237.

11. Novalis, *Schriften* (Stuttgart: W. Kohlhammer, 1960), vol. ii, p. 427.

12. Ibid., p. 418.

13. Friedrich Schlegel, "Athenaeum Fragments," no. 284, in *Friedrich Schlegel's Lucinde and the Fragments,* trans. Peter Firchow (Minneapolis: University of Minnesota Press, 1971), p. 202.

14. Ibid., no. 132, p. 178.

15. Lilian R. Furst, *Romanticism in Perspective* (New York: Humanities Press, 1970), p. 152.

16. The German Romantics' discovery of the Unconscious is treated in detail in Ferdinand Lion, *Romantik als Deutsches Schicksal* (Stuttgart: W. Kohlhammer, 1963), p. 43ff.

17. Quoted in Ilse Weidekampf, *Traum und Wirklichkeit in der Romantik und bei Heine* (Leipzig: Mayer and Müller, 1932). Reprinted by Johnson Reprint Corporation (New York: 1967), p. 4. Translation author's.

18. Novalis, "Hymnen an die Nacht," *Schriften,* vol. i, p. 32.

19. Novalis, "Heinrich von Ofterdingen," *Schriften,* p. 195.

20. Friedrich von Schiller, *Naive and Sentimental Poetry* and *On the Sublime,* trans. Julius Elias (New York: Frederick Ungar Publishing Co., 1966), p. 150.

21. Schlegel's reformulation of Schiller's ideas is discussed at length in L. P. Wessell, Jr., "Antinomic Structure of Friedrich Schlegel's Romanticism," *Studies in Romanticism* 12 (Summer 1973):648–69.

22. *The Works of Heinrich Heine,* trans. Charles G. Leland (London: William Heinemann, 1906), vol. v, p. 269.

23. Vierick.

24. H. S. Reiss, ed., *The Political Thought of the German Romantics: 1793-1815* (New York: Macmillan, 1955), p. 131.

25. Ibid., p. 171.

26. Müller's ideas in relation to the political thought of the German Romantics is summarized quite ingeniously in Anonymous, "Romantic Reaction," *Times Literary Supplement* 3401 (May 4, 1967):369–70.

27. Heine, p. 309.

28. Novalis, *Schriften,* vol. ii, p. 413. A play on words in the original German which gives the force of the irony in this aphorism is lost somewhat in English translation. Novalis says we seek the "unconditioned" *(unbedingt)* but we find only "things" *(Dinge).*

29. Jacob Böhme, *Mysterium Magnum* (Cornehill, England: M. Simmons, 1654), ch. 1.

30. See a synopsis of Böhme's thought in Richard Kroner, *Speculation and Revelation in Modern Philosophy* (Philadelphia: Westminster Press, 1961), p. 70ff.

31. Quoted in Alexander Gode-von Aesch, *Natural Science in German Romanticism* (New York: Columbia University Press, 1941), pp. 70–71.

32. Ibid., p. 180.

33. Ibid.

34. See Peter L. Thorslev, *The Byronic Hero* (Minneapolis: University of Minnesota Press, 1967), p. 10ff.

Chapter 4

1. Jacques Barzun, *Romanticism and the Modern Ego* (Boston: Little, Brown, and Company, 1943), p. 141.

2. Thomas Carlyle, *Complete Works* (New York: John W. Lovell), vol. i, p. 465.

3. R. R. Palmer, *A History of the Modern World* (New York: Alfred A. Knopf, 1965), p. 490.

4. See Robert Binkley, *Realism and Nationalism* (New York: Harper & Brothers, 1935), p. 105.

5. Thomas Carlyle, *Selected Works, Reminiscences, and Letters,* ed. Julian Symons (Cambridge, Mass.: Harvard University Press, 1957), p. 287.

6. Thomas Carlyle, *Complete Works,* vol. i, p. 484.

7. G. B. Tennyson, ed., *A Carlyle Reader* (New York: Modern Library, 1969), p. 307.

8. Ibid., p. 306.

9. Ibid., p. 305.

10. Ibid., p. 173.

11. Ibid., p. 174.

12. Carlyle, *Complete Works,* vol. ii, p. 371.

13. *A Carlyle Reader,* p. 407.

14. *Selected Works,* p. 297.

15. See Michael Moran, "Thomas Carlyle," in *English Philosophy,* vol. ii, (New York: The Macmillan Company, 1967), p. 25.

16. Albert LaValley, *Carlyle and the Idea of the Modern* (New Haven, Conn.: Yale University Press, 1968), p. 256.

17. *Selected Works,* pp. 442–43.

18. LaValley, p. 290.

19. Friedrich Nietzsche, *Gesammelte Werke* (Munich: Musarion Verlag, 1925), vol. xviii, p. 115.

20. Schopenhauer had virtually no friends and was a misanthropist who despised the company of other human beings. His only real comrade was his dog.

21. Friedrich Nietzsche, "Thoughts out of Season," trans. Adrian Collins in Oscar Levy, ed., *The Complete Works of Nietzsche* (New York: Russell and Russell, 1964), vol. v, p. 126.

22. Arthur Schopenhauer, *Gespräche,* ed. Arthur Hübscher (Stuttgart: F. Fromann, 1971), p. 126.

23. Arthur Schopenhauer, *Die Handschriftliche Nachlass,* ed. Arthur Hübscher (Stuttgart: F. Fromann, 1971), p. 126.

24. Ibid., p. 149.

25. Arthur Schopenhauer, *The World as Will and Representation,* trans. E. F. J. Payne (Clinton: The Colonial Press, 1958), vol. i, p. 100.

26. Ibid., p. 31.

27. Ibid., p. 279.

28. Ibid., p. 250.

29. Ibid., p. 315.

30. *Nachlass,* vol. iv, p. 35.

31. Arthur Schopenhauer, *Essays and Aphorisms,* trans. R. J. Hollingdale (Baltimore: Penguin Books, 1970), p. 52.

32. *World as Will and Representation,* p. 184.

33. Arthur Schopenhauer, *On the Basis of Morality,* trans. E. F. J. Payne (Indianapolis, Ind.: Bobbs-Merrill, 1965), p. 212.

34. Friedrich Nietzsche, *Gesammelte Werke,* vol. xviii, p. 189.

35. Ibid., vol. xix, p. 347.

36. Ibid., vol. xv, pp. 20–21.

37. Ibid., p. 83.

38. Ibid., vol. xiii, p. 255.

39. Ibid., p. 215.

40. Ibid., p. 108.

41. Ibid., p. 109.

42. Ibid., p. 258.

43. Ibid., pp. 254–55.

44. Ibid., vol. vi, p. 234.

45. Ibid., p. 237.

46. Ibid., vol. xviii, p. 68.

47. Ibid., vol. xvii, p. 142.

48. Ibid., vol. xix, p. 349.

49. Ibid., vol. xviii, p. 283.

50. Ibid., vol. xvii, p. 159.

51. Ibid., vol. xix, p. 373.

52. Ibid., vol. xiii, p. 281.

53. Ibid., vol. xvii, p. 158.

54. Ibid., vol. xiii, p. 408.

55. Ibid., vol. xii, p. 248.

56. Ibid., vol. xxi, p. 284.

57. A common misapprehension about Nietzsche is that he was an evolutionist thinker. Nietzsche, however, did not consider the *Übermensch* as the end product of a long process of genetic or racial evolution. Rather, the "overman" is a veritable *coup d'eclat*, a triumph of individual genius and will outside the matrix of historical and biological development.

58. Friedrich Nietzsche, *Gesammelte Werke*, vol. xiii, p. 372.

59. Ibid., vol. xv, p. 119.

60. Ibid., p. 223.

61. Ibid., vol. xviii, p. 182.

62. Goethe, indeed, was the first to use the term *Übermensch* referring to the Faustian ideal of the self-made hero, the Romantic/Promethean individual who is constantly striving toward the peaks of self-creation.

63. See Theodor Schieder, "Nietzsche and Bismarck," trans. Alexandra Hendee, *Historian* 29 (August 1967):584–604.

64. Letter #168 to Jacob Burckhardt, in *Nietzsche: A Self-Portrait from his Letters*, ed. Peter Fuss and Henry Shapiro (Cambridge, Mass.: Harvard University Press, 1971), p. 142.

65. Ibid., p. 144.

Chapter 5

1. Enid Starkie, *Arthur Rimbaud* (New York: New Directions, 1961), p. 86.

2. James Webb, *The Occult Underground* (LaSalle, Ill.: Open Court, 1974), p. 167ff.

3. Péladan, *L'Art Idéaliste et Mystique, Doctrine de l'Ordre et du Salon de Rose-Croix*, 2nd edition (Paris: 1894), pp. 17–18. Quoted in Webb, p. 181.

4. William Butler Yeats, *Explorations* (New York: Macmillan, 1962), p. 33.

5. "Each and all things in nature correspond to spiritual things; and in like manner each and all things in the human body." Emanuel Swedenborg, *A Compendium of Theological Writings* (New York: Swedenborg Foundation, Inc., 1875), pp. 98–99.

6. See F. W. Leakey, *Baudelaire and Nature* (Manchester: University of Manchester Press, 1969), p. 150.

7. Charles Baudelaire, *Artificial Paradise*, trans. Ellen Fox (New York: Herder and Herder, 1971), p. 81.

8. See Marcel Raymond, *From Baudelaire to Surrealism* (London: Methuen and Company, 1970), p. 36.

9. Arthur Rimbaud, *Illuminations* (New York: New Directions, 1946), p. 11.

10. Arthur Rimbaud, *A Season in Hell*, trans. Hannah and Matthew Josephson (New York: Maccaulay Company, 1931), p. 303.

11. Ibid., p. 283.

12. *Illuminations*, p. 29.

13. *A Season in Hell*, p. 281.

14. John Senior, *The Way Down and Out: The Occult in Symbolist Literature* (Ithaca, N.Y.: Cornell University Press, 1959).

15. *A Season in Hell*, p. 299.

16. Ibid., p. 283.

17. See Morton I. Seider, *William Butler Yeats: The Poet as Mythmaker* (East Lansing, Mich.: Michigan State University Press, 1962), p. 458.

18. See George Mills Harper, *Yeats' Golden Dawn* (London: Macmillian Press, 1974), p. 70.

19. William Butler Yeats, *Essays and Introductions* (New York: The Macmillan Company, 1961), p. 114.

20. Ibid.

21. Ibid., p. 151.

22. William Butler Yeats, *A Vision* (New York: The Macmillan Company, 1938), p. 68.

23. Ibid., p. 267.

24. See David S. Thatcher, *Nietzsche in England* (Toronto: University of Toronto Press, 1970), p. 182ff.

25. *Explorations*, p. 336.

26. Ibid., p. 335.

27. William Butler Yeats, *Letters* (London: Hart-Davis, 1914), p. 812.

28. *Explorations*, p. 312. Author's italics.

29. Quoted in Franz Calgren, *Rudolf Steiner 1861-1928* 3rd edition (Dornach, Switz.: Goetheanum School of Spiritual Science, 1972), p. 17.

30. Rudolf Steiner, *A Road to Self-Knowledge* (London: Anthroposophical Publishing Company, 1956), p. 11.

31. Rudolf Steiner, *Investigations in Occultism* (London: Rudolf Steiner Publishing Co., 1920), p. 194.

32. P. D. Ouspensky, *A New Model of the Universe* (New York: Random House, 1971), p. 111.

33. Ibid., p. 110.

34. Ibid., p. 108.

35. P. D. Ouspensky, *In Search of the Miraculous* (New York: Harcourt, Brace and World, 1949), p. 58.

36. Fritz Peters, *Boyhood with Gurdjieff* (New York: Dutton, 1964), p. 42.

37. *A New Model of the Universe*, p. 440.

38. J. G. Bennett, *Gurdjieff: Making a New World* (New York: Harper & Row, 1973), p. 245.

39. *In Search of the Miraculous*, p. 21.

40. Ibid., p. 145.

41. P. D. Ouspensky, *The Psychology of Man's Possible Evolution* (New York: Random House, 1974), p. 42.

42. *In Search of the Miraculous*, p. 157.

43. Ibid., p. 158.

44. Peters, p. 42.

45. *In Search of the Miraculous*, p. 360.

46. *New Model of the Universe*, p. 373.

47. Ibid., p. 123.

48. Ibid., p. 447.

Chapter 6

1. G. Criel, "Surrealism: Loftiest Attempt of the Mind Toward Freedom," *Books Abroad* 26 (1952):133.

2. See F. J. Hoffman, "From Surrealism to the Apocalypse: A Development in Twentieth-Century Irrationality," *English Literary History* 15 (June 1948):153.

3. *Manifestoes of Surrealism*, trans. Richard Seaver and Helen R. Lane (Ann Arbor, Mich.: University of Michigan Press, 1969), p. 18.

4. Ibid., p. 14.

5. Ibid., p. 35.

6. *Manifestoes*, p. 128.

7. Herman Hesse, "If the War Goes on Another Two Years," in *If the War Goes On: Reflections on War and Politics,* trans. Ralph Mannheim (New York: Farrar, Strauss, & Giroux, 1971), p. 20.

8. Ibid., p. 25.

9. Ibid., p. 28.

10. Rainer Maria Rilke, *Sonnets to Orpheus*, trans. C. F. MacIntyre (Berkeley: University of California Press, 1967), p. 77.

11. H. Stuart Hughes, *Consciousness and Society* (New York: Alfred A. Knopf, 1958), p. 120.

12. Henri Bergson, *Creative Evolution*, trans. Arthur Mitchell (New York: Modern Library, 1944), p. 261.

13. Ibid., p. 54.

14. Henri Bergson, *The Creative Mind*, trans. Mabelle L. Andison (New York: Philosophical Library, 1946), p. 42.

15. Henri Bergson, *The Two Sources of Morality and Religion*, trans. Ashley Audra, Cloudesley Brereton, and W. H. Carter (New York: Henry Holt and Company, 1935), p. 201.

16. Ibid., p. 212.

17. Ibid., p. 253.

18. C. G. Jung, *Letters,* ed. Gerhard Adler (Princeton, N.J.: Princeton University Press, 1973), p. 91.

19. C. G. Jung, *Modern Man in Search of a Soul,* trans. W. S. Dell and Carl F. Baynes (New York: Harcourt, Brace & World, 1933), p. 206.

20. Aniela Jaffé, "The Influence of Alchemy on the Work of C. G. Jung," in *Alchemy and the Occult,* comp. Ian Macphail (New Haven, Conn.: Yale University Press, 1968), vol. i, p. xvi.

21. *Modern Man in Search of a Soul,* p. 197.

22. C. G. Jung, *Memories, Dreams, Reflections,* recorded and edited by Aniela Jaffé, trans. Richard and Clara Winston (New York: Random House, 1961), pp. 247–48. Italics author's.

23. C. G. Jung, *Collected Works,* trans. R. F. C. Hull (New York: Bollingen Foundation, 1963), vol. IX, i, pp. 122–23.

24. Ibid., vol. IX, i, pp. 284–85.

25. Ibid., vol. IX, ii, p. 266.

26. Ibid., vol. IX, ii, p. 222.

27. Ibid., vol. VII, p. 175.

28. Ibid., vol. XII, p. 41.

29. C. G. Jung, *The Integration of Personality,* trans. Stanley Dell (New York: Farrar & Rinehart, 1939), p. 296.

30. *Memories, Dreams, Reflections,* p. 314.

31. *Collected Works,* vol. XI, p. 468.

32. Ibid., vol. XI, p. 513.

33. Ibid., vol. IX, ii, p. 194.

34. Ibid., vol. IX, ii, p. 493.

35. Ibid., vol. IX, ii, p. 503.

36. *Letters,* p. 88.

37. C. G. Jung, *The Undiscovered Self,* trans. R. F. C. Hull (New York: Little Brown and Company, 1957), pp. 21–22.

38. Volodynmyn W. Odajnyk, *Jung and Politics* (New York: Harper & Row, 1976), p. 63.

39. For Jung's disavowal of any Nazi sympathies, see his letter to the anonymous Mrs. N. (May 20, 1940), *Letters,* p. 283. However, Paul Stern has argued in his critical biography that Jung, while never an outright Nazi hanger-on, was at least constrained by his own ambivalence toward modern, bourgeois culture, by his feelings about the "Jewishness" of Freud and Freudian psychoanalysis, by his Romantic deference toward supermen and occult heroes to whiffle on the subject of Nazi extravagances. See P. Stern, *C. G. Jung: The Haunted Prophet* (New York: George Braziller, 1976), p. 217ff.

40. *Letters,* p. 129.

41. Ibid., p. 537.

42. Cited in Miguel Serrano, *C. G. Jung and Herman Hesse: A Record of Two Friendships,* trans. Frank MacShane (New York: Schocken Books, 1966), p. 94.

43. Ibid., p. 95.

44. Herman Hesse, *Demian*, trans. Michael Roloff and Michael Lebeck (New York: Bantam Books, 1965), p. 25.

45. Ibid., p. 138.

46. Ibid., pp. 140–41.

47. Herman Hesse, *Klingsor's Last Summer*, trans. Richard and Clara Winston (New York: Farrar, Strauss & Giroux, 1970), p. 190.

48. Ibid., p. 194.

49. Herman Hesse, *Siddhartha*, trans. Hilda Rosner (New York: New Directions, 1951), p. 117.

50. See Marie-Louise von Franz, *C. G. Jung: His Myth in our Time*, trans. William H. Kennedy (New York: G. P. Putnams Sons, 1975), p. 114f.

51. Heinrich Heine, *Works*, trans. Charles G. Leland (London: William Heinemann, 1906), vol. 5, i, pp. 207–8.

52. See James H. McRandle's discussion of the *Wandervögel* as forerunners of Nazism in *The Track of the Wolf* (Evanston, Ill.: Northwestern University Press, 1965), p. 56.

53. See Fritz Stern, *The Politics of Cultural Despair* (Berkeley: University of California Press, 1961), p. 146.

54. See Hitler's remarks in his *Secret Book*, trans. Salvator Attanasio (New York: Grove Press, 1961): "The foundation of the Aryan struggle for life is the soil, which he cultivates and which provides the general basis for an economy satisfying primarily its own needs within its own orbit through the productive forces of its own people.

"Because of the lack of productive capacities of its own the Jewish people cannot carry out the construction of a state, viewed in a territorial sense, but as a support of its own existence it needs the work and creative activities of other nations. Thus the existence of the Jew himself becomes a parasitical one within the lives of other peoples. . . ." p. 212.

55. A classic, though somewhat sensational and flawed study of occult influences on Hitler is Louis Pauwels and Jacques Bergier, *The Morning of the Magicians*, trans. Rollo Myers (London: Anthony Gibbs & Phillips, 1963).

56. See Jean-Michel Angebert, *The Occult and the Third Reich*, trans. Lewis A. M. Sumberg (New York: Macmillan, 1974), p. 164ff.

57. Werner Maser, *Hitler: Legend, Myth, and Reality*, trans. Peter and Betty Ross (New York: Harper & Row, 1971), p. 99.

58. Alfred Rosenberg, *Der Mythus Des 20. Jahrhunderts* (Munich: Hoheneichen Verlag, 1936), p. 30.

59. Adolf Hitler, *Mein Kampf*, ed. John Chamberlain, et al. (New York: Reynal and Hitchcock, 1940), pp. 393–94.

60. See Gerhard Ritter, "The Historical Foundations of the Rise of National Socialism," in Maurice Baumont, et al., eds., *The Third Reich* (New York: Praeger, 1955), p. 392ff.

61. See F. Gregoire, "The Use and Misuse of Philosophy and Philosophers," ibid., p. 688ff.

62. *The Integration of Personality,* p. 62.
63. *The Two Sources of Morality and Religion,* p. 317.

Chapter 7

1. Walt Whitman, "Democratic Vistas," *The Works of Walt Whitman* (New York: Funk and Wagnalls, 1968), vol. 2, p. 213.
2. Walt Whitman, "Notes Left Over," ibid., p. 347.
3. Sidney Mead, "The American People: Their Space, Time and Religion," *Journal of Religion* 34 (Oct. 1954):251.
4. Walt Whitman, "Song of Myself" *Leaves of Grass,* 46.
5. Ibid., "Song of Myself," 51.
6. Ibid., "Children of Adam," 9.
7. Perry Miller, "From Edwards to Emerson." *New England Quarterly* 13 (1940):617.
8. William Ellery Channing, "Likeness to God," in *The Transcendentalists: An Anthology,* Perry Miller, ed. (Cambridge: Harvard University Press, 1950), p. 23.
9. Ibid., p. 24.
10. Amos Bronson Alcott, "Orphic Sayings," ibid., p. 307.
11. Christopher Cranch, "Transcendentalism," ibid., p. 301.
12. David Bowers, "Democratic Vistas," in Brian M. Barbour, *American Transcendentalism: An Anthology of Criticism* (Notre Dame, Ind.: Notre Dame University Press, 1973), p. 17. Reprinted from Robert E. Spiller, et al., eds., *Literary History of the United States,* vol. 1, 3rd edition (New York: Macmillan, 1953).
13. Ralph Waldo Emerson, *Journals* (Boston and New York: Houghton Mifflin and Company, 1909-14), vol. x, p. 259.
14. See Robert Detweiler, "Over-rated Oversoul," *American Literature* 36 (March 1964):65–68.
15. *Journals,* vol. ix, p. 313.
16. Ralph Waldo Emerson, "Discipline," *Works* (Boston and New York: Houghton, Mifflin and Company, 1876), vol. i, p. 46.
17. *Journals,* vol. ix, p. 217.
18. Ibid., p. 216.
19. "Immortality," *Works,* vol. viii, pp. 330–31.
20. *Journals,* vol. vii, p. 161.
21. Ibid., p. 112.
22. Ibid., vol. ix, p. 120.
23. "Works and Days," *Works,* vol. vii. pp. 170–71.
24. "Lecture on the Mind," *Works,* vol. i, p. 273.
25. "Divinity School Address," *Works,* p. 123.
26. "The Sovereignty of Ethics," *Works,* vol. x, p. 190.

27. Ibid.

28. "Aristocracy," *Works*, p. 66.

29. "The Young American," *Works*, vol. i, p. 365.

30. "Politics," *Works*, vol. iii, p. 204.

31. "The American Scholar," *Works*, vol. i, p. 102.

32. For a discussion of the history of these movements, see Whitney R. Cross, *The Burned-Over District* (Ithaca, N.Y.: Cornell University Press, 1950).

33. *Journals*, vol. x, p. 10.

34. "Young America," *Works*, p. 365.

35. Donald Meyer, *The Positive Thinkers* (Garden City, N.Y.: Doubleday & Company, 1965), p. 83.

36. J. Stillson Judah, *The History and Philosophy of the Metaphysical Movements in America* (Philadelphia: Westminster Press, 1967), p. 53.

37. A recent and provocative study of Swedenborg's spiritual revelations is that of Wilson van Dusen, *The Presence of Other Worlds* (New York: Harper & Row, 1974).

38. Andrew Jackson Davis, *The Great Harmonia* (Boston: B. Marsh, 1852–56), vol. i, p. 13.

39. Ibid., p. 43.

40. Ibid., vol. iii, p. 14.

41. Ibid., p. 20.

42. Mary Baker Eddy, *Science and Health with Key to the Scriptures* (Boston: Allison V. Stewart, 1915), p. 113.

43. Ibid., p. 336.

44. Ibid., p. 120.

45. Ibid., p. 129.

46. Ibid., p. 90.

47. Robert Peel, *Mary Baker Eddy: The Years of Trial* (New York: Holt, Rinehart and Winston, 1971), p. 116.

48. Manicheanism was an ancient, dualistic religion originating in Persia that was associated with Gnosticism.

49. Mary Baker Eddy, *Miscellaneous Writings: 1883-1896* (Boston: Allison V. Stuart, 1914), p. 428.

50. Quoted in Charles Braden, *Spirits in Rebellion* (Dallas, Tex.: Southern Methodist University Press, 1963), p. 199.

51. Christian D. Larson, *Mastery of Fate* (Chicago: The Progress Company, 1908), p. 16.

52. Ibid., p. 52.

53. Ibid., p. 38.

54. Nellie E. Friend, *Triumphant Living* (Boston: Murray Press, 1945), p. 36.

55. Braden, p. 135.

56. Nellie E. Friend, *The Tapestry of Eternity* (New York: Philosophical Library, 1951), p. 151.

57. Egbert M. Chesley, "The Significance of the New Metaphysical Movement," in Horatio Dresser, *The Spirit of New Thought* (New York: Thomas Y. Crowell, 1917), p. 38.

58. Gertrude M. Williams, *Priestess of the Occult* (New York: Alfred A. Knopf, 1946), p. 114.

59. Helena P. Blavatsky, *Isis Unveiled* (New York: J. W. Bouton, 1888), p. 588.

60. Ibid., p. 640.

61. Leslie Bullock has written: "The objects of the Theosophical Society have little or nothing to do with the actual teaching and practice of the group. It is not universal in its appeal; it is neither scientific nor philosophical nor religious; and it poses as laws certain unproven theories, spun out of the imagination of a neurotic woman." "Theosophical Cults, the Bible and Modern Religions," *Interpretation* 12 (April 1958):219.

62. *Blavatsky,* p. 588.

63. Ibid., p. 18f.

64. For a historical overview of this utopian experiment, see Emmett A. Greenwall, *The Point Loma Community in California: 1897-1942* (Berkeley: University of California Press, 1955).

65. C. W. Leadbetter, *A Textbook of Theosophy* (Wheaton, Ill.: The Theosophical Press, 1946), p. 39.

66. William Q. Judge, *The Ocean of Theosophy* (Pasadena, Calif.: Theosophical Press, 1948), p. 116.

67. Annie Besant, *Popular Lectures on Theosophy* (Hollywood, Calif.: Theosophical Publishing House, 1919), p. 51.

68. From an address by Annie Besant to the Theosophical Society at the Parliament of Religions, Chicago, 1893. Cited in the *Proceedings,* p. 78.

69. Ibid.

70. Ibid.

71. Francis Hackett, "The Self is a Bore," *New Republic* 136 (Jan. 28, 1957):20.

72. Swami Vivekenanda, *Practical Vedanta* (Calcutta: Advaita Ashrama, 1970), p. 8.

73. Ibid., p. 109.

74. Wendell Thomas, *Hinduism Invades America* (New York: Beacon Press, 1930), p. 90.

Chapter 8

1. William James, *The Varieties of Religious Experience* (New York: New American Library, 1958), p. 58.

2. Ibid., p. 81.

3. Ibid., p. 83.

4. Ibid., p. 76.

5. Louis Pauwels and Jacques Bergier, *The Morning of the Magicians* (New York: Stein and Day, 1957), p. 168.

6. D. T. Suzuki, *Zen Buddhism,* ed. William Barrett (Garden City, N.Y.: Doubleday, 1956), p. 191.

7. Jack Kerouac, *The Dharma Bums* (New York: Viking Press, 1958), p. 78.

8. Alan Watts, *The Meaning of Happiness* (New York: Harper & Row, 1940), p. 66.

9. Ibid., p. 180.

10. Alan Watts, *The Meaning of Insecurity* (New York: Pantheon Books, 1951), p. 78.

11. David Stuart, *Alan Watts* (Radnor, Penn.: Chilton Book Co., 1976), p. 151.

12. Ibid., p. 181f.

13. Alan Watts, *In My Own Way* (New York: Pantheon Books, 1972), p. 262.

14. Ibid., p. 309.

15. Ibid., p. 273.

16. See Alan Watts, *Nature, Man and Woman* (New York: Pantheon Books, 1958), p. 33.

17. Alan Watts, *The Joyous Cosmology* (New York: Pantheon Books, 1962), p. 3.

18. Ibid., p. 39.

19. Ibid., p. 56.

20. *In My Own Way,* p. 345.

21. R. E. L. Masters and Jean Houston, *The Varieties of Psychedelic Experience* (New York: Holt, Rinehart and Winston, 1966), p. 9.

22. Theodore Roszak, *The Making of a Counterculture* (Garden City, N.Y.: Doubleday, 1969), p. 173.

23. Ibid., p. 176.

24. Ibid., p. 258.

25. Theodore Roszak, *Where the Wasteland Ends* (Garden City, N.Y.: Doubleday, 1973), p. 270.

26. Ibid., p. 324.

27. Stephen Larsen, *The Shaman's Doorway* (New York: Harper & Row, 1976), p. 81.

28. *Where the Wasteland Ends,* p. 409. Italics author's.

29. Ibid., p. 426.

30. Ibid., p. 408.

31. Alan Watts, *Beyond Theology* (New York: Random House, 1964), p. 63.

32. Ibid., p. 208.

33. See Robert Grant, *Gnosticism and Early Christianity* (New York: Columbia University Press, 1965), p. 15.

34. Alan Watts, *This Is It* (New York: Random House, 1958), p. 36.

35. Baba Ram Dass, *Be Here Now* (San Cristobal, N.M.: Lama Foundation, 1971), preface.

36. Ibid., part 1, p. 31.

37. Ibid.

38. Ibid., p. 81.

39. Ibid., p. 33.

40. Jacob Needleman, *The New Religions* (Garden City, N.Y.: Doubleday, 1970), p. 16f.

41. Charles Cameron, ed., *Who Is Guru Maharaji?* (New York: Bantam Books, 1973), p. 148.

42. A. C. Bhaktivedanta Swami Prabhupada, *The Nectar of Devotion* (New York: Bhaktivedanta Book Trust, 1970), p. 9.

43. A. C. Bhaktivedanta Swami Prabhupada, *Krsna: The Reservoir of Pleasure* (New York: Bhaktivedanta Book Trust, 1972), p. 17.

44. From the Hare Krishna magazine *Back to Godhead* 10 (1975):1.

45. *Who Is Guru Maharaji?* p. 152.

46. Ibid., p. 99.

47. Baba Ram Dass, *The Only Dance There Is* (Garden City, N.Y.: Doubleday, 1974), p. 6.

48. Charles Reich, *The Greening of America* (New York: Random House, 1970), p. 376.

49. Robert Bellah, "The New Consciousness and the Crisis in Modernity" in Charles Y. Glock and Robert Bellah, eds., *The New Religious Consciousness* (Berkeley: University of California Press, 1976), p. 342.

50. Christopher Lasch, "The Narcissist Society," *The New York Review of Books* 23 (Sept. 30, 1976):12.

51. Peter Marin, "The New Narcissism," *Harper's* 251 (Oct. 1975):46.

Index

WESTMAR COLLEGE LIBRARY